2nd Edition

Limited Liability Company

The step-by-step guide to form your own LLC in Georgia

Vincent M Cornelius II

Exigoro Books

Atlanta, Georgia

Limited Liability Company
The Step-by-Step Guide to Form Your Own LLC in Georgia
First Edition: 2014
Second Edition: 2017

Exigoro Books, LLC
P.O. Box 961144
Riverdale, GA 30296
Tel: (678) 343-7840
www.exigorobooks.com

Publisher's Cataloging-in-Publication

Cornelius, Vincent M., II, author.
    Limited liability company : the step-by-step guide to
 form your own LLC in Georgia / Vincent M. Cornelius II.
 -- 2nd edition.
    p. cm.
    ISBN 978-0-9972988-5-7
    1. Private companies--Georgia--Popular works.
 2. Private companies--Georgia--Handbooks, manuals, etc.
 3. Limited partnership--Georgia--Popular works. 4. Limited
 partnership--Georgia--Handbooks, manuals, etc. 5. Law
 for laypersons. 6. Handbooks and manuals.   I. Title.

 KFG207.5.C67 2016
 346.758'0668--dc23
                          2016946285

This publication is designed to provide accurate and authoritative information in regard to the subject matter covered. It is sold with the understanding that the publisher is not engaged in rendering legal, accounting, or other professional service. If legal advice or other expert assistance is required, the services of a competent professional person should be sought.

PRINTED IN THE UNITED STATES OF AMERICA

Acknowledgements

I am so privileged to be able to acknowledge the special people in my life that helped, encouraged, and supported me throughout the writing of this book. First, to Sandra Bettard, the woman that believed in me so much that I had to believe in myself; to Urseldra Samedi for the financial support that kept me progressing toward this finished product when I was on a ramen noodle diet; to Rasha Williams for the words of encouragement and having faith that this day would eventually come; and to Teila Cornelius for looking up to me and giving me inspiration to be a role model in her life.

Also, to Philissa Gilliard for listening to my vision daily and seeing my vision, before seeing my vision; to Brian Brazzel for forming a mastermind alliance with me and tapping into that unseen power; to Brian Tracy for teaching me to prioritize and set goals; and to Robert G. Allen for introducing me to infopreneurship.

Lastly, I would like to thank the nonbelievers and naysayers that tried to kill my dream; your desire to see me fail propelled me to succeed.

This book is dedicated to my children:

Vincent Cornelius III

Isaiah Cornelius

Josiah Cornelius

Keyshawn Cornelius

Michael Cornelius

Lamar Cornelius

Daddy loves you all.

Table of Contents

Chapter 3 – Articles of Organization

Chapter 4 – Taxes

Chapter 5 – Your Operating Agreement

Chapter 6 – Form an LLC (Step-by-Step)

Chapter 7 – Compliance

Chapter 8 – LLC Kit

Glossary

Appendix A

Appendix B

About the Author

Introduction

No matter what the economy looks like, new businesses are being started by the millions each year. In the past, a corporation was the ideal vehicle to reach this destination, but within the last ten years, the limited liability company (LLC) has gained popularity as the preferred business entity. The main reason for this is because of the flexibility it offers, and for the protection it provides to the owners; all without the added hassles of the extra paperwork and regulations required of corporations.

Other than a corporation, the LLC is the only other business entity that provides identical limited liability status, with a fraction of the cost. Limited liability status is when an owner is not personally liable for any of the debts of the company, other than the amount of their investment in that company.

This book was written to help you form your own LLC in the state of Georgia with little to no assistance from a lawyer. Most books that you will find written on the subject of limited liability companies are blanketed with information for each state in America, which takes away from the specific details relating to any particular state. This book is the opposite.

Rest assured knowing that this book is written by a Georgia resident, with the most up-to-date knowledge on the laws and statutes governing this state; he has a close relationship with local lawyers, CPAs, and the secretary of state's office. Also, the author has many years of experience with forming limited liability companies in the state of Georgia.

Documents needed to form and maintain your LLC can be found at www.exigorobooks.com/forms

Chapter 1

Business Entity Basics

A business entity is a vehicle for individuals to conduct business as a separate, legal, identifiable existence apart from themselves. Each business entity has its advantages and disadvantages. New businesses and beginning entrepreneurs should examine the many aspects of conducting a business before deciding which entity best suits their business needs. As you decide upon your business entity, you should carefully evaluate both your present and future needs for operating your business. If you do not, you risk the chances of duplicating legal expenses, licensing, and other paperwork if you choose to convert to a different business entity later.

The Four Main Business Entities

The four main business entities that we will discuss are:

- Sole Proprietorship
- Partnership
- Corporation
- Limited Liability Company

Here is a brief introduction to each:

1. Sole Proprietorship

A sole proprietorship is owned and operated by one person: the sole proprietor. The sole proprietor has unlimited personal liability for all business debts and obligations, meaning he or she is fully responsible for the debts and liabilities of the company. No paperwork is required to form a sole proprietorship. When an individual engages in business, a sole proprietorship is automatically formed.

2. Partnership

A partnership is when two or more persons go into business together and share decision-making, profits, and losses. Partners have unlimited personal liability for all business debts and obligations.

There are three types of partnerships: general, limited, and limited liability. (Limited liability partnerships will not be discussed in the book.)

3. Corporation

A corporation is a business entity that is separate from its owners. This means that corporate shareholders (owners) have limited liability of the corporation's business debts. Although shareholders own the corporation, the corporation is managed by its board of directors.

There are several types of corporations, but we will only discuss two in this book: C corporations and S corporations.

4. Limited Liability Company

A limited liability company is a business entity that combines some of the best features of a partnership and a corporation. Like a partnership, it has pass-through taxation which means the profits and losses of the LLC pass through the business and are annotated on the owners' individual tax returns. Like a corporation, it offers the benefits of limited liability.

Factors to Consider When Choosing an Entity

Given the many different ways in which business is conducted in America, selecting the most appropriate form of business for your needs involves carefully weighing a variety of factors.

Ease of Formation

Some business entities are very easy to form, such as sole proprietorships, while others are more complicated, such as corporations.

Personal Liability

The financial exposure an individual faces is one of the most critical factors to consider when choosing a business entity.

Management

Do you want to manage the business yourself? Maybe you prefer to invest in the business and have someone else manage it. This is important because if there are multiple owners, member-management could get complicated.

Taxation

Do not forget to consider applicable tax requirements. For some, the individual tax rates may be best; for others, the corporate tax rates may offer more advantages. Remember, some business entities allow pass-through taxation, while corporations are burdened with double taxation.

Sole Proprietorship

There is no difference between the sole proprietor and his or her business; they are one in the same. Depending on how you view things, this can be bad or good. It could be bad because, if your company gets sued, essentially, you are being sued. It could be good because you do not have to worry about opening a business bank account, so your customers can pay you directly.

Most people who run a sole proprietorship are running (or plan to run) family businesses. One downfall for these family-run businesses is if the owner should die, the company dissolves and is no longer able to conduct business. The primary effect of the death of a sole proprietor is that the business cannot continue in its existing form. The business must either wind down completely, have its assets sold to a third party, or be transferred to another individual or legal entity pursuant to the last will and testament of the sole proprietor.

Although there are no official documents to file with the state of Georgia to form a sole proprietorship, in some cases there may be a few formalities to follow.

For Example: If you are operating under a name other than your legal name, you will be required to register your fictitious or assumed name, also known as a DBA (doing business as), with the Secretary of State's office. This is so that people who deal with your business will know who the real owner is. Another reason for the formality is that if your business requires licensing—be it for your

It's Simple: A sole proprietorship is the simplest and most common structure with which to start a business. Most entrepreneurs start with sole proprietorships and do not know it.

Ease of Formation

Because it is so simple, this is the most common entity type for businesses that have little to no liability issues. Its setup is so simple mainly because it is governed by state and local laws, while federal laws play a very minor role (such as civil rights and taxes). Because no paperwork is required to form a sole proprietorship, if there are no licenses needed to operate and you are not subject to any local laws, then you may start operating in your prospective field at any time.

Note: You must still pay taxes for your business activities, but the sole proprietorship itself is not taxed. The profits or losses pass through the company and onto the owner's personal tax return.

Personal Liability

The biggest downside to operating a business as a sole proprietor is the liability you are subject to. If your business incurs debts that it cannot pay from the profits, you are personally liable and responsible for payment. Creditors may sue you personally to satisfy the debt. Along with liability for debts, as a sole proprietor you also have personal liability for any torts or injuries that occur as a result of any acts of your business. You may, however, be able to purchase

profession, your state, county, or even city licensing—the proper business name must appear on these.

liability insurance for your business to help eliminate the burden.

Management

A sole proprietorship is managed and owned by one person, the sole proprietor. Although a sole proprietor may hire employees for simple management, day-to-day management (as in critical business operations) must reside with the owner, or else it is more of a partnership than a sole proprietorship. An exception to the one-owner rule is in a spousal sole proprietorship. In 2007, a new law was enacted; if you and your spouse are the only owners and both of you are actively operating the business, the business is allowed to have two owners; the husband and wife.

If you meet the requirement of a spousal sole proprietorship and want to have your business treated as a sole proprietorship, you and your spouse must file separate IRS Schedule Cs, with each of you reporting your individual share of the business's income or loss. If you would like to take this route, it also means that you must each file a separate self-employment tax form (Schedule SE), reporting and paying Social Security and Medicare taxes on your separate shares of the business income.

Taxation

Reporting income from your sole proprietorship means that you must list your business's profit or loss information on

Schedule C, which you are to submit to the IRS along with Form 1040.

You will be taxed on all profits of the business—that is total income minus expenses—regardless of how much money you actually withdraw from the business. In other words, even if you leave money in the company's bank account at the end of the year (for instance, to cover future expenses or expand the business), you must pay taxes on that money.

As the owner of a sole proprietorship, you are allowed to deduct much of the money you spend in pursuit of profit—just like any other business—including operating expenses, product and advertising costs, travel expenses, and some of the cost of business-related meals and entertainment. You can also write off certain start-up costs and the cost of business equipment and other assets you purchase for your business.

Therefore, you will need to keep accurate records for your business that are clearly separate from your personal expenses. One approach is to pay for all of your business expenses out of the business checking account.

Note: If your business is expanding to the point that you need to hire additional help, you may want to consider changing your sole proprietorship into a limited liability company for liability purposes.

Advantages

- Simple and inexpensive to form
- Not governed or regulated by federal or state statutes

- The owner makes all business decisions
- Pass-through taxation

Disadvantages

- Unlimited personal liability
- Dissolves if owner dies
- Limited in ways to raise capital
- Limit on number of owners

General Partnership

A general partnership, usually referred to simply as a partnership, is another common business entity. A general partnership is formed when two or more persons decide to go into business together. The persons in a partnership may consist of an individual, a business entity, another partnership, or any combination of these.

Ease of Formation

Similar to a sole proprietorship, forming a general partnership does not require any formal documents to be filed or state regulations to be followed. Although it is not recommended, a general partnership may be formed with as little as a firm handshake and a verbal agreement. However, even with close relatives, it is always a good idea to put partnership details in writing. At the very least, you should consider having a written agreement outlining the inner workings of the business and how the profits and losses will be dispersed.

Personal Liability

Remember, each partner can make decisions on behalf of the company that could adversely affect the business itself or the individual owners. Each partner has unlimited personal liability for the debts and obligations of the partnership. Also, a creditor has the option to sue all partners, the partnership itself, or any individual partner.

For Example: Brandon, Tanisha, and Mark form a company that sells candy apples. While away on a business trip, Mark finds what he believes to be a great deal on candy apple sticks. On his own, he signs a contract on behalf of the company for a year's worth of product. Good idea, right? Well, not quite. The sticks were poorly constructed, and are entirely too small. Once the partnership received their first batch of sticks, they decided they no longer wanted to do business with the shoddy candy apple stick company.

The candy apple stick company was unwilling to release Mark and his company from their contract; therefore, the partnership was liable for the full amount due. The creditor is now allowed to pursue any one partner, or all partners, for its debt. If one partner's pockets are deeper than the others' (in this case, Brandon's), then the whole debt can be taken from that partner. Later, Brandon may sue the other partners to recoup his loss and evenly distribute the debt if he decides to.

Management

Each partner shares the management and decision making within the business. One partner can bind the partnership and their co-partners, in a contract or other obligations, resulting in personal liability for an act that the other partners may have not been aware of, nor approved. One way around this is the use of partner votes to limit certain partners' managing authority; if this process is to be used, it must be written in the partnership agreement.

Note: Georgia partnerships are governed by the Uniform Partnership Act (UPA). This is only considered in cases where a partnership has a dispute and there is not a written agreement to cover the situation.

Uniform Partnership Act

The UPA states that each partner has a fiduciary relationship to the partnership and must act in good faith and for the benefit of the partnership. In management decisions, each partner has one vote, and most decisions are based on a majority vote. However, certain major decisions, such as a decision to merge with another partnership, require a unanimous vote.

Taxation

A partnership must file an annual information return to report the business's income, deductions, gains, losses, etc., from its operations, but it does not pay income tax. Instead, any profits or losses are "passed through" to its partners. Each partner includes his or her share of the partnership's income or loss on his or her tax return. However, a general partnership may be required to send income tax deposits on behalf of one or more partners under certain circumstances. (Check with the Department of Labor). Partnerships are also generally required to register with the state's

Department of Revenue for the collection and remittance of sales and to use taxes, payroll taxes, or any other applicable state or local taxes.

When a Partner Leaves or Dies

Without a partnership agreement, if a partner leaves or dies, the partnership dissolves—even in a partnership of more than two partners. To cover situations like this, a buy–sell agreement needs to be added. Buy–sell agreements are beyond the scope of this book, but here's a brief explanation: They are binding contracts between co-owners of a business that govern what will happen when an owner wants to leave or a new owner wants to join.

Advantages

- Can be formed easily
- No written agreement required
- Relatively inexpensive
- Other partners can contribute capital
- Pass-through taxation

Disadvantages

- Unlimited personal liability
- Dissolution if other partners leave or die
- Each partner is responsible for other partners' decisions

Raising Capital

Raising money for your business is one of the basic necessities to operate. This presents disadvantages to most sole proprietorships. Unlike a corporation, a sole proprietorship cannot sell shares of the business, because there are none. Also, banks are hesitant to lend to sole proprietors because of a perceived lack of credibility when it comes to repayment if the business fails.

Although it may be difficult, it is not impossible to acquire capital for a sole proprietorship. Friends and family can loan or invest in your company. If you have a strong business plan, angel investors may be a good choice. You may also apply for a Small Business Administration loan. The SBA offers guaranteed loan programs to small business owners. Their Microloan program is a common option for start-ups, and it offers low interest rates and easy payment terms. The maximum amount you can get under this loan program is $50,000.

Limited Partnership

The main difference between a general partnership and a limited partnership is that in a limited partnership, one or more of the partners retain limited liability (limited partner) while the other partner or partners have none (general partner). Unlike general partnerships, a limited partnership must file a Certificate of Limited Partnership with the Secretary of State.

Ease of Formation

Limited partnerships are slightly more complex than general partnerships. Limited partnerships are required to file with the Secretary of State's office and are governed by a Limited Partnership Agreement. If the limited partnership wants to operate under a name other than the last names of the owners, then it has to apply for a fictitious name. Also, it must comply with any local and state licenses or permits.

Personal Liability

General partners have full management responsibility and control of the business and also accept full personal responsibility for partnership liabilities. Limited partners have no personal liability beyond their investment in the partnership interest. Limited partners cannot participate in the general management and daily operations of the partnership business without being considered general partners in the eyes of the law.

In other words, partners with limited liability have no say in the day-to-day decisions and do not participate in the company's operations. If they do, they risk losing their limited liability status. These partners usually invest in or contribute capital to the business (the money needed to start or operate the business), called capital contributions. If done correctly, limited partners only risk their initial investment in the company.

This form of business may be well suited for a silent partner/investor or someone seeking capital for a low-risk business.

Management

As stated previously, a limited partnership is managed by the general partner or partners. This responsibility cannot be designated or assigned to outside management. If this is not ideal for the type of business you operate, there are many other entities to choose from that allow more flexibility such as a limited liability company or a corporation.

Taxation

Limited partnerships are pass-through tax entities. Like in a sole proprietorship, the profits and losses pass through the company and onto the partners' personal tax returns.

Advantages

- Limited partners only risk their money, or whatever investment they have contributed
- General partners maintain full control of the business operations
- Pass-through taxation

Disadvantages

- General partners are personally responsible for the debts and liabilities of the company
- Limited partners are not allowed to participate in the daily operations of the business
- If one of the business's general partners dies, the company dissolves unless partners have previously agreed that the business will continue in such cases

C Corporation

There are two types of corporations that will be discussed in this book, C corporations and S corporations. Corporations are considered tax-paying entities separate from the people who create them. This is the main difference between the other business entities and the corporation. A C corporation can survive the death of one or more of the owners and not have its existence affected. Depending on your business's needs, this may be ideal.

A corporation can have as few as one owner, but no more the 100. The owner of a one-person corporation must abide by certain formalities in order to obtain true C corporation status. For example, he or she may need to hold annual shareholders' meetings, maintain corporate records, draft bylaws, assign officers, separate personal funds from corporate funds, and issue stock, to name a few.

Note that in the state of Georgia, a C corporation must publish a "notice of incorporation," a public announcement of the new entity.

Insight: A shareholder working as an officer is considered an employee and must be paid a wage subject to payroll taxes.

Ease of Formation

Creating a C corporation is more complicated than forming a limited liability company, partnership, or sole proprietorship. More paperwork is required and it also takes more time and more money. A C corporation is established with state authorities and must abide by corporate laws. To form a C corporation, you will need to register your business name, file a certificate of incorporation (also called Articles of Incorporation), and pay a fee. You will also need to draft corporate bylaws and hold a board of directors' meeting. Staying in compliance and following the state regulations is the hardest part of maintaining a corporation for most people that form their own corporation. Hiring a professional to handle this process is highly recommended.

Personal Liability

A major advantage of a C corporation is that its owners have limited liability. Thus, they do not stand personally liable for debts incurred by the corporation; they cannot be sued individually for corporate wrongdoings.

While a C corporation is an attractive way of forming a business due to the limited liability of its owners, there are certain circumstances wherein the limited liability will not be able to protect the owners' personal assets. An owner will be held personally liable if he or she:

- Personally/directly injures someone
- Personally guarantees a bank loan or a business debt on which the corporation defaults
- Fails to deposit taxes withheld from employees' wages
- Intentionally does something fraudulent, illegal, or reckless that causes harm to the company or to someone else
- Treats the corporation as an extension of his or her personal affairs, rather than as a separate legal entity
- The courts rule that a corporation ceases to exist, as the proper formalities have not been adhered to

Management

A corporation is owned by the people who own its shares (shareholders) but is operated by its board of directors. The shareholders conduct meetings and vote on who will be on the board of directors. The corporation adopts bylaws, which govern the inner workings of the company—similar to a partnership agreement in a partnership.

Taxation

The C corporation structure does have its drawbacks. For instance, a C corporation's profits are taxed when earned and taxed again when distributed as shareholders' dividends. This is what is known as "double taxation." Shareholders in a C corporation also cannot deduct any corporate losses from their personal tax return. To avoid these concerns, many small business owners choose to form S corporations instead.

Note: Although C corporations are subject to double taxation, they also have greater tax flexibility. In a C corporation, you can use income shifting to take advantage of lower income tax brackets.

For Example: To illustrate, let's use a company that earns $100,000 a year as an example. With a sole proprietorship, a business owner who is married and filing jointly would be in the 25% income tax bracket. With a corporation, assuming the business owner takes $50,000 in salary and leaves $50,000 in the corporation as corporate profit, the federal corporate tax rate would be 15% on the first $50,000. Furthermore, the business owner is now in the 15% tax bracket for his or her personal income tax. This can reduce overall tax liability by over $8,000.

Advantages

- Shareholder liability is limited to the amount of property or income they have invested in the corporation
- A shareholder can sell his/her interest and the corporation will still continue to exist
- The death of a shareholder will not result in the dissolution of the business
- Unlimited lifespan

Disadvantages

- Taxed separately from the owners which causes double taxation
- Complicated to form and maintain alone
- Requires a tremendous amount of paperwork

- Most expensive business entity to form

S Corporation

An S corporation is more of a special tax election than a separate type of corporation. What is called an "S sub-chapter tax election" allows a corporation to be taxed as a partnership and still enjoy the benefits of a corporation. In other words, the S corporation does not pay corporate income taxes.

Ease of Formation

S corporations are formed in the same manner as C corporations. One difference is that owners of an S corporation must file Form 2553 with the IRS within 75 days of incorporating to take advantage of the special S sub-chapter tax election.

A few other rules that an S corporation must adhere to are:

- It cannot have more than 100 shareholders
- All shareholders must be US citizens or resident aliens
- It can only have one class of stock
- All shareholders must agree on the S corporation status election

Personal Liability

The S corporation has the same liability protection as a C corporation. To maintain this limited liability, an S corporation must hold special meetings of directors and shareholders.

Management

Shareholders only have the right to elect the directors and vote on major extraordinary business of the corporation (for example, on a merger, complete sale of the corporation, dissolution, or amendments to the Articles of Incorporation). The directors' role is much wider. They have the power to authorize the corporation to enter into contracts, purchase property, open bank accounts, borrow or loan money, and enact other such significant actions.

The board can also delegate this authority to its officers, but it must do so in writing. In many corporations, in fact, much of the actual operations are handled by the officers. However, all of the officers' authority to operate on behalf of the corporation stems directly from the board of directors.

Taxation

While employee Medicare and FICA taxes, as well as state taxes, are not affected by a company's corporate structure, federal income tax treatments are different for LLCs and S corporations than for other entities. The corporate tax rate allowed for LLCs and S corporations is usually lower than the personal income tax rate.

Advantages

- An S corporation is treated as a pass-through entity that allows the owners of the business to report their portion of the company's profits and losses directly on their personal income tax returns

- Owners of the company have limited liability protection from the corporation's liabilities, debts, and obligations
- S corporations benefit from the ability to issue stock to potential investors
- Unlimited lifespan

Disadvantages

- Ongoing fees, such as annual report and/or franchise tax fees
- An S corporation can have only one class of stock
- Closer IRS scrutiny (e.g., wages may be characterized as dividends, costing the corporation a deduction for compensation paid)
- Less flexibility in allocating income and loss

Limited Liability Company

A limited liability company is one of the newest business entities enacted by Georgia state law. It combines the best aspects of corporations and partnerships. It has tax benefits, like those of a partnership, and it has limited liability protection, like a corporation, meaning the personal assets of the individual owners are not in jeopardy if the company gets sued and loses.

Ease of Formation

LLCs are very much like corporations. Paperwork must be filed with the Secretary of State to establish your LLC. The paperwork required to form your LLC, called the Articles of Organization, is similar to the Articles of Incorporation required for corporations.

The information needed to fill out the forms includes:

- Name of the LLC
- Name of the person filing for the LLC
- The principal office mailing address
- Registered agent's name and address
- Names and addresses of the owners

Note: An LLC can have as few as one owner, and there is no limit on the maximum amount of owners it is allowed to have.

Personal Liability

Like shareholders of a corporation, all LLC owners are protected from personal liability for business debts and claims. This means that if the business itself cannot pay a creditor (such as a supplier, a lender, or a landlord), the creditor cannot legally come after an LLC member's house, car, or other personal possessions. Because only LLC assets are used to pay off business debts, LLC owners stand to lose only the money that they have invested in the LLC.

Also, an LLC will protect its owners from personal liability for any wrongdoing committed by the co-owners or employees of an LLC during the course of business. If the LLC is found liable for the wrongdoing of its owner or employee, the LLC's money or property can be taken by creditors to satisfy a judgment against the LLC, but the LLC's owners would not be personally liable for that debt. The owner or employee who committed the act might also be personally liable for his or her actions, but the people who were not involved in the wrongdoing would not be.

However, an LLC has the same exceptions as a corporation. That is, an LLC owner can be held personally liable if he or she:

- Personally/directly injures someone
- Personally guarantees a bank loan or a business debt on which the LLC defaults
- Fails to deposit taxes withheld from employees' wages
- Intentionally does something fraudulent, illegal, or reckless that causes harm to the company or to someone else
- Treats the LLC as an extension of his or her personal affairs, rather than as a separate legal entity

Management

The owners of an LLC are called members, and instead of shares, the owners hold LLC membership interest, or LLC interest. Using LLC interest is a great way to raise capital, but the downside is that this interest cannot be traded on the public stock exchange.

An LLC can be member-managed or manager-managed. Member-managed is when all of the owners play an integral role in the management of the LLC. Manager-managed is when an individual or individuals other than the owners manage the LLC. These individuals can be members or nonmembers. (More on this in Chapter 2.)

Taxation

One of the greatest features of an LLC is that it is a pass-through tax entity, meaning that the LLC itself is not taxed, but the profits or losses pass through onto the individual owners' personal tax returns. This is unlike a C corporation, in which the profits are taxed twice, once by the company and then once again by the owners.

Another great thing that sets LLCs apart from other business entities is that, while an LLC is a pass-through tax entity by default, it can choose any taxation structure that benefits the company the most.

Advantages

- Flexibility in the management structure
- Personal liability protection for the members
- Ability to choose taxation structure
- Limited compliance requirements
- Unlimited lifespan

Disadvantages

- Cannot go public on the stock exchange
- Responsible for paying self-employment tax
- State regulations are involved when adding a new member

Business Entity Comparison	Sole Proprietorship	General Partnership	Limited Partnership	Limited Liability Company	S Corporation	C Corporation
Formation	No state filing required.	No state filing required.	State filing required.	State filing required.	State filing required.	State filing required.
Duration of Existence	Dissolves if sole proprietor stops doing business or dies.	Depends on partnership agreement. Usually dissolves upon death or withdrawal of a partner.	Perpetual	Perpetual	Perpetual	Perpetual
Number of Owners	Minimum: 1 Maximum: 1	Minimum: 2 Maximum: ∞	Min: 1 GP & 1 LP Max:: 1 GP & ∞ LP	Minimum: 1 Maximum: ∞	Minimum: 1 Maximum: 100	Minimum: 1 Maximum: ∞
Liability	Sole proprietor is fully liable.	All partners are equally liable unless the partnership agreement states otherwise.	General Partner is fully liable.	Owners have Limited Liability	Owners have Limited Liability	Owners have Limited Liability

Business Entity Comparison	Sole Proprietorship	General Partnership	Limited Partnership	Limited Liability Company	S Corporation	C Corporation
Operational Requirements	Few legal requirements.	Few legal requirements.	Moderate legal requirements.	Moderate legal requirements.	Extensive legal requirements.	Extensive legal requirements.
Taxation	Taxed on earnings at the personal income tax level.	No federal tax is paid at the partnership level.	No federal tax is paid at the partnership level.	No federal tax is paid at the partnership level unless LLC elects to be taxed as a corporation	No federal tax is paid at the S corporation level, but built in gains taxes may apply.	Taxed on earnings at the corporate level.
Pass-through Taxation	Yes	Yes	Yes	Yes	Yes	No
Interest Transferability	No	No	Depends on partnership agreement	Depends on the operating agreement	Yes	Yes

Business Entity Comparison	Sole Proprietorship	General Partnership	Limited Partnership	Limited Liability Company	S Corporation	C Corporation
Raising Capital	Typically owner funded	Typically funded by partners	Typically funded by partners	By selling membership interest	By selling stock	By selling stock
Double Taxation	No	No	No	No	No	Yes
Subject to Securities Law	No	No	Yes	Yes, if investors are not members	Yes	Yes
Dissolution	Easiest	Easy	Moderate	Complex	Most complex	Most complex

Business Entity Comparison	Sole Proprietorship	General Partnership	Limited Partnership	Limited Liability Company	S Corporation	C Corporation
If Owner Dies/Quits	Dissolves	Default: Dissolves	Default: Dissolves	Depends on the operating agreement	Depends on the bylaws	Depends on the bylaws
Management	Sole proprietor is in control of managing operations	All partners have equal managing rights unless the partnership agreement states otherwise.	Limited partners are excluded from management unless they serve on the board of directors.	Operating agreement outlines management	Managed by directors who are elected by the shareholders	Managed by directors who are elected by the shareholders

Chapter 2

Members and Management

Members Defined

The owners of an LLC are called members. A member of an LLC is similar to a shareholder in a corporation. Instead of stocks or shares, members own membership units, or membership interest, which determine their percentage of ownership.

There are two ways to become a member of an LLC. The first is to be listed in the Articles of Organization as a founding member. The second is by being added later in accordance to the operating agreement drafted by the founding members, or in absence of an operating agreement, the state's default rules. This normally includes a majority vote and the new member contributing capital in return for membership interest.

Membership Interest

A membership interest in an LLC is personal property and holds economic rights. Economic rights are the rights to a certain percentage of the profits of the limited liability company. Typically, this right is equal to the percentage of membership interest the member owns. For example, if a member owns 30 Membership Units and there are a total of 100 Membership Units issued to all members, that member would get 30% of the profits. Unless otherwise stated in the operating agreement, those rights also include transferability, the ability to sell and to receive distributions of the LLC's assets.

Note: Voting rights and management rights are not included as they are classified as non-economic rights.

Admitting a New Member

After approval, the LLC should make sure that the issuance of membership interest to the new member is in compliance with any applicable state securities laws. Securities laws are beyond the scope of this LLC book, but generally, if the member being admitted has a preexisting relationship with you and the LLC and will be active in the management and operations of the LLC, there should be no state limitations. On the other hand, if the member is more like an investor and will be contributing substantial money or other property in exchange for membership interest without actively managing or operating the LLC, please check with a local attorney to determine if there are any securities-related obligations.

Membership Flexibility

There is no limit on the number of members an LLC is allowed to have, but the minimum requirement is one. This is more of a benefit than a requirement, because in the past, before LLCs were enacted, in order for an individual to start a company alone, they had to form a sole proprietorship or corporation.

Also, LLC membership is not limited to individuals; LLC members may consist of foreign businesses, corporations, partnerships, trust, other LLCs, or any combination of the sort.

Capital Contributions

Capital contributions are contributions in the form of money, property, or service to a business by the owners or outside investors, usually in return for membership interest. Property and service contributions must be listed and described within the operating agreement, and the members must agree on the fair market value of the non-cash contributions. Initial capital contributions on formation of the LLC may be any amount. Members usually contribute enough to pay for startup expenses and assets.

Caution: In some cases, inadequate capitalization could be a factor in disregarding an LLC and finding the members personally liable for the debts or obligations of the LLC. If your LLC has particularly significant risks or liabilities, it may be necessary to have a greater capital contribution.

Additional capital contributions may be made periodically in accordance with a schedule set by the entity's budget or business plan or pursuant to a particular capital call after the initial issuance of the LLC interest. For this reason, operating agreements usually contemplate the possibility that the members will need to make additional capital contributions. Because this requires a commitment from the members to put up more capital, the provisions governing additional capital contributions can be quite detailed and heavily negotiated. This is particularly the case when a managing member has the authority to make capital calls that the non-managing members must abide by.

Member Capital Accounts

A Limited Liability Company capital account is a way to keep track of an individual member's investment in the business. If the business is sold or the member wanted to sell their share of the business back to the LLC, the capital account is a measure of what they will receive in return. The account represents a combination of the member's initial investment, additional contributions made to the business, the share of the LLC's profits and losses, and any cash or property distributions they received from the business.

Establishing Capital Accounts

Step 1: Establish the beginning balance of each capital account.

When an LLC is created, the members contribute money or property so the business can begin operation. The initial balance of each capital account is equal to the market value of the property or cash contributed to the LLC. If member A contributes $50,000 in cash and member B contributes $50,000 in machinery, both have capital accounts equal to $50,000.

Step 2: Adjust the account for the member's share of the annual gains or losses of the business.

The LLC's operating agreement will normally dictate how the profits or losses will be divided amongst the members each year. Assume members A and B agree to share equally in the business's income and losses, and the LLC suffers a $50,000 loss in the first year but generates $100,000 in income the second year. Both A and B's capital accounts would increase over that two year period by $25,000, or minus $25,000 for year one and plus $50,000 for year two.

Step 3: Subtract the amount of any distributions made by the LLC to the owner.

If the business distributes cash to its members, the capital account needs to be decreased by the amount of the distribution. If members A and B receive a $15,000 distribution, their capital accounts decrease by $15,000 each.

Step 4: Add the value of any additional contributions the members made to the LLC after the initial investment.

Using the same guidelines that established the initial balance, the capital accounts must be increased by the value of the property or cash the members contribute. So, if member A contributes $25,000 worth of raw material inventory and member B contributes $25,000 in cash, both accounts need to be increased by $25,000.

Note: Unless otherwise stated in the operating agreement, profits and losses are dispersed equally in relation to each member's percentage of contribution.

For example: If the total capital contribution from all members equal $10,000 in which one member contributed $2,000, another member $4,000, another $1,000, and another contributed services and property that was equivalent to $3,000, the percentage would look like this:

$2,000 = 20%

$4,000 = 40%

$1000 = 10%

$3000 = 30%

Contribution percentages can be different from distribution percentages. Initial member percentages of ownership can be set by the operating agreement and the agreement can set different percentages of share of the profits/losses. The members can do anything they want concerning their profit and loss disbursement as long as it is not in conflict with state law, it is agreed upon, and the agreement is stated in the operating agreement. Changing contribution percentages can be very tricky and often raises red flags to the IRS. Consult an experienced attorney if you decide to use this method.

Voting Rights

Voting rights in an LLC have to be specifically addressed in the operating agreement. Unlike a corporation, owners of an LLC do not have to vote in proportion to their ownership percentage. LLCs get to decide upon how member voting rights are distributed. Therefore, voting rights can be more important than majority ownership in some cases.

Voting rights are commonly broken down into two types:

1. Voting power that is in relation to the member's ownership percentage. (This is the default according to Georgia state statutes.) If there is no voting provision in your operating agreement, this will be the governing factor.

2. Voting power where each member gets one vote.

What is voted upon?

There are a plethora of business issues that can be settled by member voting. Some issues could include the rules on accepting or dismissing members from the LLC, the roles and responsibilities of the members, or business transactions that require significant investments such as purchasing an office building or buying a company. You decide; but always create the power to vote.

After Forming Your LLC

To prove ownership of interest in an LLC, members issue what are known as membership certificates. They are not required by Georgia state law, but it is a good idea to issue them because it adds an extra layer of protection when liability issues are a concern. Also, some people like to hold or see something tangible concerning a purchase of property. Furthermore, it adds a sense of professionalism to your company.

Upon formation, corporations must designate the number of outstanding shares and the par value of stock and then issue stock certificates. An LLC's operating agreement defines the base value of its membership interests. LLC members' ownership derives from the agreement between the company and its members, not from the possession of a certificate.

Issuing Certificates

After issuing certificates to members and investors, record the interest and certificates issued in the transfer ledger. The transfer ledger will be kept in the LLC Kit, also known as the Corporate Kit or Records. On the face of a certificate, there is normally the LLC's name, the state it was organized in, how many members it has, the name of the member holding the certificate, the percentage of interest the member owns, the benefits the member is entitled to, and a witness signature.

Management

Within your LLC, members will need to decide upon how it will be managed. There are only two methods: member-managed and manager-managed. In a member-managed LLC, all the members have full rights in managing the company. This is the default option, but this can be modified in the operating agreement if all members agree. Then, there is the manager-managed LLC where one or more people are decided upon (by the members) to act as a manager of the company.

Selecting your management structure

This can be done in a variety of ways:

1. You can select certain members to be managers. This works out well when some of the members are passive investors. In this case, the active members (members that handle day-to-day operations) may be chosen as the managers.

2. You can choose to be managed by only nonmembers. This is best for LLC owners who have no expertise in their company's business but wish for it to be operated by professionals in their prospective fields.

3. You may decide to be managed by some members and some nonmembers. There are several reasons why some would take this approach. If that works for your type of business, feel free to choose this type.

Management Authority

All management has the right to legally bind the company to a contract as long as the action committed is within the company's normal scope of business. So unless the act is authorized by the other members, an act of a manager whose purpose is not to carry on the business of a limited liability company in the usual way, does not bind the company.

Management Responsibility

While the operating agreement may limit the authority of the managers and require a member's approval on key business decisions, managers have day-to-day control of the LLC. Management has moral and legal responsibilities to uphold. Management should ensure that the commingling of funds never happens. This means LLC funds should not be used for the personal matters of the LLC's members or the LLC's management team. Also, management should not personally guarantee any debt or financial obligation. If a manager does this, that manager throws his or her limited liability protection out the window. Not adhering to any of these responsibilities will most likely lead to the piercing of the LLC's corporate veil. Management should strictly follow the principles outlined within the operating agreement to be sure that all actions will be performed in the best interest of the LLC.

Piercing the Corporate Veil

When an LLC is a sham; engages in fraud or other wrongful acts; or is used solely for the personal benefit of its members, managers, or investors; courts may disregard the separate corporate existence and impose personal liability on the members, managers, or investors. In other words, courts may pierce the "veil" that the law uses to divide the LLC (and its liabilities and assets) from the people behind the company. This veil is what creates a separate, legally recognized corporate entity and shields the people behind the LLC from personal liability.

Courts may disregard the separate corporate existence when an LLC fails to follow the formalities required by LLC state statutes. In addition, courts traditionally require fraud, illegality, or misrepresentation before they will pierce the corporate veil. Courts often cite the lack of corporate formalities in finding that an LLC has become the alter ego or instrumentality of the owners.

For Example: a court may justify piercing the corporate veil if an LLC began to conduct business before its articles of incorporation was completed, failed to hold meetings, failed to file an Annual Report or tax return, or directed the LLC's business receipts straight to owner's or managers' personal accounts. Also, courts may refuse to recognize a separate corporate existence when doing so would violate a clearly defined statutory policy.

Economic Rights

Members of an LLC are taxed at their individual tax rate on their personal tax returns. The profits and losses of the LLC "pass through" the business entity. The LLC itself does not pay federal income taxes. If the LLC is a single member LLC, then the IRS treats it as a sole proprietorship unless that member elects to be taxed otherwise.

Taxes are assessed on the member's full distributive share. According to the IRS, each LLC member must pay taxes on their full distributive share each year whether they receive it or not, even if LLC members need to leave profits of the business within the company; for example, to buy inventory or to expand the business.

Fiduciary Duties

All managers, whether a member or non-member, must adhere to their jurisdiction's minimum standards of conduct. These standards include fiduciary duties such as the duty of care and loyalty. A duty of loyalty requires the manager to conduct business and make management decisions with the best interests of the LLC in mind. A manager who seeks personal gain from potential business opportunities or competes with the LLC is personally liable for the resulting damage and loss of profits to the LLC. The duty of care requires a manager to refrain from acting in a grossly negligent manner. To be grossly negligent, the manager must act with flagrant disregard of the law or acceptable business practices, or act with indifference to the safety of others. A manager is personally liable to the LLC for grossly negligent acts that result in loss or damage to the business.

Adding Members & Managers

Adding a new member in a member-managed LLC, by default statutes, can only be allowed by a vote of all the LLC's existing members.

Removing Members and Managers

It may sometimes become necessary to remove a member or manager of an LLC, particularly if the management of the LLC has irretrievably broken down. However, the default provision of the Uniform Limited Liability Company Act does not allow LLC members to vote out other LLC members. Unless the LLC's operating agreement allows members to vote out other members, an LLC member may only be removed if he or she submits written notice of withdrawal to the LLC. There are other ways to leave an LLC. Leaving an LLC is usually referred to as withdrawal or dissociation.

Member's Dissociation

ULLCA SECTION 601
MEMBER'S POWER TO DISSOCIATE; WRONGFUL DISSOCIATION.

(a) A person has the power to dissociate as a member at any time, rightfully or wrongfully, by withdrawing as a member by express will under Section 602(1).

(b) A person's dissociation from a limited liability company is wrongful only if the dissociation:

(1) is in breach of an express provision of the operating agreement; or

(2) occurs before the termination of the company and:

(A) the person withdraws as a member by express will;

(B) the person is expelled as a member by judicial order under Section 602(5);

(C) the person is dissociated under Section 602(7)(A) by becoming a debtor in bankruptcy; or

(D) in the case of a person that is not a trust other than a business trust, an estate, or an individual, the person is expelled or otherwise dissociated as a member because it willfully dissolved or terminated.

(c) A person that wrongfully dissociates as a member is liable to the limited liability company and, subject to Section 901, to the other members for damages caused by the dissociation. The liability is in addition to any other debt, obligation, or other liability of the member to the company or the other members.

ULLCA SECTION 602.
EVENTS CAUSING DISSOCIATION.

A person is dissociated as a member from a limited liability company when:

(1) the company has notice of the person's express will to withdraw as a member, but, if the person specified a withdrawal date later than the date the company had notice, on that later date;

(2) an event stated in the operating agreement as causing the person's dissociation occurs;

(3) the person is expelled as a member pursuant to the operating agreement;

(4) the person is expelled as a member by the unanimous consent of the other members if:

(A) it is unlawful to carry on the company's activities with the person as a member;

(B) there has been a transfer of all of the person's transferable interest in the company, other than:

(i) a transfer for security purposes; or

(ii) a charging order in effect under Section 503 which has not been foreclosed;

(C) the person is a corporation and, within 90 days after the company notifies the person that it will be expelled as a member because the person has filed a certificate of dissolution or the equivalent, its charter has been revoked, or its right to conduct business has been suspended by the jurisdiction of its incorporation, the certificate of dissolution has not been revoked or its charter or right to conduct business has not been reinstated; or

(D) the person is a limited liability company or partnership that has been dissolved and whose business is being wound up;

(5) on application by the company, the person is expelled as a member by judicial order because the person:

(A) has engaged, or is engaging, in wrongful conduct that has adversely and materially affected, or will adversely and materially affect, the company's activities;

(B) has willfully or persistently committed, or is willfully and persistently committing, a material breach of the operating agreement or the person's duties or obligations under Section 409; or

(C) has engaged in, or is engaging, in conduct relating to the company's activities which makes it not reasonably practicable to carry on the activities with the person as a member;

(6) in the case of a person who is an individual:

(A) the person dies; or

(B) in a member-managed limited liability company:

(i) a guardian or general conservator for the person is appointed; or

(ii) there is a judicial order that the person has otherwise become incapable 87 of performing the person's duties as a member under [this act] or the operating agreement;

(7) in a member-managed limited liability company, the person:

(A) becomes a debtor in bankruptcy;

(B) executes an assignment for the benefit of creditors; or

(C) seeks, consents to, or acquiesces in the appointment of a trustee, receiver, or liquidator of the person or of all or substantially all of the person's property;

(8) in the case of a person that is a trust or is acting as a member by virtue of being a trustee of a trust, the trust's entire transferable interest in the company is distributed;

(9) in the case of a person that is an estate or is acting as a member by virtue of being a personal representative of an estate, the estate's entire transferable interest in the company is distributed;

(10) in the case of a member that is not an individual, partnership, limited liability company, corporation, trust, or estate, the termination of the member;

(11) the company participates in a merger under [Article] 10, if:

(A) the company is not the surviving entity; or

(B) otherwise as a result of the merger, the person ceases to be a member;

(12) the company participates in a conversion under [Article] 10;

(13) the company participates in a domestication under [Article] 10, if, as a result of the domestication, the person ceases to be a member; or

(14) the company terminates.

Chapter 3

Articles of Organization

The document needed to form an LLC is called the Articles of Organization. This is the document you must file with the Secretary of State to establish your LLC as a legal business entity. In the state of Georgia, there are only a few items to cover within this document. Other provisions may be included, but are not required.

It is better to add the other provisions in the operating agreement, because it costs nothing but the ink used and the paper it is printed on to amend. Amending through the Secretary of State includes paying fees; filing paperwork; obtaining signatures; and in some cases, a vote of the members.

Georgia's Secretary of State's website provides a comprehensive, easy to use, insert box that allows you to submit your registration information online. Once all of your information has been submitted, the website will generate a printable form that you will use as your Articles of Organization. There is also a sample Articles of Organization provided on their website. In their sample there are only two articles; this may be to imply that those are the minimum requirements for filing, and the other articles that are common in most states will be listed on the Transmittal form 231 (see Chapter 6).

Preparing Your Articles

In order, we will discuss the information needed from you about your company to complete your LLC registration with your Articles of Organization and the Data Transmittal Form 231. Although it is not mandatory, name reservations should be filed prior to filing your articles. If you can afford to spend an additional $25, it is recommended that you apply for a name reservation. You will be able to secure the name in advance of applying for your LLC, and it also speeds up the process of the Secretary of State accepting your articles and forming your LLC. After applying for your name reservation, you will be given a number within 24 hours that remains in effect for 30 days that you will need to place on the Transmittal Form 231.

1. Name Reservation Number

If you have decided to apply for a name reservation number, once it has been issued, place this number on line one.

2. The Agent

This is the person that is setting up your LLC. This individual's name, phone number, and address is required.

3. Principal Office Mailing Address

This is the location of the head office of the business; where the books and records are kept (LLC/Corporate Kit).

4. Registered Agent

The registered agent is the person or business that accepts service of process on behalf of your LLC. Their name and address is needed here.

5.   Name and address of each organizer

These are the members/owners of the LLC.

6.   Sign & date the Transmittal form 231

Naming Your LLC

The Secretary of State will not accept your LLC registration if the name you choose to operate under is the same as, or too similar to, a name already registered with them. This is covered in more detail within Chapter 6.

One of the first steps to creating a name for your LLC is to choose something that speaks about the nature of your company. The name should convey what it is your company sells or does. It should also be easy to pronounce, spell, and remember. Also, use creativity to come up with something unique. There are certain types of companies that will not necessarily have to follow these guidelines, but for most, this is the foundation of how to name your business.

There are professional companies out there that will create a company name for you using proven techniques, and will charge anywhere from $1000 to $30,000. If you have more time on your hands than money, sit down and brain storm until you come up with three or four names. After you have chosen a few names, your name search begins to see if any of the names are available for use. If you plan to stay local and only operate in the state of Georgia, there are only a few avenues to check. But, if your plan is to someday grow and expand outside the state, then there are many other paths to consider

when checking the availability of a chosen name.

For Example: Locally - you may use the phone book, the Secretary of State's website, Google, and online company directories.

Nationally - you may use the USPTO, Google, and other states' Secretary of State's websites.

This is not a fully exhaustive list of resources, so be creative. Remember to be safe; some companies choose not to incorporate or register their names. This is one of the reasons a name search is so critical.

Brand Names

What's in a name? A lot when it comes to small-business success. The right name can make your company the talk of the town. The wrong one can doom it to obscurity and failure. Ideally, your name should convey the expertise, value, and uniqueness of the product or service you have developed.

Some experts believe that the best names are abstract, a blank slate upon which to create an image. Others think that names should be informative so customers know immediately what your business is. Some believe that coined names are more memorable than names that use real words.

Name Availability

Trademark Law

To stay out of trouble, understand the basics of trademark law. Trademark law prevents a business from using a name that is likely to be confused with the name of a competing business. If you choose a business name that is too similar to a competitor's name, you might find yourself accused of violating the competitor's legal rights (called "trademark infringement" or "unfair competition"), and you could be forced to change your business's name and possibly pay monetarily for damages.

There's only one way to ensure that you won't violate someone else's trademark rights: do some digging to find out whether or not another business is already using a name that's identical or similar to the one you want to use.

Conducting a Name Search

Doing a name search for competing businesses is not always an easy task. While it would be nice to say that there is one place that you can visit to find out all the trademarked names in use, this is just not the truth. Under the laws that apply in the United States, a business can establish a trademark just by using the name. Because of this, you have to be clever in order to find all the registered and unregistered trademarks. Here are some suggestions:

1. Basic Screening Search

One of the best steps that you can take before jumping into an extensive search is to do a simple screening search to make sure that doing a more in-depth search is worth it.

A great way of doing a basic screening search is to plug the proposed name of your business into your favorite search engine and examine the results. By doing this, you can quickly and easily see whether someone is already using your name (or a very similar name) and is marketing a similar product. This is a quick way to determine your name's availability.

2. Look at the Fictitious Name Databases

The next step in your search should be to go through the fictitious name database that is kept by your county. Their database will contain all the registered fictitious business names, or "Doing Business As" (DBA) names, that are in use in your county.

This is a great next step to take after using a search engine. Many small businesses often register a fictitious business name without ever registering it as a trademark or putting it online. If you find a name that is the same as, or very similar to, the business name you have chosen, you should think twice about using it.

3. Databases Containing Names of Corporations, LLCs and Limited Partnerships

If you are planning on operating your business as an LLC, you need to check with Georgia's Secretary of State's filing office to see if the name that you are planning on using is already in use by another corporation or LLC. If the name you want has already been taken or another name that is very similar is already in use, you should go back to the drawing board and find a new business name that you like for your LLC.

4. Find Unregistered Business Names

ThomasNet (www.thomasnet.com) is another great place to find more unregistered trademarks. The Thomas Register is a cross-industry website that contains thousands of registered and unregistered trademarks and service marks. However, you should always keep in mind that there is no "one, complete source" that you can use to be sure that the business name you have chosen is available for use. It is always best to use more than one search method and be as thorough as possible.

Network Solutions is another great online tool that you can use to potentially find out the availability of your chosen business name. When you go to Network Solutions, you should plug in your desired business name, along with variations, and see if someone else has already reserved a domain name that includes your business name. If you find one, you may not be able to use your business name if the person that has reserved the domain name and is using it commercially.

5. Registered Trademarks

The last place that you should look when conducting your business name search is the database of registered trademarks that is kept by the federal government; however, this is not to say that you should not check it. Indeed, you should always check it, but only if you get to this last step. This database will include every trademark that has been registered by the United States Patent and Trademark Office (USPTO).

The first benefit that you will get from checking the database kept by the USPTO is that you will avoid claims of willful infringement of trademark rights. If you do not check the database and it turns out that you did infringe on someone's trademark rights by choosing your business name, you may face a lawsuit that contains a claim that you willfully infringed the trademark rights. If you are found to have willfully infringed another's trademark rights, you will face steeper penalties. Do yourself a favor and check the database—it really is quite easy and it can save you a whole lot of trouble.

The best way to search the USPTO's database is to use their online services. To do this, navigate to www.uspto.gov and then go to their "Trademark" section. Once there, you should see a link that says "Search." Simply click on this link and follow the helpful instructions that the website will lay out for you.

In addition to checking the federal database of registered trademarks, it is also a good idea to check your state's database of registered trademarks. It often happens that a small business will only need trademark protection within its home state. Because of this, many small businesses do not apply for federal trademark protection. If you do not check your state's database of registered trademarks, you again run the chance of being found liable for willful infringement. If you plan on doing business in other states, make sure you check their databases as well.

Name Infringement

Trademark infringement is when a trademark or service mark is used without the approval of the owner. Infringement automatically ensues upon use, especially in the case of attempting to manipulate a potential customer into believing that said product or service if from the trademark or service mark holder.

Once infringement has been committed, the trademark or service mark owner has the right to file a lawsuit against the infringer. This lawsuit aids the infringed to stop their mark from being used further by the infringer and allows the infringed to seek restitution.

Putting Your Search Results Together

So, you've finally finished your long search. If you are satisfied that the name you want to use is unique within your industry, then you should feel pretty safe about using it. However, if you have found evidence that there may be another business that is already using your business name, or a very similar name, then you should be careful. Depending on the circumstances, you may or may not be able to use the name you like.

Times When You Cannot Use a Similar or Identical Name

The first rule that you should always apply is that if the name you want is identical or similar to the name of a major player in your industry, stay away from it. Always remember that the larger the player is, the more likely it is that they have the resources and the reasons to come after you for trademark infringement.

In addition, if the name you have chosen is similar to, or the same as, a name that has been registered as a trademark (especially if it is a registered federal trademark), then stay away from it. This is true even if you have given the name of your business a different sound. A federal trademark gives the owner of the mark the right to use the trademarked name exclusively in every state in the country.

Times When It May Be OK to Use a Similar or Identical Name

There are a few situations in which it may be okay to use a name that is already in existence; just be sure that the name you are using is not famous! For example, if the name that you want to use is already being used by another company but the other company sells a drastically different product than you plan on selling, then you may be able to move forward with using your chosen name. In addition, geographic location is another factor that would determine if you can use an identical name. If the business that already has your name is far away and serves only a small population, this makes it safer for you to use the name.

The key question that you have to answer is "Is it likely that a customer would be confused about the origins of the product or service if I used the same, or a similar name?" For example, suppose that a business called "X-Y-Z" already exists and sells candy in Florida. If you want to open a business called "X-Y-Z" that repaired computers, it would be allowed in most cases because it is in a totally different industry.

Name Establishment

Registering Your Own Trademark

If you have found the name that you want and have started using it, you may want to think about using federal or state laws to protect it. Although it is not required that you register a trademark in order to "have" a trademark, it definitely helps if you ever have to enforce your trademark rights in court.

Name Reservation

In some cases, you may not be ready to form your LLC but would like to reserve your business name. This is when Georgia's LLC name reservation comes in handy. It allows you to reserve the business name you intend to use for a period of 30 days.

A name reservation may be filed online at http://www.sos.ga.gov/Corporations/. The application fee is $25. You may also download the Name Reservation Form and mail it in with the $25 fee. Remember, a name reservation is effective for 30 days or until the filing of your Articles of Organization is submitted, whichever is sooner. If the requested name is not available, a rejection notice will be sent (the $25 charge still applies) and will include instructions on submitting another request at no additional charge. Online name reservation requests are responded to within 24 hours of receipt. Mail-in name reservation requests are responded to within 36 hours of receipt.

If the name is available, the name will be reserved and a name reservation number will be sent to the applicant. Up to three name preferences may be submitted on the mail-in name reservation request form; if the first choice is available, it will be reserved, and the second and third choices will not be reviewed.

Name Availability Standards

Georgia law provides that a limited liability company's name must be distinguishable upon the records of the Secretary of State from the names of other LLCs filed with the Secretary of State. This is the standard in nearly 40 states and is a more "liberal" standard than "deceptively similar" or "likelihood of confusion."

Names are not distinguishable if the only difference is "a," "an," or "the" at the beginning of the name. "The Auto Store, Inc." is not distinguishable from "Auto Store, Inc."

Names are not distinguishable if the only difference is the entity type. "The Auto Store, LLC" is not distinguishable from "The Auto Store, Inc."

"&" and "and" do not make names distinguishable. "A & B, Inc." is not distinguishable from "A and B, Inc.", and "A and B, Inc." or "A & B, Inc." is not distinguishable from "AB, Inc." or "A.B., Inc."

Punctuation does not make names distinguishable. "A.B.C., Inc." is not distinguishable from "ABC, Inc."

Plural forms of the same word do not make names distinguishable.

A suffix added to a word or any other deviation from or derivative of the same word does not make names distinguishable.

Names are not distinguishable if the only difference is the abbreviation of a word in the name. "Ga. Auto Store, Inc." is not distinguishable from "Georgia Auto Store, Inc."

Names are not distinguishable if the only difference is a phonetic spelling of the same word. "Boyz, Inc." is not distinguishable from "Boys, Inc."

Restricted Word Usage

The use of some words is controlled by laws not administered by the Secretary of State. Customers who wish to form entities using these words should submit a letter of approval from the appropriate agency along with the filing of your Articles of Organization.

Entities that include the word "insurance," "assurance," or "surety" require approval from the Office of Commissioner of Insurance for filing.

Entities that include the words "bank," "credit union," or "trust" require approval from the Department of Banking and Finance for filing.

Entities that include the word "college" or "university" require approval from the Georgia Nonpublic Postsecondary Education Commission.

Certain "professional" terms require approval from the professional licensing board for filing.

Name Designators

All Limited Liability Companies must designate its status in one of many ways. (This is similar to a corporation adding Inc. to the end of its name to designate "incorporated.") The designators accepted by the state of Georgia are:

- Limited Liability Company
- Limited Company
- Ltd. Co.
- L.L.C
- LLC

Registered Agent

All limited liability companies in the state of Georgia are required by law to designate and maintain a registered agent. A registered agent is a business or an individual that is chosen by the LLC to receive service of process on its behalf. Service of process is the act of giving legal notice to a business entity of a claim against it such as litigation, legal proceedings, or any other official government correspondence. Also included in service of process are tax notifications and other types of compliance documents. Once a registered agent receives service of process, it is then their responsibility to forward these documents on to you, the LLC owner or manager.

To be considered a legitimate registered agent, the requirements are:

- The registered agent must be 18 years old or older.
- The registered agent has to have a registered office located in the jurisdiction that your LLC conducts business.
- The registered office must be a physical street address and not a P.O. Box or mailbox service.
- The registered agent must be available during normal business hours, normally Monday through Friday 8am-5pm, to receive service of process.

Represent Yourself

If you can fulfill these obligations, legally, you may serve as your own registered agent. The down side to this is that your personal information will be recorded on the Secretary of State's website and made available to anyone willing to search the database.

Anonymity

A lawyer or petitioner may attempt to use this information to pierce your corporate veil and seek you personally. Having a registered agent other than yourself will help to shield your personal information and the true owners of the LLC in some cases.

Be Aware of Penalties

Whatever route you take, be sure to assign and maintain a registered agent; failure to do so may result in the dissolution of your LLC which will stop you from being able to conduct business within the state. You will also be out of compliance and lose your state of "good standing," which in order to reestablish, will involve substantial fines and penalties that can last for a period of time before it can be reinstated.

Chapter 4

Taxes

One of the many advantages of LLC formation is the ability to choose a tax classification. As an LLC, the owners may decide upon which type of tax classification they want to be taxed under. They may be taxed as a sole proprietorship, partnership, S corporation, or C corporation depending on which suits their needs best.

Generally, the IRS classifies an LLC as a pass-through tax entity. Pass-through taxation is a tax classification in which the taxes of the business are "passed through" onto the members of the LLC rather than the business itself. The members then pay taxes on their portion of the profits or deduct their portion of the business losses. This process of taxation eliminates double taxation. Double taxation is when a corporation is taxed on its profits, and then the owners are taxed again on the dividends they receive from those same earnings.

Pass-through taxation is beneficial for most people who decide to form a LLC because the final tax burden may be less than it would be with the double taxation associated with corporations. Although the LLC does not file a tax return, the LLC does file an information return. The information return lists each member's share of the LLC's profits or losses, which the IRS then reviews to make sure each LLC member is reporting their income.

Federal Income Tax

If your LLC decides not to be taxed according to the default taxation method, it can choose to be taxed like an S corporation or a C corporation. For this to happen, the LLC must qualify under these conditions:

- Be a domestic corporation
- Have only allowable shareholders including individuals, certain trust, and estates and may not include partnerships, corporations, or non-resident alien shareholders
- Have no more than 100 shareholders
- Have one class of stock
- Not be an ineligible corporation, e.g., certain financial institutions, insurance companies, and domestic international sales corporations.

Also, if an LLC does not want to accept its default federal tax classification or wishes to change its classification, it must use Form 8832 (Entity Classification Election) to elect how it will be classified for federal tax purposes. Generally, an election specifying an LLC's classification cannot take effect more than 75 days prior to the date the election is filed, nor can it take effect later than 12 months after the date the election is filed. An LLC may be eligible for late election relief in certain circumstances.

Note: More information is listed in Form 8832's General Instructions.

Single member LLCs are taxed as sole proprietorship by default. The owner of the LLC reports profits or losses on a form 1040 schedule C, E, or F. Although some companies may choose to leave some profits in the bank at the end of the year, income tax must be paid on that money as well.

Multiple member LLCs are taxed as partnerships by default. Each LLC owner pays taxes on their share of the profits or deducts their share of the losses (distributive shares) on their personal income tax returns or the schedule E that will accompany their 1040 or 1065.

Most operating agreements provide that a member's distributive share is in proportion to his or her percentage interest in the business.

For Example: If Lynn owns 60% of the LLC and Rodrique owns the other 40%, Lynn will be entitled to 60% of the LLC's profits and losses and Rodrique will be entitled to 40%. If you would like to split up profits and losses in a way that is not proportionate to the members' percentage of interest in the business, you would need to set up a "special allocation." Special allocations within the operating agreement are covered in Chapter 5.

Self-Employment Tax

You are self-employed if you are an active member of a single member, or multiple member LLC. You must pay self-employment tax if you had net earnings from self-employment of $400 or more. Generally, the amount subject to self-employment tax is 92.35% of your net earnings from self-employment. Net earnings are calculated by subtracting ordinary and necessary trade or business expenses from the gross income you derived from your trade or business.

Note: You can be liable for paying self-employment tax even if you are currently receiving social security benefits.

The self-employment tax rate is a percentage set by law of your net earnings from self-employment. This rate consists of 10.4% for Social Security and 2.9% for Medicare for 2012. The maximum amount of net earnings subject to the social security tax is set by law and changes annually. All of your net earnings are subject to the Medicare tax.

However, members who are not active in the day-to-day operations of the LLC and are more-so investors are normally exempt from paying self-employment taxes on their share of profits. This has been the case for the last few years. There are also legal ways of not paying income taxes or self-employment taxes on most of the money that your company spends. You can deduct your legitimate business expenses from your business income, which will greatly reduce the profits you must report to the IRS.

State Income Tax

Being that LLCs are pass-through entities, they are not required to pay income tax to either the federal government or the State of Georgia. Instead, income from the business is distributed to individual LLC members, who then pay federal and state taxes on the amounts allocated to them.

While, by default, LLCs are classified for tax purposes as partnerships (or, for single member LLCs, "disregarded entities"), it is possible to elect to have your LLC classified as a corporation. In that case, the LLC would also be subject both to Georgia's 6% corporate income tax and the corporation net worth tax.

For Example: For the latest tax year, your multi-member LLC, which has the default tax classification of a partnership, had federal taxable income of $500,000. The $500,000 in net income will be divvied up between you and your fellow LLC members, and you will each pay tax on your respective portions on your respective individual Georgia tax returns. Rates will vary depending on overall taxable income.

Tax Identification Number

A Tax Identification Number (TIN) is also known as a federal Employer Identification Number, and is used to identify a business entity. It is the social security number of the business. Some banks require this along with your LLC control number. The IRS issues TIN's to individuals and companies; it can be done online, by phone, by fax, or by mail by filling out the Form SS-4. If done online, it can be issued and printed in as little as 15 minutes, and the best part is that it is free.

Tax Records

To incorporate another layer of protection within your LLC, you should hold on to your tax records for at least seven years. Tax returns and financial records show the legitimacy of your LLC, and it shows the courts that you are, in fact, operating as a real business. Bank statements and receipts are also a great way to provide evidence when needed. Financial documents such as these show that funds are not being commingled and will keep you safer from the alter ego doctrine used by the courts.

Chapter 5

Your Operating Agreement

An operating agreement is similar to the bylaws of a corporation or the partnership agreement of a partnership. It lays out the inner workings of your LLC such as holding meetings, voting, quorums, elections, and the powers of members and managers. Operating agreements are usually about 5 to 10 pages, but for a more elaborate LLC setup, operating agreements can be up to 30 pages. LLC operating agreements also cover financial dispersions and allotments. This document is second in importance to your articles of incorporation. Once this document is signed by the members, it acts as an official contract binding them to its terms.

Why is it so important?

The operating agreement protects your company's limited liability status. Without it, your LLC can look too much like a sole proprietorship or partnership, jeopardizing your personal liability. Operating agreements are a great way to annotate verbal agreements; even if members have orally agreed to certain terms, misunderstandings can still arise. It is always best to have the operational conditions of your business in writing so they can be referred to in the event of any conflict.

An operating agreement is not required by Georgia state law, but it would be unwise not to draft one on that account. If you choose not to create one for your LLC, Georgia's default rules will govern your LLC.

The state of Georgia outlines default rules within its statutes that apply to businesses that do not sign operating agreements. These rules are general in nature and don't necessarily pan out for the benefits of an LLC or its owners, and it is highly unlikely that the state's default laws will reflect what you and your members have in mind for your business.

Common issues concerning Georgia's default rules

Ownership – allows you to control who owns what and in what percentages.

Voting - allows you to control voting thresholds for certain actions such as how voting works, what actions need a certain level of approval, and even how much individual member's votes count.

Management - allows you to pass management on to appointed mangers instead of the members who own the LLC.

Allocations and Distributions - allows you to control when distributions are made by the company to members and also the order of the distributions. Also, it allows you to choose how the profits and losses of the LLC will be distributed among the members and in what order, if need be.

Dissolution – allows you to choose the event(s) that will dissolve the company.

Transfers of Ownership – allows you to control how the members approve transfers of the owner's membership interest to other members. Including this provision will also control the process.

Dispute Resolution - allows you to choose arbitration or mediation to settle disputes arising out of the agreement, which can be faster and cheaper than going to court.

Operating Agreement Provisions

Top 10 provisions to address

1. Member Managed vs. Manager Managed - If you do not specifically address whether the LLC is managed by the members or a manager, then by default, it is deemed managed by all the members. A member-managed entity means that each of the members has management rights. If this is not what you want, then it needs to be changed in the operating agreement. The simple solution is to state in the operating agreement that the entity is manager-managed and then expressly state the name(s) of the manager(s).

2. Having a Vote - Even when the LLC is manager-managed (by the majority member), the minority member(s) should try to negotiate to retain a right to veto financial and business decisions. The manager can still make day-to-day decisions, but major issues would require approval of a majority of the members. Important issues that typically require a majority approval are (a) a change in the business of the company; (b) a merger, sale of the business or significant assets, dissolution, bankruptcy, or reorganization; (c) transactions in excess of a certain amount; (d) amendments to the operating agreement; (e) incurring loans in excess of a defined amount; (f) entering into transactions with

the LLC members or officers; (g) redemption of membership interests; (h) employment or consulting agreements or increases in compensation of employees/consultants in excess of a certain amount; and (i) admission of new members.

3. Membership Percentage - If the intention is to allocate profits and losses in a way other than based on the percentage of interests a member owns in the LLC or to create separate classes of voting rights, then define the terms in the operating agreement. The operating agreement can vary the financial rights of members and create different classes of members, giving partners the flexibility to grant interests in the business that are not strictly defined by percentage of ownership.

4. Tax Provisions - The members can choose to include (or not to include) several significant tax provisions and elections affecting treatment of contributions of property, capital accounts, allocations and distributions, and other tax issues. These tax provisions should not be overlooked and should be discussed with an accountant.

5. Transfer of Membership Interests - The operating agreement should address restrictions on transfer of membership interests and will often include:

(a) A right of first refusal, giving other members the right to purchase offered interests pro-rata based on a member's percentage interest in the LLC. The right of first refusal prevents a member from selling their shares to a third party without giving the other members an opportunity to purchase the shares. The right is as much about a chance for members to increase their ownership as it is about excluding the transfer of interests to an undesirable new partner. If you include a right of first refusal, make sure the operating agreement clearly sets forth the procedure and time periods relating to exercise or waiver of the right.

(b) Co-sale rights give members the right to sell a percentage of their interests alongside a selling member so that a partner cannot liquidate its interests without giving other members an opportunity to sell some of their shares as well. As with the right of first refusal, be sure to define what is necessary to meet each member's obligations under the co-sale terms.

(c) An exception for transfers made to related parties since an operating agreement will generally require a member obtain approval for any transfer; however, you may not want your partner's son or husband as a partner, so before agreeing to such a provision, consider if transfer to a related partner is acceptable.

(d) Although technically not a transfer, a restriction on the pledge or encumbrance of a member's interests. The restriction prevents an involuntary transfer of a partner's interest to a lender or other lien holder that would otherwise occur if the member defaults on its obligations to the lien holder.

Note: The restrictions on transfer of a member's interests in an operating agreement boils down to the simple point that you entered into a business relationship with a partner (or partners), and you do not want a partner to hand over their interests to someone you do not know, or worse, do not like.

6. Buy/Sell Provision - Business partners can grow apart, their involvement or desire to be involved in the business can change, a partner can fail to meet expectations, or a number of other issues can arise in which a partner wants to leave the business or the other partners want a partner outside of the LLC. A Buy/Sell provision will avoid the disputes, distractions, and also legal costs that otherwise will inevitably arise during a business split. The Buy/Sell provision should set the terms under which the LLC or other partner can buyout a partner or a partner can require the LLC to buy its interests. The structure and mechanisms of a Buy/Sell provision are beyond the scope of this book, but the importance of clear terms as to when the provision can be invoked, how the selling interests to be valued, and the procedure for completing the transaction should be looked through with a knowledgeable.

7. Termination - Include the grounds for termination/dissolution of the LLC. If you are a minority or equal partner in the LLC, a court will not grant an application to dissolve the entity simply because you cannot "get along" with your business partner. In fact, a dysfunctional partnership that still manages to be a successful business generally will not be dissolved by judicial decree. Therefore, the operating agreement should clarify the circumstances under which dissolution of the LLC can occur including (without limitation) a defined time period, the occurrence of a certain event, or a vote of a majority of interests. Indeed, if you include a buy/sell provision (as discussed above) and one partner wants to end the business while another does not, then there will be an avenue to address the issue through a buyout.

8. Non-Compete - You may want to include a non-compete clause, and if so, it must comply with Georgia law in terms of geographic scope and time scope.

9. Dispute Resolution - The dispute resolution clause should set forth the body that will decide any dispute (e.g., a court or arbitration), the venue the matter will be tried (including not only the geographic location, but also the arbitral institution), and perhaps that the losing party will be responsible for the legal fees of the prevailing party.

10. Indemnification – This covers how the LLC will handle liabilities awarded against an LLC member or manager for something he or she did while acting in good faith.

The operating agreement is an extremely flexible document and is limited only by what is expressly prohibited or required by the Georgia Uniform Limited Liability Company Act (ULLCA). As such, there are a number of other financial and control terms that can be addressed in the operating agreement, so be sure to take advantage of this flexibility in structuring the rights and obligations of the members when drafting your operating agreement.

Operating Agreement Template

This operating agreement is made and entered into this 1st day of January, 2016, by and between the Members whose signatures appear on the signature page hereof.

Now, therefore, the parties agree as follows:

ARTICLE I

Definitions

Definitions used in this Operating Agreement shall have the respective meanings set forth below unless otherwise expressly provided:

1.1   "**Assigning Member**" means a Member who has assigned his or her Membership Interest.

1.2   "**Capital Accounts**," as of any given date, shall mean the Capital Contribution to the Company by a Member as adjusted up to such date. Upon a dissolution event, as determined in this Operating Agreement, capital will be determined as of the date of the dissolution event. If Capital Accounts are determined and maintained through the date of the dissolution event in accordance with the Capital Accounting rules of §1.704-1(b)(2)(iv) of the Income Tax Regulations, then capital determined as of the date of the dissolution event represents the Capital Account balances determined on that date.

1.3   "**Capital Contribution**" shall mean any contribution to the capital of the Company in cash or property by a Member whenever made.

1.4   "**Company**" means the Limited Liability Company, a Limited Liability Company created under the state of Georgia.

1.5   "**Distributable Cash**" shall mean all cash, revenues and funds received by the Company from Company operations, less the sum of the following to the extent paid or set aside by the Company: (i) all principal and interest payments on indebtedness of the Company and all other sums paid to lenders; (ii) all cash expenditures incurred in the normal operation of the Company's business; and (iii) such reserves as the – Members – Managers deem reasonably necessary for the proper operation of the Company's business.

1.6   "**Manager**" shall mean one or more Managers, elected by the Members. References to the Manager in the singular or as him, her, it, itself, or other like references shall also, where the context so requires, be deemed to include the plural or the masculine or feminine reference, as the case may be deemed to include the singular, or the masculine or feminine reference, as the case may be.

1.7   "**Majority Interest**" shall mean one or more interest of Members which in aggregate exceed fifty percent (50%) of all interest held in the Company.

1.8   "**Member**" shall mean each of the parties who execute this Operating Agreement or its counterpart as a Member and each of the parties who may hereafter become Members. A Person is a Member immediately upon the purchase or other acquisition by such Person of an interest, such Person shall have all the rights of a Member with respect to such purchased or otherwise acquired interest.

1.9   **"Membership Interest"** shall mean a Member's entire interest in the Company including such Member's economic and participatory interest.

1.10   **"Net Income"** means the net income of the Company computed in accordance with generally accepted accounting principles for federal income taxes under the Internal Revenue Code.

1.11   **"Net Profits"** and "Net Losses" shall mean the income, gain, loss, deductions and credits of the Company in the aggregate or separately stated, as appropriate, determined in accordance with generally accepted accounting principles employed under the cash method of accounting at the close of each fiscal year on the Company's tax return filed for federal income tax purposes.

1.12   **"Notice"**

    a.   A writing, delivered by first class mail, addressed to the last address known to the sender; or

    b.   A writing, delivered to the recipient in person.

1.13   **"Operating Agreement"** means this Limited Liability Company Operating Agreement.

1.14   **"Percentage Interest"** shall mean for any Member of the Company the percentage of ownership interest in the Company as set forth in this Operating Agreement, as may be changed from time to time by the unanimous vote of the Members or pursuant to the terms hereof.

1.15   **"Person"** means any individual or entity (partnership, joint venture, association, corporation, limited liability company, etc.) and the heirs, executors, administrators, legal representatives, successors, and assigns of such "Person" where the context so permits.

1.16   **"Property"** means anything of value.

1.17   **"Profits,"** upon a dissolution event as determined in this Operating Agreement, are determined and allocated based on any reasonable estimate of profits from the date of the dissolution event to the projected termination of the Company agreement that is in effect as of the date of the dissolution event.

1.18   **"State"** means the state in which the Limited Liability Company is formed, unless indicated otherwise.

ARTICLE II

NAME, PLACE, PURPOSE, AND DURATION

2.1   **Formation**.   The Parties have formed a Limited Liability Company pursuant to the Limited Liability Company Act of the state of Georgia (the act"). The Members have executed and caused to be filed the Articles of Organization as required under the Act.

2.2   **Name**.   The business of the Company shall be conducted under the name of the Limited Liability Company.

2.3   **Purpose**.   The business and purpose of the Company shall be to engage in any lawful act or activity in which a Company may engage.

2.4   **Place**.   The principle place of business of the Company shall be at _____, or at such other place as the Company Members may from time to time designate.

2.5   **Registered Office and Agent**.   The Company's initial registered office shall be at the office of its registered agent. The name of its initial registered agent shall be _____ located at _____ Riverdale, GA 30303. The registered office and registered agent may be changed by filing the address of the new registered office and/or the name of the new registered agent with the state pursuant to the Act.

2.6   **Term**.   The Limited Liability Company shall commence on the date first above written and shall continue for _____ years, unless sooner terminated by law or as herein provided.

2.7   **Amendments**. This Operating Agreement may be amended upon the unanimous vote of the Members. Each Member shall receive written Notice of any amendment within thirty 30 days following the amendment.

ARTICLE III

RIGHTS AND DUTIES OF MANAGERS

3.1   **Management**. The company shall be managed by the Managers, who shall be elected to direct, manage and control the business of the Company. Except for situations in which the approval of the Members is expressly required by this Operating Agreement or by non-waivable provisions of the Act, the Managers shall have full and complete authority, power and discretion to manage and control the business, affairs and properties of the Company, to make all decisions regarding those matters and to perform any and all other acts or activities customary or incident to the management of the Company's business.

3.2   **Number, Tenure, and Qualifications**.   The company shall initially have two (2) Managers (herein referred to as Managers) elected by the Members. A Manager's rights to act as a Manager shall terminate upon earlier of the sale by Manager of its entire Membership

Interest, or upon such Manager's resignation or termination by majority vote of the Members. Upon the resignation or termination of a Manager's right to act as a Manager, Members shall have the right to appoint a new Manager. The Managers and their addresses are as follows:

***John L. Doe 277 North University Avenue Riverdale, GA 30274

Joseph R. Williams 275 North University Avenue Riverdale, GA 30274***

[This provision can be customized several ways to give the members more control over the manager and the manager's appointment. However, giving the members more control may reduce the asset protection potential of the LLC. If the manager has more control and the members can't readily replace the manager, charging order protection will be increased. Customizing this provision will depend upon who the members are. For example, a husband and wife LLC will be written one way and a group of business "partners" who are unrelated will be written differently.]

3.3   **Duties and Authority of Managers**. Subject to the restrictions upon Managers under this Operating Agreement, Managers may exercise any powers necessary to provide all needed services with respect to the operation and management of the Company, including, without limitation, those referenced below:

a.   To obtain, sell, convey, mortgage, encumber, lease, exchange, pledge, partition, plat, subdivide, improve, repair, surrender, abandon or otherwise deal with or dispose of any and all real property of whatsoever character and where ever situated at such time or times an in such manner and upon such terms as the Managers deem expedient and proper. To give options therefore, to execute deeds, transfers, leases, pledges, mortgages, and other instruments of any kind. Any leases and contracts may extend beyond the term of the Company.

b.   To acquire any personal property for the use of the Company.

c.   To purchase, invest in, or otherwise acquire, and to retain, any and all stocks, bonds, notes, or other securities, or any variety of real or personal property, including stocks or interests in investment trusts and common trust funds operated and managed by a corporate trustee.

d.   To sell, transfer, assign, convey, lease, exchange, or otherwise dispose of any or all of the assets of the Company upon such terms and conditions as the Members deem advisable, including a deferred payment sale or exchange for other assets of any kind.

e.   To place record title to, or the right to use, Company assets in the name of a Manager or the name of the nominee for any purpose convenient or beneficial to the Company.

f.   To open and to close checking accounts, savings accounts and safety deposit boxes in banks or similar financial institutions, with or without indication of any fiduciary capacity. To deposit cash in and withdraw cash from such accounts and boxes, with or without any indication of any fiduciary capacity. To hold such accounts and securities in bearer form, or in the name of a Manager or in the name of a nominee, with or without indication of any fiduciary capacity.

g.   To borrow money upon terms acceptable to the Managers from any person or entity, to pledge or mortgage any property as security therefore and to renew any indebtedness incurred by the Managers.

h.   To employ brokers, consultants, attorneys, accountants, architects, engineers, property managers, leasing agents and other agents, persons or entities deemed appropriate to the conduct of the Company business, including, without limitation, any persons or entities related to a Manager or in which a Manager has an interest.

i.   To adjust, arbitrate, compromise, sue, defend, settle, abandon or otherwise deal with any and all claims in favor of or against the Company.

j.   To acquire and enter into any contract of insurance which the Managers deem necessary and proper for the protection of the Company, for the conservation of its assets, or for any purpose convenient of beneficial to the Company.

k.   To execute and deliver on behalf of the Company such documents or instruments as the Managers deem appropriate in the conduct of the Company business. No person, firm or corporation dealing with the company shall be required to inquire into the authority of the Managers to take any action or make any decisions.

l.   To make employment contracts, to pay pensions and to establish pension and other incentive plans of any or all of its employees.

m.   To establish, invest and maintain reserves for the benefit of the Company in such amounts as the Managers, in their sole discretion, shall determine, and to expend such reserves in such amounts and for such purposes as the Managers shall determine.

n.   Managers shall supervise the establishment and maintenance of all other records relative to the operation of the Company and cause to be provided to the Members such reports or summaries, including any internal audit reports prepared by Managers, with respect to such records, as Members with a Majority Interest may from time to time reasonably request.

o.   Managers shall prepare and file, or cause to be prepared and filed, all periodic reports and tax returns and perform other related administrative services.

p.   Managers shall establish and maintain all accounting, bookkeeping, cash management and financial systems and records relating to the Company in accordance with generally accepted accounting principles, standards and procedures. Managers shall prepare and furnish to the Members not later than fifteen (15) days after the close of each monthly accounting period monthly financial reports and statements which shall include an income statement for the month, a statement of cash flows for the month and a balance sheet dated as of the end of the month, and such other reports related to the Company as reasonably requested by a majority interest of the Members. Managers shall prepare and file, on the Company's behalf, all periodic reports and tax returns in respect of income of the Company attributable to the Members of the Company.

q.   Each Manager may authorize any persons to act for him by proxy on all matters in which Manager is entitled to participate. Every proxy shall be valid after the expiration of eleven (11) months from the date thereof unless otherwise provided in the proxy. Every proxy shall be revocable at the pleasure of such Manager executing it. A Manager may change its representative and appoint a successor representative at any time by giving written Notice of such change to the other Managers.

3.4   **Standard of Care**.   Each Manager shall perform its duties as a Manager in good faith, in a manner it reasonably believes to be in the best interests of the Company, and with such care as an ordinarily prudent person in a like position would use under similar circumstances. No Manager shall be liable to the Company or to any Member for any loss or damage shall have been the result of fraud, deceit, gross negligence, willful misconduct or a wrongful taking by the Manager.

3.5   **Managers Have No Exclusive Duty to Company**. No Manager shall be required to manage the Company as its sole and exclusive function and each Manager may have other business interest and engage in activities in addition to those relating to the Company. Neither the Company nor any Member shall have other investments or activities of any Managers or to the income or proceeds derived therefrom.

3.6   **Annual Report**.   Managers shall cause an annual report to be sent to the Members no later than ninety (90) days after the close of the fiscal year or the calendar year adopted by the Company. This annual report shall be sent at least 15 days before the annual meeting of Members to be held during the next fiscal year and in the manner specified in this Operating Agreement for giving Notice to the Members of the Company. The annual report shall contain a balance sheet as financial position for the fiscal year, accompanied by any report of independent accounts or, if there is no such report, the certificate of a Manager that the statements were prepared without audit from the books and records of Company.

Nothing herein shall be interpreted as prohibiting the Managers from issuing other reports to the Members.

3.7   **Indemnity of the Managers, Employees and Other Agents**.   The Company shall, to the maximum extent permitted, indemnify and make advances for expenses to each Manager, its employees, and other agents.

3.8   **Resignation**. Any Manager may resign at any time by giving written Notice to the Members of the Company. The resignation of any Manager shall take effect upon receipt of

Notice thereof or at such later date specified in such Notice; and, unless otherwise specified therein, the acceptance of such resignation shall not be necessary to make it effective. The resignation Manager who is also a Member shall not affect the Manager's rights as a Member and shall not constitute a withdrawal of a Member.

3.9   **Vacancies**.   Any vacancy occurring for any reason in the position of Managers of the Company may be filled by the affirmative vote of Members holding a Majority Interest. Any Manager's position to be filled by reason of an increase in the number of Managers shall be filled by election at a meeting of Members called for that purpose or by the Members' unanimous written consent. A Manager elected to fill a vacancy shall be elected for the unexpired term of his predecessor in office until the expiration of such term and until his successor shall be elected and qualified or until his earlier death, resignation or removal. A Manager chosen to fill a position resulting from an increase in the number of Managers shall hold office until his successor shall be elected and qualified, or until his earlier death, resignation or removal.

ARTICLE IV

RIGHTS AND OBLIGATIONS OF MEMBERS

4.1   **Names and Addresses**.   The names and addresses of the original Members are set forth in this operation Agreement. The names, addresses, and Percentage Interest of all Members shall be set forth in Schedule B. Upon the written request of any Member, the Managers shall provide a list showing the names, addresses and interests of all Members.

4.2   **Limitation of Liability**.   Each Member's liability shall be limited as set forth in this Operating Agreement, the Act and other applicable law.

4.3   **Company Debt Liability**.   A Member will not be personally liable for any debts or losses of the Company beyond his respective Capital Contributions, or as otherwise required by law.

4.4   **Member Approval**.   A vote of the Members holding a Majority Interest shall be required to approve the following:

a.   to approve all operating budgets and capital budgets for the Company;

b.   to approve all leases and other long term agreements between the Company and any other Person or entity;

c.   to approve all borrowing (whether pursuant to loan or credit agreements, notes, leases or otherwise) by the Company;

d.   to approve the sale, exchange, or other disposition of all, or substantially all, of the Company's assets which is to occur as part of a single transaction or plan;

e.   to direct Managers to take such other actions as Members with a Majority Interest deem, in their sole discretion, to be in the best interest of the Company and its Members; and

f.   to approve any major act or decision of the Company.

[The length of the list of items requiring member approval is an important issue in asset protection. Many statutes will not allow a unanimous vote, so the things voted on will determine how easy it is for someone with a charging order to control your LLC. The make-up of the members and their personal liability issues will play a big factor in determining what approvals the members should be given.]

4.5   **Company Books**.   Each Member shall have the right upon a reasonable written request, at a time during ordinary business hours, as reasonably determined by the Managers, to inspect and/ or copy (at the requesting Member's expense) the account, books, and other relevant Company documents. The Member shall maintain all such copied material as confidential.

4.6   **Priority and Return of Capital**.   Except as may be expressly provided herein, no Member shall have priority over any other Member, either as to the return of Capital Contributions or as to Net Profits, Net Losses or distributions; provided that this section shall not apply to loans which a Member has made to the Company.

4.7   **Liability of a Member to the Company**.   A Member who receives a distribution or the return in whole or in part of its contribution is liable to the Company only to the extent provided by the Act.

4.8   **Member Sale, Assignment or Exchange**.   A Member or a Member's legal representative has the power to sell, assign or exchange such Member's Membership Interest.

4.9   **Member Incompetence or Death**.   If a Member, who is an individual, dies or a court of competent jurisdiction, decrees him to be incompetent to manage his person or his property, such Member's executor, administrator, guardian, conservator, or other legal representative has:

a.   Power to exercise all of the rights of the Member for the purpose of settling or administering the Member's property;

b.   Power to assign the Member's interest in accordance with this Operating Agreement and the Articles of Organization for the Company;

4.10   **Member Loan**.   Any Member may loan money to the Company. Such a loan to the Company shall be at a reasonable rate of interest. Except as provided by law, the lending Member has the same rights and risks as any person making a loan to the Company who is not a Member.

ARTICLE V

MEETING OF MEMBERS

5.1   **Meetings**.   There shall be an annual meeting of Members to be held within ninety (90) days of the close of the Company's tax year.

5.2   **Special Meetings**.   Special meetings of the Members, for any purpose or purposes, may be requested by any Manager or by any Member or Members holding a Majority Interest in the Capital Account of the Company. Such requests shall be noticed as required herein and shall state the purpose of the purposed meeting. No special meeting of the Members shall be held within thirty (30) days of the previous special meeting without the unanimous consent of all Members and Managers.

5.3   **Place of Meetings**.   If a meeting is called, the place of meeting shall automatically be the principal place of business of the Company, unless the Manager and Members unanimously designate and give Notice to all Members and Managers of another place, either within or outside the state which is designated as the principal place of business for the Company.

5.4   **Notice of Meetings**.   Except as provided in the following paragraph, written Notice stating the place, day and hour of the meeting and the purpose or purposes for which the meeting is called shall be delivered not less than five nor more than thirty days before the date of the meeting, either personally or by mail, to each Member entitled to vote at such meeting. If mailed, such Notice shall be deemed to be delivered five (5) calendar days after being deposited in the United States mail, addressed to the Member at its address as it appears on the books of the Company, with postage thereon prepaid.

5.5   **Meeting of All Members**.   If all of the Members shall meet at any time or place, and consent to the holding of a meeting at such time and place, such meeting shall be valid without call or Notice, and at such meeting lawful action may be taken.

5.6   **Record Date**.   For the purpose of determining Members entitled to Notice, or to vote at any meeting, or Members entitled to receive payment of any distribution, or in order to make a determination of Members for any other purpose, the date on which Notice of the meeting is mailed or the date on which the resolution is declared, shall be the record date for such determination of Members. When a determination of Members entitled to vote at any meeting of Members has been made as provided herein, such determination shall apply to any adjournment thereof.

5.7   **Quorum**.   Members holding at least a Majority Interest, represented in person or by proxy, shall constitute a quorum at any meeting of Members. In the absence of a quorum at any such meeting, a majority of Members so represented may adjourn the meeting for a period not to exceed sixty (60) days. A notice of the adjourned meeting and the new fixed record date shall be given to each Member. At such adjourned meeting at which a quorum shall be present or represented, any business may be transacted which might have been transacted at the meeting as originally Noticed. The Members present at a duly organized meeting may continue to transact business until the adjournment, notwithstanding the withdrawal of members which would cause less than a quorum.

5.8 **Manner of Acting**.   If a quorum is present, the affirmative vote of Members holding a Majority Interest shall be considered the act of the Members, unless the vote of a greater of lesser proportion or number is otherwise required by the Act or by this Operating Agreement. Unless otherwise expressly provided herein or required under applicable law, only Members may vote or give consent upon any matter and their vote or consent, as the case may be, shall be counted in the determination of whether the matter was approved by the Members.

[or]

5.8 **Manner of Acting**.   If a quorum is present, the unanimous affirmative vote of Members holding an Interest shall be considered the act of the Members, unless the vote of a lesser proportion or number is otherwise required by the Act or by this Operating Agreement. Unless otherwise expressly provided herein or required under applicable law, only Members may vote or give consent upon any matter and their vote or consent, as the case may be, shall be counted in the determination of whether the matter was approved by the Members.

[The affirmative vote verses a unanimous vote of the members will influence the strength of the asset protection your LLC offers you. The statute will control, but the Manner of Acting clause should be customized to insure the maximum asset protection. The make-up of the members will also play a factor in drafting this clause.]

5.9 **Proxies**.   At any or all meetings, any Member may be represented in person or by proxy or proxies executed in writing by the Member or by a duly authorized attorney-in-fact. Such proxy shall be filed with the Managers of the Company before or at the time of the meeting. No proxy shall be valid after eleven (11) months from the date of its execution, unless otherwise provided in the proxy.

5.10 **Action by Members without a Meeting**.   Action required or permitted to be taken at a meeting may be taken without a meeting if the action is evidenced by one or more written consents describing the action taken, signed by each Member entitled to vote and delivered to the Managers of the Company for inclusion in the minutes or for filing with the Company records. Action taken under this Section is effective when all Members entitled to vote have signed the consent, unless the consent specifies a different effective date.

5.11 **Waiver of Notice**.   When any Notice is required to be given to any Member, a waiver thereof in writing signed by the person entitled to such Notice, whether before, at, or after the time stated therein, shall be equivalent to the giving of such Notice.

ARTICLE VI

CAPITAL CONTRIBUTIONS

6.1   **Initial Capital Contributions**.   The initial Capital Contributions of the Members in cash or in other assets is shown on the attached Schedule A. Based on the initial contributions, each original Member is shown as having the following Percentage Interest in the Company:

Members	Percentage Interest
John L. Doe	50%
Joseph R. Williams	50%

[Note: Some states will presume a majority interest upon foreclosure following a successful charging order attack if there is a 50%-50% split of interest. Although we have left the even split here for the sake of convenience, in reality you would usually want one party or the other to have a majority ownership interest unless foreclosure of a member's interest is not a risk in your state. The customized version of the LLC operating agreement will go through the issues and/ or see Georgia's state laws to find out more.]

6.2   **Allocation of Profit and Losses**.   All profits and losses of the Company and each item of income, gain, loss, deduction or credit entering into the computation thereof shall be allocated among the borne by the Members based on their Percentage Interest as shown on the table above.

[LLC distributions can be divided in a number of ways. For example, membership interests can be the determining factor. Charging order protection can be substantially weakened or strengthened by what this clause says. The decisions will rest on the trust the members have for each other and their individual exposures to liabilities.]

6.3   **Additional Capital Contributions**.   From time to time a Member may be required to make additional Capital Contributions as shall be determined reasonably necessary to meet the expenses and obligations of the Company. Except as provided below, such additional Capital Contributions shall not affect the Members' relative Percentage Interest. In the event that any Member fails to make its required Capital Contributions and thereby defaults, then the non-defaulting Members, on a pro rata basis, shall have the right, exercisable in their sole discretion, to make the Capital Contribution that the defaulting Member failed to make. In such event, the relative Percentage Interest of the Members shall be adjusted such that each contributing non-defaulting Member's Percentage Interest shall be increased, in respect to each defaulting Member's Percentage Interest.

6.4   **Return of Capital Contributions**.   Each Member irrevocably waives any statutory, equitable or other rights he or she may have to withdraw or demand the return of his or her Capital Contribution except as provided herein.

6.5   **No Interest on Capital Contributions**.   Capital Contributions to the Company shall not bear interest.

6.6   **Nature of Interest**.   All property owned by the Company, whether real or personal, tangible or intangible, shall be deemed to be owned by the Company as an entity. No Member shall have any direct ownership of any Company property.

6.7   **Limitation on Liability foe Members**.   No Member shall personally be liable for any of the debts or losses of the Company beyond such Member's capital account in the Company.

6.8   **Rights of Priority**.   Except as herein provided, the individual Members shall have no right to any priority over each other as to the return of Capital Contributions.

6.9   **Distribution of Profits**.   Distributions to the Members of net operating profits of the Company shall be made at least annually except that earnings may be retained by the Company and transferred to Company capital for the reasonable needs of the Company as determined in the sole discretion of the Managers. Distributions shall be made to the Members simultaneously.

6.10   **Federal Income Tax Treatment**.   The items of income, gain, loss, deduction or credit allocated among the Members shall, for federal income tax purposes, be deemed to retain their character as ordinary income, short-term or long-term capital gain or loss, depreciation, income or receipts entitled to tax-free or non-recognition treatment or other federal tax characterization in the hands of the Member to whom allocated in the same proportion as each Member's proportionate share.

[Not to be used if you are taxing your LLC as a C corporation.]

6.11   **Federal Income Tax Elections**.   The Company shall elect to treat as an expense, for federal tax purposes, all amounts incurred for taxes, interest, and other fees, charges and expenses to the extent that such expenditures are permitted or required to be currently deductible expenses in accordance with applicable laws and regulations. The Members agree that no election shall be made under Section 761 of the Internal Revenue Code of 1954, as amended, to exclude the Company from application of any provisions of Subchapter K, Chapter 1, thereof. It is the intent of the Members to have the Company treated as an S Corporation for tax purposes to the fullest extent possible.

[This provision is for LLCs taxed as a Subchapter S corporation.]

ARTICLE VII

CAPITAL ACCOUNTS

7.1   **Separate Capital Accounts**. A separate Capital Account will be maintained for each Member. The initial balance of the Capital Account of each Member shall be that Member's proportionate share of the total Capital Contributions. The Capital Account of each Member:

a.   Shall be increased at the end of each taxable year by the amount of the Company's income and gain allocated to the Member for the taxable year,

b.   Shall be decreased at the end of each taxable year by the amount of the Company's deductions and losses allocated to the Member for that taxable year, and

c.   Shall be decreased at the time of any distributions by the amount of that distribution.

7.2   **Determination of Profits and Losses**.   The profits and losses of the Company shall be the Net Profits or Net Losses of the Company for federal income tax purposes as determined by the Company's accountant in accordance with the accounting principles employed by the Company for federal tax purposes.

7.3   **Liquidation**.   Upon liquidation of the Company, liquidating distributions will be made in accordance with the Members' respective Percentage Interests. A member shall not receive any distribution until all liabilities of the Company have been paid or there remains property of the Company sufficient to pay them.

The Company may offset damages for breach of this Operating Agreement by a Member whose interest is liquidated (either upon the withdrawal of the Member or the liquidation of the Company) against the amount otherwise distributable to such Member.

7.4   **Deficit Balance**.   No Member shall have any liability to restore all or any portion of a deficit balance in such Members' Capital Account.

7.5   **Withdrawal or Reduction of Members' Contribution to Capital**. No Member shall be entitled to withdraw or borrow any amount from his Capital Account without the consent of the Managers. A Member has only the right to demand and receive cash in return for its Capital Contribution.

ARTICLE VIII

BOOKS, RECORDS AND ACCOUTING

8.1   **Accounting Year.**   The Company's fiscal year shall commence on January 1st of each year and shall end on December 31st of each year.

8.2   **Method of Accounting.**   The Company shall use a cash basis method of accounting and maintain its accounting records in accordance with generally accepted accounting principles employed for federal income tax purposes.

8.3   **Books and Records.** The Managers shall maintain the books and records of the Company at the principal places of business. Each Member shall have access to such books and records and shall be entitled to examine them at any time during the Company's ordinary business hours. Such records include:

   a.   A current list in alphabetical order if the full name and last known business street address of each member;
   b.   A copy of the Articles of Organization and all Certificates of Amendments to them;
   c.   A copy of the Company's federal, state, and local income tax returns ad reports, for the three most recent years; and
   d.   A copy of the Company's Operating Agreement.

8.4   **Annual Statements.**   At the end of the year, the Managers shall cause the Company's accountant to prepare a balance sheet setting forth the financial position of the Company and a statement of operations (income and expenses) for that year. The Managers shall provide to each Member a report of the financial position and operations of the Company no later than ninety (90) days from the end of the fiscal year. The report shall contain a financial report showing the Company's profit or loss for the year and the allocation thereof among the Members, together with the applicable tax information of the Company. Copies of all income tax returns filed by the Company shall be furnished to all Members upon request.

8.5   **Member Objections.** Each Member shall be deemed to have waived all objections to any transactions or other facts about the operation of the Company disclosed in the balance sheet, statement of operations and income tax returns unless he or she shall have notified the Manager in writing of his or her objections within sixty (60) days of the date on which each such documents is mailed.

ARTICLE IX

DISSOLUTION OR TERMINATION OF THE COMPANY

9.1   **Dissolution**.   The Company shall be dissolved upon the occurrence of any of the following events:

    a.   When the period fixed for the duration of the Company shall expire;
    b.   By the unanimous written agreement of all Members;
    c.   The occurrence of an event which makes it unlawful for Company business to be continued
    d.   The sale or disposition of all or substantially all of the Company assets; or
    e.   The Company is no longer able to engage in the purpose for which it was created.

9.2   **Winding Up, Liquidation and Distribution of Assets**.   Upon dissolution, an accounting shall be made by the Company's independent accountants or the accounts of the Company and of the Company's assets, liabilities, and operations, from the date of the last previous accounting until the date of dissolution. The Managers shall immediately proceed to wind up the affairs of the Company, complying with all requirements of applicable law pertaining to the winding up of the affairs of final distributions of its assets. The Managers shall:

    a.   Sell or otherwise liquidate all of the Company's assets as promptly as practicable (except to the extent the Managers may determine to distribute any assets to the Members in kind).
    b.   Allocate any profit of loss resulting from such sales to the Member's Capital Accounts as described herein. If there is a deficit in a Capital Account, no Member shall have any liability to restore all or any portion of a deficit balance in such Member's Capital Account.
    c.   Discharge all liabilities of the Company, including liabilities to Members who are creditors, to the extent otherwise permitted by law, other than liabilities to Members for distributions, and establish such reserves as may be reasonably necessary to provide for contingent liabilities of the Company (for purposes of determining the Capital Accounts of the Members, the amounts of such reserves shall be deemed to be an expense of the Company).
    d.   Distribute the remaining assets to the Members in accordance with their respective Percentage Interests. Members shall look solely to assets of the Company for the return of its Capital Contribution. If the Company property remaining after the payment or discharge of the debts and liabilities of the Company is insufficient to return the cash contribution of one or more Members, such Members shall have no recourse against any other Member, except as otherwise provided by law.

9.3   **Company Terminated**.   Upon completion of the winding up, liquidation and distribution of the assets, the Company shall be deemed terminated.

ARTICLE X

MISCELLANEOUS PROVISONS

10.1   **Amendments**. This Operating Agreement may not be amended except in writing by the affirmative vote of Members holding a Majority Interest. Any amendment changing the Percentage Interest of the Members requires the unanimous vote of the Members.

[The ability to amend an LLC operating agreement seems like a straight forward issue. However, this is one of the most important issues in determining asset protection. If you are in trouble with a creditor, one of the most important things you can do is amend the operating agreement. On the other hand, if a creditor is successful in their charging order bid, their ability to amend could cost you your entire LLC. There are several ways to word this provision, based upon a number of factors.]

10.2   **Execution of Additional Instruments**.   Each Member hereby agrees to execute such other and further statements of interest and holding, designations and other instruments necessary to comply with any laws, rules or regulation.

10.3   **Construction**. Whenever the singular number is used in this Operating Agreement and when required by the context, the same shall include the plural and vice versa, and the masculine gender shall include the feminine and neuter genders and vice versa.

10.4   **Headings**.   The heading in the Operating Agreement are inserted for convenience only and are in no way intended to describe, interpret, define, or limit the scope, extent or intent of this Operating Agreement of any provision hereof.

10.5   **Waivers**.   The failure of any party to seek redress for default of or to insist upon the strict performance of any covenant or condition of this Operating Agreement shall not prevent a subsequent act, which would have originally constituted a default, from having the effect of an original default.

10.6   **Rights and Remedies Cumulative**. The rights and remedies provided by this Operating Agreement are cumulative and the use of any one right or remedy by any party shall not preclude or waive the right to use any other remedy. Said rights and remedies are given in addition to any other legal rights the parties may have.

10.7   **Severability**.   If any provisions of this Operating Agreement or the application thereof to any person or circumstance shall be invalid, illegal or unenforceable to any extent, the remainder of this Operating Agreement and the application thereof shall not be affected and shall be enforceable to the fullest extent permitted by law.

10.8   **Heirs, Successors and Assigns**.   Each and all of the covenants, term, provisions and agreements herein contained shall be binding upon and inure to the benefit of the parties hereto and, to the extent permitted by this Operating Agreement, their respective heirs, legal representatives, successors and assigns.

10.9 **Creditors**.   None of the provisions of the Operating Agreement shall be for the benefit of or enforceable by any creditors of the Company.

10.10 **Counterparts**. This Operating Agreement may be executed in counterparts, each of which shall be deemed an original but all of which shall be constitute one and the same instrument.

10.11 **Company Agrees to Be Bound**.   The Limited Liability Company hereby accepts the terms of the operating agreement and agrees to be bound thereby.

IN WITNESS WHEREOF, the Undersigned hereby execute this Operating Agreement the ***1st day of January, 2016***.

MANAGER: MEMBERS:

_____   _____

John L. Doe   John L. Doe

_____   _____

Joseph R. Williams   Joseph R. Williams

SCHEDULE "A"

The below listed property is hereby transferred, conveyed, assigned ad delivered to the Limited Liability Company, subject to the terms and conditions of the Limited Liability Company Operating Agreement dated the ***1st of January, 2016***, and signed by the Undersigned as Grantors and Managers:

1. All present and future interest of the Undersigned in the following real estate, where ever located, together with all present and future improvements, thereon, and all present and future water and water rights thereunto belonging and also including all present and all future property located thereon:

2. The following accounts in the following institutions together with all future additions, interest or accumulation therein and also including all new accounts and the

accumulation and the future additions of interest or the accumulation in any and all other financial institution in which new accounts are opened in the future:

3. The following securities, stocks, and other investments:
4. The following other non-real estate assets:

Dated this the ***1st day of January, 2016***

_____

John L. Doe, Manager

_____

Joseph R. Williams, Manager

STATE OF ***GEORGIA***)

COUNTY OF ***CLAYTON***)

   BEFORE ME, the undersigned, a Notary Public in and for said County and State, personally appeared ***John L. Doe and Joseph R. Williams***, personally known to me or proved to me on the basis of satisfactory evidence to be the persons whose names are subscribed to the within instrument and acknowledged to me the they executed the same in their authorized capacities, and that, by their signature on the instrument, the persons executed the instrument.

_____

NOTARY PUBLIC

SCHEDULE "B"

This Schedule B is attached to the Limited Liability Company Operating Agreement, dated the ***1st day of January, 2016***.

The following is a list of the names, addresses, and Percentage Interests of the Members of the Company.

***John L. Doe   50%

277 North University Avenue

Riverdale, GA 30274

Joseph R. Williams   50%

275 North University Avenue

Riverdale, GA 30274***

Memorandum of Items to Review

The following is a list to review periodically and be aware of concerning your LLC.

ITEM	INSTRUCTIONS
1. Tax Return	An LLC can be a separate entity for tax purposes; therefore, it may file its own yearly 1065 tax return with K-1 forms. [Partnership taxation]
2. Financial Statements	Financial statements for the LLC Should be prepared annually
3. Meetings	There should be an LLC meeting at least annually to review the records and business activities of the LLC
4. Gifting	Gifting of interests in the LLC can be an excellent estate and income tax planning move. We recommend that you meet with your LLC attorney of tax expert yearly for proper gifting of interests in your LLC to others.
5. Accountant	Please advise your accountant or tax preparer immediately of the creation of your LLC if there are any questions or needed clarification. Also, be sure to apply for your Federal LLC identification number (SS-4).
6. Amended Certificate	An Amended Certificate of LLC must be filed when certain changes occur such as the addition or removal of a Member.

Chapter 6

Form an LLC Step by Step

Step 1. Conduct a name search

The first step to conducting a name search is to create the perfect name. (Download the free E-book *How to Create the Perfect Business Name* at www.georgiallcdirect.com/perfectname.) To conduct a proper name search, you should come up with at least three names to choose from in case your first choice is not available. Once you have a few strong business names, it's time to get started. The next, and simplest, step to take when conducting a name search is to Google the names. Google has an extensive bank of reliable information about new and established businesses. Just type the proposed business name in the search bar and examine the results. Be sure to check slight variations for potential ways the name could be spelled. Google is the most comprehensive search engine, but Bing, Yahoo, or any of the other top five search engines will work just as well. If everything is clear and the name does not appear to be taken, you are free to move on to the next phase. If this is not the case, continue this process until you find a name you can use.

Now, take that name and add a ".com" after it. The key to choosing the best name is to own all rights to the name you have created. In order to do this, you should create a domain name based on your business's name. In this new information era, when people hear about a new company and are interested in learning more about it, they tend to type that company's name into their address bar, followed by ".com," to see what they can find. Once your company begins to gain popularity, you'll want potential customers to find you the same way. So remember "to own the domain is to own the name." If the domain is available, chances are the name is available also, but don't stop there.

The next step is to search your local phonebook and online directories. A few common online directories include Yelp, Manta, DexKnows, and MerchantCircle. New companies are being created every day, many of which are sole proprietorships. Phonebooks and online directories allow sole proprietors to list their company names without any formal documentation, so don't be discouraged if you spot the name that you desire to use one of these two ways; just be aware of that company's existence. There is a possibility that the company could be out of business or has never formally established a legal presence.

Next, you'll want to search the online database of the Secretary of State's website. In order to do an in-depth search, an account may be required. Don't worry, setting up an account is still free for now. Visit Georgia's Secretary of State's website at http://sos.ga.gov/ and find the section labeled "Business Search." If you have searched the full company name and found that no one has used the name, a useful tip is to search one word at a time. For example, suppose you're doing a name search on the name "Great Popcorn Carnival." After searching for "Great Popcorn Carnival," you would then search for just the word "Great" and view all the business names with "Great" listed within them to find a similarity. Next, try "Popcorn," and so on. Continue this process until you've searched each part of the name individually. This process can be time-consuming, but the effort is well worth it. After completing this phase, you may want to pay to reserve your business name to protect it on a state level. They will hold your name for a maximum of thirty days. If you have not finalized the name by the time the 30 days have passed, you can pay an additional fee to reserve the business name again.

If you only plan to conduct business within your current state and do not plan to expand, you can stop your search at the Secretary of State's office. Otherwise, you will need to conduct a more in-depth search. In this case, the final step is to conduct a name search within the database of the United States Patent and Trademark Office (USPTO). Names on the USPTO are protected on a national level. The USPTO uses the Trademark Electronic Search System (TESS). This program is very technical and there are no guides on how to proficiently use the system, but there are lawyers and other professionals that have mastered the process. If your budget doesn't allow for professional help, you can always do it yourself. It may be difficult, but it is doable.

That's all you need to know in order to conduct a business name search!

Step 2. Determine Company Organizer Name and Address

Decide who will be listed as the company's Organizer. Remember the Organizer is the person(s) or entity that signs the LLC's formation application. By signing the Articles of Organization, the Organizers affirm that the information contained in the application is true. The signature also confirms that the

applicant will pursue business activities allowed by the state's LLC rules. Individuals acting as Organizers sign and print their names, and they also provide their addresses. If the Organizer is a business entity, they must provide the entity's exact name and the name and title of the individual signing on its behalf. Using someone other than one of the members of the LLC can add great anonymity to protect your private information from the public, being that all information submitted to the Secretary of State is in the public domain. Also, you will not have to worry about nearly as much junk mail from business-to-business type solicitors.

Step 3. Establish Principal Office Mailing Address

Your principal office mailing address is typically your actual place of business. In the event that you may be working from a home office and would prefer for this information to be anonymous, this address can be a P.O. Box. The purpose of having this address on file is just for state records; no correspondence goes out to this address.

Step 4. Choose a Registered Agent

When forming an LLC, you must identify the person or company who will act as the registered agent. Your registered agent will receive all legal documents on behalf of your company and forward them to you. This includes service of process as well as annual reports and tax documents. The registered agent's address should be a business address where mail is regularly received and reviewed, even when the individual named as the registered agent is on vacation, ill, or otherwise unavailable. The registered agent's address must be in the state where you are forming the LLC and must be a physical street address, rather than a box number.

Step 5. Elect Members

It's very important to decide who will be active owners and who will be passive investors/owners. Members of an LLC usually play a vital role in the day-to-day operations of the LLC. In some cases, LLCs have owners that participate only in the net gain or losses of the LLC. If the members are considered passive investors, these members do not have to be listed within the original filing of the LLC, but can be written in later in the operating agreement. Once everyone has a firm grasp on which members are active and which are passive, then you can elect the members by listing them with the Secretary of State on the Transmittal Form 231.

Step 6. File Articles of Organization

Once the Transmittal Form 231 is complete, there are several different ways to file it with the Secretary of State.

1. Online
2. Snail mail
3. In person

The quickest, most convenient, way is to file online. To do this, access the Secretary of State's website at www. ecorp.sos.ga.gov, click "Online services," and set-up an account. Once you are logged in on the dashboard, click on the "Create or Register a Business" tab. After you have gotten in to the application, there will be a few self-explanatory questions to answer concerning your business.

The last steps in this process are to review your application and verify that all questions have been answered correctly, pay the fee, and submit it.

To file in person, first obtain the required documents, either by accessing them online

and printing them; calling (404) 656-2817 and requesting that copies be sent to you; or by going to the office located at 2 MLK Jr. Dr. Suite 313, Floyd West Tower Atlanta, GA 30334 and picking up a copy. Once the documents are filled out completely, take the documents to 2 MLK Jr. Dr. Suite 313, Floyd West Tower Atlanta, GA 30334. One of the receptionists will timestamp your application and accept your payment. Cash is not accepted, but all other forms of payment are.

For snail mail, write a check or money order payable to the Secretary of State Corporations Division to 2 MLK Jr. Dr. Suite 313, Floyd West Tower Atlanta, GA 30334-1530. Include a self-addressed, postage-paid, manila envelope.

Step 7. Apply for an Employer Identification Number

Remember, you need an Employer Identification Number (EIN) to open a business account. Currently there is no charge to file for and obtain an EIN. To apply for an EIN, you must first go to www.irs.gov. Once there, under the "Tools" category, click "Apply for an Employer ID Number." Next, click on "Apply Online Now." Lastly, click "Begin Application" and fill out the information using the instructions listed on the web page.

Step 8. Decide Tax Filing Status and Apply

As we discussed earlier, an LLC can choose to be taxed as a sole proprietorship or a partnership depending on the number of members, or it may elect to be taxed as an S corporation or a C corporation. After you have consulted a tax professional and decided which tax filing status most benefits you and your LLC, you can notify the IRS.

If your LLC has only one owner, then there is nothing extra that you must do to be considered sole proprietorship filing status. Likewise, if your LLC has only two owners, there is nothing extra that you must do to be considered partnership filing status. Otherwise, you will have to file Form 2553 to elect to be taxed as an S corporation. To elect to be taxed as a C corporation, you must file Form 8832. The easiest way to find these forms is to go to the IRS website and search either "Form 2553" or "Form 8832."

Step 9. Establish Capital Contributions

A capital contribution is when a member transfers money, property, or services to an LLC in exchange for membership interest. The LLC then uses the funds invested to capitalize the company. Adequate capitalization provides enough money for a business to cover its financial obligations and acquire assets. The specific amount of money needed to capitalize a business adequately differs with each business.

If the LLC pulls in enough money to pay its bills and acquire assets, the owners have nothing to worry about. Otherwise, the company must withdraw the funds needed from the capital contributions to pay for its obligations. If the LLC is undercapitalized, then the owners risk their limited liability protection.

For Example: if an LLC runs out of money; closes its doors; and declares bankruptcy, the courts would then have to decide upon the amount of money that specific company would have needed to properly fund the venture. If the courts decide a proper amount was $100,000 and the owners only contributed $10,000, that's an automatic disqualification; the corporate veil will be pierced and the owners' personal assets will be attacked.

Step 10. Open Business Bank Account

Limited liability protection is only possible if LLC owners take certain precautions; otherwise, all that protection goes out the window. Creditors and plaintiffs are constantly looking for ways to bypass the business entity and attack the business owners' personal assets. Always separate your personal endeavors from your company's. One way to do that is to by opening a business account.

Commingling funds automatically negates your limited liability protection. Commingling is when an individual mixes their personal funds with that of their business funds. So, if you're using the same bank account for your personal and business needs, you're commingling. If you're paying your gym membership fees with a business check, you're commingling. And the most common, if you're transferring money between your business and personal account without properly documenting each transaction, you're commingling.

Step 11. Draft an Operating Agreement

As you learned in chapter five, operating agreements are a great way to annotate verbal agreements; even if members have orally agreed to certain terms, misunderstandings can still arise. It is always best to have the operational conditions of your business in writing so they can be referred to in the event of any conflict. The resources within this book will help you draft your own operating agreement. If you need a more comprehensive draft, feel free to contact your local attorney.

Step 12. Issue Membership Interest Certificates

As you now know, membership interests of an LLC are evidence of ownership and sometimes, control of the company. It is a good idea to issue membership certificates to those who have ownership of interest in your LLC.

In issuing membership certificates, first get a blank stock or certificate form and a ledger. You can find these documents at most office supply stores. Once you have obtained your membership ledgers and membership certificates, you will need to fill them out.

This is similar to getting a stock ledger and stock certificates to issue in a corporation. To do this, you must put your name at the side or on the top of the paper, depending on the style of certificate. Then, you will put the value of the certificate in the number of membership interests. You could have the membership interests worded as a percentage of the LLC or as a specific number of membership interests. Next, annotate this same information within the ledger. Repeat this process for each owner.

Membership certificates are usually filled out in the name of the individual(s) that owns an interest in the LLC. That's okay, but it is not fully protected that way; being that the certificate is an asset, just like a stock certificate is an asset, and you should protect it. When issuing membership certificates, you should put the "ownership" of your LLC, which is probably your most valuable asset (your company), in the name of your living revocable trust. That way your company won't be caught in a probate proceeding if you die.

Step 13. Obtain Business Licenses and Permits

In some industries, it is required that the owner obtain a license in order to start their business. Professional licensing is monitored by the Professional Licensing Boards Division of the Secretary of State's office. If your company operates in a field such as Athletic Training, Chiropractic Examination, Optometry, or Cosmetology, then you must apply to the proper department for your industry.

If your industry is not governed by a professional licensing board, the next step is to contact your county's Business License Division. This is the place for all other licenses and permits, unless your company operates solely online. In the case of your company operating mostly or solely online, contact a local lawyer for more detailed information. In some cases, you will save more money by seeking professional help in this area.

Step 14. Hold Organizational Meeting

Organizational meetings are held to appoint officers, elect or appoint directors, issue membership interest, approve operating agreements, set up minute books, etc.

Other issues that may be addressed:

- Setting a budget
- Choosing a bank
- Designating key professional service providers, such as accountants and attorneys
- Resolving to obtain tax-exempt status
- Purchasing insurance

You do not need to make a regulatory filing for your organizational meeting minutes with the state. The organizational meeting minutes are for your own records. The organizational meeting minutes should be stored in your corporate minute books (LLC Kit) for safekeeping.

Step 15. Log Minutes of the Meetings

An LLC's minutes of meetings are where the results of votes, records of resolutions, and summaries of proposed ideas for the company are kept. A director, usually the secretary, should keep a record of what went on at the meeting. The minutes are not required to contain any specialized language, but should accurately reflect what was said and done at the meeting.

Information to include in the minutes are the time, location, and members present at the meeting; any pertinent company issues raised and a summary of some of the key issues raised in response to that issue; the results of any votes conducted, including who voted for or against; and any other important information about what happened at the meeting.

A good rule of thumb is to include all information that a director who was unable to attend the meeting would need to know. Minutes should be filed with all other important company documents.

Step 16. Compile a Company Records Book

The Company Records Book is better known as the LLC Kit. It holds the records an LLC needs to keep in order to show that it is functioning in the manner required by the Internal Revenue Service and the laws of the state in which the business was formed. Company records are needed to show that the corporation is functioning appropriately and show that it is a separate entity in order to maintain its liability protection.

Some documents that should be kept within it are:

- Formation documents
- Compliance documents
- IRS documents
- Blank Membership Interest certificates
- Operating Agreement
- Ledger
- Minutes of meetings
- Any other key documents that you deem important to your business

These are all the steps that you need to follow to form your LLC and be ready for business. Follow these sixteen steps, and you will have an LLC.

Chapter 7

Compliance

Many small business owners recognize the benefits of incorporating or forming a Limited Liability Company (LLC) for their business. Among the advantages, limiting personal liability is key. That is, if your company happens to be sued, the company (and not you personally) is responsible for its debts and liabilities.

While incorporating a business or forming an LLC is a critical step, your work isn't done after submitting those initial forms. You have got to make sure that your LLC remains in good standing, because if your business happens to get sued, the plaintiff may attempt to show that you have not complied with your state's compliance laws on a yearly basis to keep your LLC in compliance. If they are successful, your corporate veil is pierced and the plaintiff can seek recovery against your personal assets.

Maintain Your LLC

Maintaining an LLC is an ongoing process. Here is what you need to know to make sure your LLC stays in compliance for years to come...

1. File your annual reports: Georgia requires an annual report filing by April 1st of each year. Missing this deadline can result in penalties and late fees—in the worst-case scenario, your company can be subject to suspension or dissolution.

2. Keep up to date with your corporate minutes and resolutions: For extra protection, you will need to record Minutes of Meetings whenever a corporate meeting is held. You will need to note every action or decision for the company in these minutes. Minutes content typically includes: time and place of meeting, attendance and chair of the meeting, any actions (purchases, elections, etc.), the signature of the recorder, and the date. Keeping these minutes, even if you are a sole owner of your LLC, can help you stand up in court and protect your limited liability shield if needed.

3. Record any changes to your LLC by filing "Articles of Amendment": Did you change your address? Drop the ".com" from your official company name (or implement any other name change)? Authorize more shares? Did a board member or director leave the business? Any time you make a change to your LLC, you can basically count on having to file an official notification (referred to as an "Amendment") with your state. In many states, these are called Articles of Amendment.

4. Make sure you're legal when conducting business out of state: If you'll be conducting business in a state other than the state where you formed your LLC, you will need to obtain authority or permission to do so. In most cases, this entails qualifying as a Foreign LLC within the state that you will be doing business within. Specific licenses and permits may also be required for certain types of businesses as well.

5. Do not commingle your personal and business finances: Small business owners often invest so much of their personal time, work, and money in their company that their personal and business finances become indistinguishable; however, you should maintain separate checking and credit card accounts for business and personal use. This simple step will also help you during tax time, as all your income and expenses related to the business will be in one place.

6. File a "Doing Business As" for any name variations: For an LLC, DBAs must be filed under the LLC whenever you conduct business using a name that is different than your LLC name; i.e., if SmallBizness, Inc. is doing business as SmallBizness.com or SmallBizness, then a DBA needs to be filed by SmallBizness, Inc. doing business as SmallBizness.com or SmallBizness. Depending on where you live, DBAs are filed at the county level.

7. Don't forget to close an inactive business by dissolving your LLC: Maybe you moved your focus from an LLC or corporation you formed years ago. You have not promoted your business and it has no revenue or customers. You still need to file a formal termination (called "Articles of Dissolution" or "Certificate of Termination") for that LLC. Otherwise, you can still be charged fees associated with the business. You will still be expected

to file an annual report (where applicable). You will also still be required to submit tax returns to the IRS and state.

As a small business owner, your schedule is consistently busy, but be sure to set aside some time to address your administrative and legal obligations. Know your deadlines and get your paperwork in on time. It's a relatively easy task and will help ensure your LLC remains in compliance and continues to shield your personal assets.

Understand the Consequences of Noncompliance

Business owners must comply with ongoing government rules and regulations after forming an LLC. You should understand the potential consequences of noncompliance to your business:

When an LLC fails to meet government obligations, the state may revoke the company's good standing, levy penalties, or even dissolve the company.

Additionally, when a business owner fails to follow the steps required to maintain their limited liability protection, the owner's personal assets will no longer be protected from lawsuits.

Chapter 8

LLC Kit

What is an LLC Kit?

An LLC is required to keep a company records book. The company records book of a corporation is known as a corporate kit. The company records book of an LLC is known as an LLC Kit. In its simplest form, an LLC Kit is basically a three ring binder that contains the governing documents of the company. A well maintained records book is a time saver for attorneys and paralegals.

Documents included within the kit

Typically, an LLC kit will contain some version of the following documents:

- Articles of Organization and any amendments as filed with the Secretary of State
- A copy of the operating agreement and any amendments
- IRS filings such as the SS-4 (EIN/TIN)
- Membership records
- Annual registration
- Membership Certificates
- Membership Ledger
- Minutes of Meetings
- Compliance Documents

Besides documents, your LLC Kit is customized with the name of your business, usually in gold foil lettering. In addition, it comes with your very own company seal, inscribed with your company's name, the state of formation, and the date it was formed. Use this embosser to emboss your company seal and validate important company papers. All of these items depend on the company you choose to order from. In some cases, everything mentioned is included, and with other companies it is considered an add-on.

Types of binders

LLC kits have changed a lot in the form of fashion over the past few years. Firstly, the range of colors now available are now as diverse as the colors in the rainbow. Some have slipcovers, some are secured with Velcro, and others secure with magnets or zippers. The list goes on and on regarding aspects such as shape and the material in which they are made.

Glossary

Amendment - the modification of the articles of organization by the addition of supplemental information; the deletion of unnecessary, undesirable, or outdated information; or the correction of errors existing in the text.

Articles of Organization - a document required to be filed with an appropriate state or local government agency, in order to establish legal recognition of a Limited Liability Company.

Buy/sell agreement - a contract among the owners of a business which provides terms for their purchase of a withdrawing member's membership interest in the enterprise.

Bylaws - the rules and regulations enacted by an association or a corporation to provide a framework for its operation and management.

C Corporation - any corporation that, under the United States federal income tax law, is taxed separately from its owners.

Capital - the initial funding of a business through services, money, or equipment.

Capital Account - an account stating the amount of funds and assets invested in a business by the owners, including retained earnings.

Capital Contribution - the initial contribution of capital, in the form of money, property, or service to an LLC by a member.

Charging Order - obtaining a court order for an LLC to pay its creditor all the money due.

Company Kit - see (LLC Kit)

Corporation - a legal entity that is separate and distinct from its owners.

Dissolution - the last stage of liquidation, the process by which an LLC is brought to an end and the assets and property of the company are redistributed.

Distributions - a company's payment of cash, stock, or physical products to its owners.

Double Taxation - a taxation principle referring to income taxes that are paid twice on the same source of earned income.

Employer Identification Number - a unique nine-digit number assigned by the Internal Revenue Service (IRS) to business entities operating in the United States for the purposes of identification.

Entity - a person, department, team, corporation, cooperative, partnership, or other group with whom it is possible to conduct business.

Fictitious Name - the name under which a business operates that is not the legal name of the owner(s) of the business.

Fiduciary Duties - the responsibility in which a party owes a duty of good faith to another or others.

Fiscal Year - a period of time a company uses for accounting purposes and preparing financial statements. The fiscal year may or may not be the same as a calendar year.

General Partner - owners of a partnership who have unlimited liability.

General Partnership - a business with more than one owner that has not filed papers with the state to become a corporation or limited liability company.

Incorporate - to form a legal corporation.

Liability - the state of being legally responsible for something.

Limited Liability Protection - a type of liability that does not exceed the amount invested in a limited liability company.

Limited Partner - a partner in a partnership whose liability is limited to the extent of that partner's share of ownership.

Limited Partnership - Two or more partners united to conduct a business jointly, and in which one or more of the partners is liable only to the extent of the amount of money that partner has invested.

Manager - a person chosen by LLC members to manage the LLC; similar to a director of a corporation.

Manager-Managed LLC - an LLC in which all members participate in the decision-making process of the LLC.

Member - owner(s) of an LLC.

Membership Interest - a member's ownership of an LLC is represented by "interests" just as a partner has an interest in a partnership and shareholders own stock in a corporation.

Membership Interest Certificate - a document providing evidence of interest/ownership in an LLC.

Minority Interest Owners - a significant but non-controlling ownership of less than 50% of an LLC's voting interest by either an investor or another company.

Minutes - decisions made by members of a limited liability company, usually annotated on a template or typed/handwritten document.

Name Reservation - to reserve a prospective name of an LLC to be used once verified as available.

Operating Agreement - the agreement between the members that governs the affairs of the LLC.

Pass-through Tax Status - taxation to which a company itself is not taxed but "passed through" onto the owners' individual tax returns.

Piercing The Veil - when the courts pierce the "veil" that the law uses to divide the company (and its liabilities and assets) from the people who own the company.

Provisions - terms of a legal document.

Quorum - the minimum number of members to be present at a meeting in order to conduct business or pass a voting decision (usually a majority).

Registered Agent - a person or entity that receives important legal and tax documents on behalf of a business. They can also receive services of process when a business entity is a party in a legal action, like a lawsuit or summons.

Registered Office - the official address of the registered agent.

S Corporation - a type of corporation that is taxed under subchapter S of the Internal Revenue Code (26 U.S.C.A. § 1 et seq.).

Service of Process - Delivery of a writ, summons, or other legal papers to the person required to respond to them.

Single-Member LLC - a limited liability company which is owned by a single person or entity.

Sole Proprietorship - a type of business entity that is owned and run by one individual, and in which there is no legal distinction between the owner and the business.

Trademark - a symbol, word, or words legally registered or established by use as representing a company or product.

Uniform Limited Liability Company Act (ULLCA) - is a uniform act, proposed by the National Conference of Commissioners on Uniform State Laws ("NCCUSL") for the governance of limited liability companies within the United States.

Georgia State Statutes

TITLE 14. CORPORATIONS, PARTNERSHIPS, AND ASSOCIATIONS

CHAPTER 11. LIMITED LIABILITY COMPANIES

ARTICLE 1. GENERAL PROVISIONS

§ 14-11-100. Short title

This chapter may be cited as the "Georgia Limited Liability Company Act."

§ 14-11-101. Definitions

As used in this chapter, unless the context otherwise requires, the term:

(1) "Articles of organization" means the articles filed under Code Section 14-11-203 and such articles as amended or restated.

(2) "Business entity" means a limited liability company, a foreign limited liability company, a limited partnership, a foreign limited partnership, a general partnership, a corporation, or a foreign corporation.

(3) "Conflicting interest" with respect to a limited liability company means the interest a member or manager of the limited liability company has respecting a transaction effected or proposed to be effected by the limited liability company (or by a person in which the limited liability company has a controlling interest), with respect to which the member or manager has the power to act or vote, if:

(A) Whether or not the transaction is brought before the members or managers responsible for the decision, as the case may be, of the limited liability company for action, to the knowledge of the member or manager at the time of commitment, he or she or a related person is a party to the transaction or has a beneficial financial interest in or so closely linked to the transaction and of such financial significance to the member or manager or a related person that it would reasonably be expected to exert an influence on the member or manager's judgment if he or she were called upon to vote on the transaction; or

(B) The transaction is brought (or is of such character and significance to the limited liability company that it would in the normal course be brought) before the members or managers responsible for the decision, as the case may be, of the limited liability company for action and, to the knowledge of the member or manager at the time of commitment, any of the following persons is either a party to the transaction or has a beneficial financial interest so closely linked to the transaction and of such financial significance to that person that it would reasonably be expected to exert an influence on the member or manager's judgment if he or she were called upon to vote on the transaction: an entity (other than the limited liability company) of which the member or manager is a director, general partner, member, manager, agent, or employee; an entity that controls, is controlled by, or is under common control with one or more of the entities specified in the preceding clause; or an individual who is a general partner, principal, or employer of the member or manager.

(4) "Contribution" means a contribution to the capital of a limited liability company authorized by Code Section 14-11-401.

(5) "Corporation" means a corporation incorporated under Chapter 2 of this title.

(6) "Distribution" means a direct or indirect transfer of money or other property (except its own limited liability company interests) by a limited liability company to or for the benefit of its members or their assignees in respect of any of its limited liability company interests. A distribution may be in the form of a transfer of money or other property; a purchase, redemption, or other acquisition of a limited liability company interest; a distribution of indebtedness; or otherwise.

(6.1) "Electronic transmission" or "electronically transmitted" means any process of communication not directly involving the physical transfer of paper that is suitable for the retention, retrieval, and reproduction of information by the recipient.

(7) "Event of dissociation" means an event that causes a person to cease to be a member, as provided in Code Section 14-11-601 or 14-11-601.1.

(8) "Foreign corporation" means a corporation for profit formed under the laws of a jurisdiction other than this state.

(9) "Foreign limited liability company" means a limited liability company formed under the laws of a jurisdiction other than this state.

(10) "Foreign limited partnership" means a limited partnership formed under the laws of a jurisdiction other than this state.

(11) "General partnership" means a partnership (other than a limited partnership) existing under the laws of this state or the laws of any other jurisdiction.

(12) "Limited liability company" means a limited liability company formed under this chapter.

(13) "Limited liability company interest" means a member's share of the profits and losses of a limited liability company and a member's right to receive distributions.

(14) "Limited partnership" means a limited partnership formed under the laws of this state.

(15) "Manager" means a person in whom management is vested in accordance with subsection (b) of Code Section 14-11-304.

(16) "Member" means a person who has been admitted to a limited liability company as a member as provided in Code Section 14-11-505 and who has not ceased to be a member as provided in Code Section 14-11-601 or 14-11-601.1.

(17) "Member or manager's conflicting interest transaction" with respect to a limited liability company means a transaction effected or proposed to be effected by the limited liability

company (or by a person in which the limited liability company has a controlling interest) respecting which a member or manager of the limited liability company having the power to act or vote has a conflicting interest.

(18) "Operating agreement" means any agreement, written or oral, of the member or members as to the conduct of the business and affairs of a limited liability company. In the case of a limited liability company with only one member, a writing signed by that member stating that it is intended to be a written operating agreement shall constitute a written operating agreement and shall not be unenforceable by reason of there being only one person who is a party to the operating agreement. A limited liability company is not required to execute its operating agreement and, except as otherwise provided in the operating agreement, is bound by its operating agreement whether or not the limited liability company executes the operating agreement. An operating agreement may provide enforceable rights to any person, including a person who is not a party to the operating agreement, to the extent set forth therein.

(19) "Person" means an individual, business entity, business trust, estate, trust, association, joint venture, government, governmental subdivision or agency, or any other legal or commercial entity.

(20) "Proceeding" means any threatened, pending, or completed action, suit, or proceeding, whether civil, criminal, administrative, or investigative and whether formal or informal.

(21) "Related person" of a member or manager means:

(A) A child, grandchild, sibling, parent, or spouse of, or an individual occupying the same household as, the member or manager or a trust or estate of which an individual specified in this subparagraph is a substantial beneficiary; or

(B) A trust, estate, incompetent, conservator, or minor of which the member or manager is a fiduciary.

(22) "Required disclosure" means disclosure by the member or manager who has a conflicting interest of (A) the existence and nature of his or her conflicting interest, and (B) all facts known to him or her respecting the subject matter of the transaction that an ordinarily prudent person would reasonably believe to be material to a judgment as to whether or not to proceed with the transaction.

(23) "State" means the District of Columbia or the Commonwealth of Puerto Rico or any state, territory, possession, or other jurisdiction of the United States.

(24) "Time of commitment" respecting a member's or manager's conflicting interest transaction means the time when the transaction is consummated or, if made pursuant to contract, the time when the limited liability company (or the person in which it has a controlling interest) becomes contractually obligated so that its unilateral withdrawal from the transaction would entail significant loss, liability, or other damage.

§ 14-11-102. Evidence of filing

A certificate attached to a copy of a document or electronic transmission filed by the Secretary of State, bearing his or her signature, which may be in facsimile, and the printed or embossed seal of this state, or its electronic equivalent, is prima-facie evidence that the original document has been filed with the Secretary of State.

ARTICLE 2. FORMATION

§ 14-11-201. Purpose

(a) A limited liability company may be formed under this chapter for any lawful purpose. If the purpose for which a limited liability company is formed makes it subject to a special provision of law, the limited liability company shall also comply with that provision.

(b) A limited liability company formed under this chapter has, unless a more limited purpose is set forth in the articles of organization or a written operating agreement, the purpose of engaging in any lawful activity.

§ 14-11-202. Powers

Each limited liability company formed in this state shall have the same powers as any person has to do all things necessary to carry out its purpose, business, and affairs.

§ 14-11-203. Formation

(a) One or more persons may act as the organizer or organizers of a limited liability company by delivering articles of organization to the Secretary of State for filing and supplying to the Secretary of State, in such form as the Secretary of State may require, the following information:

(1) The name and address of each organizer;

(2) The street address and county of the limited liability company's initial registered office and the name of its initial registered agent at that office; and

(3) The mailing address of the limited liability company's principal place of business.

(b) An organizer need not be a member of the limited liability company at the time of formation or thereafter.

(c) A limited liability company is formed when the articles of organization become effective pursuant to Code Section 14-11-206.

(d) The Secretary of State's filing of the articles of organization is conclusive proof that the organizers satisfied all conditions precedent to formation, except in a proceeding by the state to cancel or revoke the formation.

(e) During any period when a limited liability company has any members it may have one or more members.

§ 14-11-204. Articles of organization

(a) The articles of organization shall set forth the name of the limited liability company, which name must satisfy the requirements of Code Section 14-11-207.

(b) The articles of organization may set forth:

(1) That management of the limited liability company is vested in one or more managers; and

(2) Any other provisions not inconsistent with law.

§ 14-11-205. Execution of documents

(a) Unless otherwise specified in any other Code section of this chapter, any document required or permitted by this chapter to be delivered to the Secretary of State for filing shall be executed:

(1) By any member;

(2) By any manager if management of the limited liability company is vested in one or more managers;

(3) By any organizer if the limited liability company has been formed but it has no members or managers; or

(4) If the limited liability company is in the hands of a receiver, trustee, or other court-appointed fiduciary, by that fiduciary.

(b) The person executing the document shall sign it and state beneath or opposite his or her signature his or her name and the capacity in which he or she signs.

(c) The person executing the document may do so as an attorney-in-fact. Powers of attorney relating to the execution of the document do not need to be shown to or filed with the Secretary of State.

§ 14-11-206. Filing by the Secretary of State

(a) A signed original and one exact or conformed copy of any document required or permitted to be filed pursuant to this chapter shall be delivered to the Secretary of State; provided, however, that if the document is electronically transmitted, the electronic version of such person's name may be used in lieu of a signature. Unless the Secretary of State finds that the document does not conform to the filing provisions of this chapter, upon receipt of all filing fees and additional information required by law, he or she shall:

(1) Stamp or otherwise endorse his or her official title and the date and time of receipt on both the original and copy;

(2) File the original in his or her office; and

(3) Return the copy to the person who delivered the document to the Secretary of State or the person's representative.

(b) If the Secretary of State refuses to file a document, he or she shall return it to the limited liability company or its representative within ten days after the document was delivered, together with a brief written explanation of the reason for his or her refusal.

(c) The Secretary of State's duty to file documents under this chapter is ministerial.

(d) If the Secretary of State finds that any document delivered for filing does not conform to the filing provisions of this chapter at the time such document is delivered to the Secretary of State, such document is deemed to have been filed at the time of delivery (or such later time and date as is authorized by paragraph (2) of subsection (e) or subsection (f) of this Code section) if the Secretary of State subsequently determines that:

(1) The document as delivered so conforms to the filing provisions of this chapter; or

(2) Within 30 days after notification of nonconformance is given by the Secretary of State to the person who delivered the documents for filing or that person's representative, the documents are brought into conformance.

(e) Except as provided in subsection (d) of this Code section, a document accepted for filing is effective:

(1) At the time of filing on the date it is filed, as evidenced by the Secretary of State's date and time endorsement on the original document; or

(2) At the time specified in the document as its effective time on the date it is filed.

(f) A document may specify a delayed effective time and date, and, if it does so, the document shall become effective at the time and date specified. If a delayed effective date but no effective time is specified, the document shall become effective at the close of business on that date. A delayed effective date for a document may not be later than the ninetieth day after the date on which it is filed.

(g) A certificate attached to a copy of a document filed by the Secretary of State, bearing his or her signature, which may be in facsimile, and the printed or embossed seal of this state, or its electronic equivalent, is prima-facie evidence that the original document has been filed with the Secretary of State.

(h) Notwithstanding the provisions of this chapter, the Secretary of State may authorize the filing of documents by electronic transmission, following the provisions of Chapter 12 of Title 10, the "Uniform Electronic Transactions Act," and the Secretary of State shall be authorized to promulgate such rules and regulations as are necessary to implement electronic filing procedures.

§ 14-11-207. Name

(a) The name of each limited liability company shall be as set forth in its articles of organization and:

(1) Must contain the words "limited liability company" or "limited company" (it being permitted to abbreviate the word "limited" as "ltd." and the word "company" as "co.") or the abbreviation "L.L.C.", "LLC", "L.C." or "LC";

(2) Must be distinguishable on the records of the Secretary of State from the name of any corporation, limited liability company, or limited partnership; any foreign corporation, foreign limited liability company or foreign limited partnership having a certificate of authority to transact business in this state; any nonprofit corporation, professional corporation, or professional association, domestic or foreign, on file with the Secretary of State pursuant to this title; or any name reserved or registered under this title; and

(3) Shall not in any instance exceed 80 characters, including spaces and punctuation.

(b) This chapter does not control the use of fictitious or trade names. Issuance of a name under this chapter means that the name is distinguishable for filing purposes on the records of the Secretary of State pursuant to paragraph (2) of subsection (a) of this Code section. Issuance of a limited liability company name does not affect the commercial availability of the name.

§ 14-11-208. Reservation of name; transfer of reserved name

(a) A person may apply to reserve a name for the purpose of forming a limited liability company by paying the fee specified in Code Section 14-11-1101. If the Secretary of State finds that the limited liability company name applied for is available, he or she shall reserve the name for the applicant's use for 30 days or until articles of organization are filed, whichever is sooner. If the Secretary of State finds that the name applied for is not distinguishable for filing purposes upon the records of the Secretary of State, he or she shall notify the applicant who may then submit another reservation request within ten days of the date of the rejection notice without payment of an additional reservation fee.

(b) Upon expiration of a name reservation after 30 days without the filing of articles of organization, the name may again be reserved for another 30 day period by the same or another applicant under the same guidelines of subsection (a) of this Code section.

(c) A person who has in effect a name reservation under subsection (a) of this Code section may transfer the reservation to another person by delivering to the Secretary of State a signed notice of the transfer that states the name and address of the transferee.

§ 14-11-209. Registered office and registered agent

(a) Each limited liability company shall continuously maintain in this state:

(1) A registered office which may, but need not, be a place of its business in this state; and

(2) A registered agent for service of process on the limited liability company. The address of the business office of the registered agent shall be the same as the address of the registered office referred to in paragraph (1) of this subsection.

(b) A registered agent must be an individual resident of this state, a corporation, or a foreign corporation having a certificate of authority to transact business in this state.

(c) A limited liability company may change its registered office or its registered agent, or both, by filing an amendment to its annual registration that sets forth:

(1) The name of the limited liability company;

(2) The street address and county of its then registered office;

(3) If the address of its registered office is to be changed, the new street address and county of the registered office;

(4) The name of its then registered agent; and

(5) If its registered agent is to be changed, the name of its successor registered agent.

(d) A registered agent of a limited liability company may resign as such agent by signing and delivering to the Secretary of State for filing a statement of resignation, which may include a statement that the registered office is also discontinued. On or before the date of the filing of the statement of resignation, the registered agent shall deliver or mail a written notice of the registered agent's intention to resign to the limited liability company at the most recent mailing address of the limited liability company's principal place of business in this state listed in the records of the Secretary of State. The agency appointment is terminated, and the registered office discontinued if so provided, on the earlier of the filing of the limited liability company's annual registration or a statement designating a new registered agent and registered office if also discontinued or the thirty-first day after the date on which the statement of resignation was filed.

(e) A registered agent may change the agent's office and the address of the registered office of any limited liability company of which the agent is the registered agent to another place within this state by filing a statement, as required in subsection (c) of this Code section, setting forth the required information for all limited liability companies for which he or she is the registered agent, except that it need be signed only by the registered agent and need not be responsive to paragraph (5) of subsection (c) of this Code section and must recite that a copy of the statement has been mailed to the limited liability company at the most recent mailing address of the limited liability company's principal place of business listed on the records of the Secretary of State.

(f) Whenever a limited liability company shall fail to appoint or maintain a registered agent in this state or whenever its registered agent cannot with reasonable diligence be found at the registered office, then the Secretary of State shall be an agent of such limited liability company upon whom any process, notice, or demand may be served. Service on the Secretary of State of any such process, notice, or demand shall be made by delivering to and leaving with him or her or with any other person or persons designated by the Secretary of State to receive such service two copies of such process, notice, or demand. The plaintiff or his or her attorney shall certify in writing to the Secretary of State that the limited liability company failed either to maintain a registered office or appoint a registered agent in this state and that he or she has forwarded by registered or certified mail or statutory overnight delivery such process, notice, or demand to the most recent registered office listed on the records of the Secretary of State and that service cannot be effected at such office.

(g) The Secretary of State shall keep a record of all processes, notices, and demands served upon him or her under this Code section and shall record therein the time of such service and his or her action with reference thereto.

(h) This Code section does not prescribe the only means, or necessarily the required means, of serving any process, notice, or demand required or permitted by law to be served on a limited liability company.

§ 14-11-210. Amendment of articles of organization; restatement

  (a) A limited liability company amending its articles of organization shall deliver to the Secretary of State for filing articles of amendment setting forth:

  (1) The name of the limited liability company;

  (2) The date the articles of organization were filed;

  (3) The amendment to the articles of organization; and

  (4) The effective date and time of the amendment if later than the date and time the articles of amendment are filed.

(b) The articles of organization may be amended in any and as many respects as may be desired so long as the articles of organization as amended contain only provisions that may be lawfully contained in articles of organization at the time of making the amendment.

(c) Articles of organization may be restated to include only those provisions then in effect, or amended and so restated, at any time. Restated articles of organization shall be delivered to the Secretary of State for filing and shall be specifically designated as such in the heading.

§ 14-11-211. Correcting filed document

  (a) A limited liability company or foreign limited liability company may correct a document filed by the Secretary of State if the document:

  (1) Contains an incorrect statement; or

  (2) Was defectively executed.

(b) A document is corrected:

  (1) By preparing articles of correction that:

    (A) Describe the document (including its filing date);

    (B) Specify the incorrect statement and the reason it is incorrect or the manner in which the execution was defective; and

    (C) Correct the incorrect statement or defective execution; and

(2) By delivering the articles to the Secretary of State for filing.

(c) Articles of correction that are filed by the Secretary of State are effective on the effective date of the document they correct except as to persons relying on the uncorrected document and adversely affected by the correction. As to those persons, articles of correction are effective when filed.

§ 14-11-212. Conversion to limited liability company

(a) A corporation, foreign corporation, foreign limited liability company, limited partnership, foreign limited partnership, general partnership, or foreign general partnership may elect to become a limited liability company. Such election shall require (1) compliance with Code Section 14-2-1109.1 in the case of a Georgia corporation, or (2) the approval of all of its partners, members or shareholders (or such other approval or compliance as may be sufficient under applicable law or the governing documents of the electing entity to authorize such election) in the case of a foreign corporation, foreign limited liability company, limited partnership, foreign limited partnership, general partnership, or foreign general partnership.

(b) Such election is made by delivering a certificate of conversion to the Secretary of State for filing. The certificate shall set forth:

(1) The name and jurisdiction of organization of the entity making the election;

(2) That the entity elects to become a limited liability company;

(3) The effective date, or the effective date and time, of such election if later than the date and time the certificate of conversion is filed;

(4) That the election has been approved as required by subsection (a) of this Code section;

(5) That filed with the certificate of conversion are articles of organization that are in the form required by Code Section 14-11-204, that set forth a name for the limited liability company that satisfies the requirements of Code Section 14-11-207, and that shall be the articles of organization of the limited liability company formed pursuant to such election unless and until modified in accordance with this chapter; and

(6) A statement setting forth either (A) the manner and basis for converting the ownership interests in the entity making the election into interests as members of the limited liability company formed pursuant to such election or canceling them, or (B)(i) that a written operating agreement has been entered into among the persons who will be the members of the limited liability company formed pursuant to such election, (ii) that such operating agreement will be effective immediately upon the effectiveness of such election, and (iii) that such operating agreement provides for the manner and basis of such conversion or cancellation.

(c) Upon the election becoming effective:

(1) The electing entity shall become a limited liability company formed under this chapter by such election except that the existence of the limited liability company so formed shall be deemed to have commenced on the date the entity making the election commenced its

existence in the jurisdiction in which such entity was first created, formed, incorporated, or otherwise came into being;

(2) The ownership interests in the entity making the election shall be converted or canceled on the basis stated or referred to in the certificate of conversion in accordance with paragraph (6) of subsection (b) of this Code section;

(3) The articles of organization filed with the certificate of conversion shall be the articles of organization of the limited liability company formed pursuant to such election unless and until amended in accordance with this chapter;

(4) The governing documents of the entity making the election shall be of no further force or effect;

(5) The limited liability company formed by such election shall thereupon and thereafter possess all of the rights, privileges, immunities, franchises, and powers of the entity making the election; all property, real, personal, and mixed, all contract rights, and all debts due to such entity, as well as all other choses in action, and each and every other interest of or belonging to or due to the entity making the election shall be taken and deemed to be vested in the limited liability company formed by such election without further act or deed; and the title to any real estate, or any interest therein, vested in the entity making the election shall not revert or be in any way impaired by reason of such election; and none of such items shall be deemed to have been conveyed, transferred, or assigned by reason of such election for any purpose; and

(6) The limited liability company formed by such election shall thereupon and thereafter be responsible and liable for all the liabilities and obligations of the entity making the election, and any claim existing or action or proceeding pending by or against such entity may be prosecuted as if such election had not become effective. Neither the rights of creditors nor any liens upon the property of the entity making such election shall be impaired by such election.

(d) A conversion pursuant to this Code section shall not be deemed to constitute a dissolution of the entity making the election and shall constitute a continuation of the existence of the entity making the election in the form of a limited liability company. A limited liability company formed by an election pursuant to this Code section shall for all purposes be deemed to be the same entity as the entity making such election.

(e) A limited liability company formed by an election pursuant to this Code section may file a copy of such certificate of conversion, certified by the Secretary of State, in the office of the clerk of the superior court of the county where any real property owned by such limited liability company is located and record such certified copy of the certificate of conversion in the books kept by such clerk for recordation of deeds in such county with the entity electing to become a limited liability company indexed as the grantor and the limited liability company indexed as the grantee. No real estate transfer tax under Code Section 48-6-1 shall be due with respect to recordation of such election.

ARTICLE 3. AGENCY; MANAGEMENT; DUTIES; LIABILITY

§ 14-11-301. Agency of members and managers

(a) Except as provided in subsection (b) of this Code section, every member is an agent of the limited liability company for the purpose of its business and affairs, and the act of any member, including, but not limited to, the execution in the name of the limited liability company of any instrument for apparently carrying on in the usual way the business and affairs of the limited liability company of which he or she is a member, binds the limited liability company, unless the member so acting has, in fact, no authority to act for the limited liability company in the particular matter, and the person with whom he or she is dealing has knowledge of the fact that the member has no such authority.

(b) If the articles of organization provide that management of the limited liability company is vested in a manager or managers:

(1) No member, acting solely in the capacity as a member, is an agent of the limited liability company; and

(2) Every manager is an agent of the limited liability company for the purpose of its business and affairs, and the act of any manager, including, but not limited to, the execution in the name of the limited liability company of any instrument for apparently carrying on in the usual way the business and affairs of the limited liability company of which he or she is a manager, binds the limited liability company, unless the manager so acting has, in fact, no authority to act for the limited liability company in the particular matter, and the person with whom he or she is dealing has knowledge of the fact that the manager has no such authority.

(c) An act of a manager or a member that is not apparently for the carrying on in the usual way the business or affairs of the limited liability company does not bind the limited liability company unless authorized in accordance with a written operating agreement at the time of the transaction or at any other time.

(d) No act of a manager or member in contravention of a restriction on authority shall bind the limited liability company to persons having knowledge of the restriction.

§ 14-11-302. Limitations on authority to convey real property

Limitations on the authority of any or all members or managers that are set forth in a limited liability company's articles of organization shall be conclusively presumed in favor of the limited liability company and against a grantee of the limited liability company, or a person claiming through such grantee, with respect to limited liability company real property located in a county of this state if a copy of the articles of organization certified by the Secretary of State is filed in the office of the clerk of the superior court of the county where the real property is located and recorded in the book kept by such clerk for statements of partnership pursuant to Code Section 14-8-10.1.

§ 14-11-303. Liability to third parties

(a) A person who is a member, manager, agent, or employee of a limited liability company is not liable, solely by reason of being a member, manager, agent, or employee of the limited liability company, under a judgment, decree, or order of a court, or in any other manner, for a debt, obligation, or liability of the limited liability company, including liabilities and obligations of the limited liability company to any member or assignee, whether arising in contract, tort, or otherwise, or for the acts or omissions of any other member, manager, agent, or employee of the limited liability company, whether arising in contract, tort, or otherwise. Notwithstanding the provisions of this subsection, a member, manager, or employee may be personally liable for tax liabilities arising from the operation of the limited liability company as provided in Code Section 48-2-52.

(b) Notwithstanding the provisions of subsection (a) of this Code section, under a written operating agreement or under another written agreement, a member or manager may agree to be obligated personally for any or all of the debts, obligations, and liabilities of the limited liability company.

§ 14-11-304. Management

(a) Unless the articles of organization or a written operating agreement vests management of the limited liability company in a manager or managers, management of the business and affairs of the limited liability company shall be vested in the members, and, subject to any provisions in the articles of organization or a written operating agreement, the members shall have the right and authority to manage the affairs of the limited liability company and to make all decisions with respect thereto. The articles of organization or a written operating agreement may contain any provision relating to any phase of managing the business or regulating the affairs of the limited liability company.

(b) If the articles of organization or a written operating agreement vests management of the limited liability company in one or more managers, then such persons shall have such right and authority to manage the business and affairs of the limited liability company as is provided in the articles of organization or a written operating agreement. Unless otherwise provided in the articles of organization or a written operating agreement, such persons:

(1) Shall be designated, appointed, elected, removed, or replaced by the approval of more than one half by number of the members;

(2) Need not be members of the limited liability company or natural persons; and

(3) Unless they have been earlier removed or have earlier resigned, shall hold office until their successors shall have been elected and qualified.

(c) A written operating agreement may provide that (1) a member or manager who fails to perform in accordance with, or to comply with the terms and conditions of, the written operating agreement shall be subject to specified penalties or specified consequences, and (2) at the time or upon the happening of events specified in a written operating agreement, a member or manager shall be subject to specified penalties or specified consequences.

(d) A person who is both a manager and member has the rights and powers, and is subject to the restrictions and liabilities, of a manager and, except as provided in the articles of organization or a written operating agreement, also has the rights and powers, and is subject to the restrictions and liabilities, of a member to the extent of his or her participation in the limited liability company as a member.

§ 14-11-305. Duties

In managing the business or affairs of a limited liability company:

(1) A member or manager shall act in a manner he or she believes in good faith to be in the best interests of the limited liability company and with the care an ordinarily prudent person in a like position would exercise under similar circumstances. A member or manager is not liable to the limited liability company, its members, or its managers for any action taken in managing the business or affairs of the limited liability company if he or she performs the duties of his or her office in compliance with this Code section. Except as otherwise provided in the articles of organization or a written operating agreement, a person who is a member of a limited liability company in which management is vested in one or more managers, and who is not a manager, shall have no duties to the limited liability company or to the other members solely by reason of acting in his or her capacity as a member;

(2) A member or manager, as the case may be, is entitled to rely on information, opinions, reports, or statements, including but not limited to financial statements or other financial data, if prepared or presented by:

(A) One or more members, managers, or employees of the limited liability company whom the member or manager reasonably believes to be reliable and competent in the matter presented;

(B) Legal counsel, public accountants, or other persons as to matters the member or manager reasonably believes are within the person's professional or expert competence; or

(C) A committee of members or managers of which he or she is not a member if the manager reasonably believes the committee merits confidence;

(3) In the instances described in paragraph (2) of this Code section, a member or manager is not entitled to rely if he or she has knowledge concerning the matter in question that makes reliance otherwise permitted by paragraph (2) of this Code section unwarranted; and

(4) To the extent that, pursuant to paragraph (1) of this Code section or otherwise at law or in equity, a member or manager has duties (including fiduciary duties) and liabilities relating thereto to a limited liability company or to another member or manager:

(A) The member's or manager's duties and liabilities may be expanded, restricted, or eliminated by provisions in the articles of organization or a written operating agreement; provided, however, that no such provision shall eliminate or limit the liability of a member or manager:

(i) For intentional misconduct or a knowing violation of law; or

(ii) For any transaction for which the person received a personal benefit in violation or breach of any provision of a written operating agreement; and

(B) The member or manager shall have no liability to the limited liability company or to any other member or manager for his or her good faith reliance on the provisions of a written operating agreement, including, without limitation, provisions thereof that relate to the scope of duties (including fiduciary duties) of members and managers.

§ 14-11-306. Indemnification

Subject to such standards and restrictions, if any, as are set forth in the articles of organization or a written operating agreement, a limited liability company may, and shall have the power to, indemnify and hold harmless any member or manager or other person from and against any and all claims and demands whatsoever arising in connection with the limited liability company; provided, however, that no limited liability company shall have the power to indemnify any member or manager for any liability that may not be eliminated or limited by the articles of organization or a written operating agreement by reason of division (4)(A)(i) or (ii) of Code Section 14-11-305.

§ 14-11-307. Conflicting interest transactions

(a) The provisions of this Code section shall apply to a limited liability company unless its articles of organization or a written operating agreement provides that they shall not apply. If the provisions of this Code section apply to a limited liability company, its articles of organization or a written operating agreement may limit, expand, or modify, in any manner whatsoever, the effect thereof. If the provisions of this Code section do not apply to a limited liability company, its articles of organization or a written operating agreement may, but is not required to, contain any provision whatsoever relating to transactions that might give rise to conflicts of interest for members or managers.

(b) A transaction effected or proposed to be effected by a limited liability company (or by a person in which the limited liability company has a controlling interest) that is not a member's or manager's conflicting interest transaction may not be enjoined, set aside, or give rise to an award of damages or other sanctions, in an action by a member or by or in the right of the limited liability company, on the ground of a conflicting interest in the transaction of a member or manager or any person with whom or which he or she has a personal, economic, or other association.

(c) A member's or manager's conflicting interest transaction may not be enjoined, set aside, or give rise to an award of damages or other sanctions, in an action by a member or by or in the right of the limited liability company, on the ground of a conflicting interest in the transaction of the member or manager, as the case may be, or any person with whom or which he or she has a personal, economic, or other association, if:

(1) The member's or manager's action respecting the transaction was at any time taken in compliance with this Code section; or

(2) The transaction, judged in the circumstances at the time of commitment, is established to have been fair to the limited liability company.

(d) A member's or manager's action respecting a transaction is effective for purposes of paragraph (1) of subsection (c) of this Code section if the transaction received the approval of a majority of those qualified members or managers who expressed approval or disapproval of the transaction after either required disclosure to them (to the extent the information was not known by them) or compliance with subsection (e) of this Code section.

(e) If a member or manager has a conflicting interest respecting a transaction, but neither he or she nor a related person of the member or manager specified in paragraph (21) of Code Section 14-11-101 is a party thereto, and if the member or manager has a duty under law or professional canon, or a duty of confidentiality to another person, respecting information relating to the transaction such that the member or manager cannot, consistent with that duty, make the disclosure contemplated by paragraph (22) of Code Section 14-11-101, then disclosure is sufficient for purposes of subsection (d) of this Code section if the member or manager:

(1) Discloses to the members or managers voting on the transaction the existence and nature of his or her conflicting interest and informs them of the character of and limitations imposed by that duty prior to their vote on the transaction; and

(2) Plays no part, directly or indirectly, in their deliberations or vote.

(f) A majority of all the qualified members or managers constitutes a quorum for purposes of action that complies with this Code section. Members' or managers' action that otherwise complies with this Code section is not affected by the presence or vote of a member or manager who is not a qualified member or manager.

(g) For purposes of this Code section, "qualified member or manager" means, with respect to a member's or manager's conflicting interest transaction, any member (if management of the limited liability company is not vested in a manager or managers) or manager (if management of the limited liability company is vested in a manager or managers) who does not have either a conflicting interest respecting the transaction or a familial, financial, professional, or employment relationship with a second member or manager who does have a conflicting interest respecting the transaction, which relationship would, in the circumstances, reasonably be expected to exert an influence on the first member's or manager's judgment when voting on the transaction.

§ 14-11-308. Approval rights of members and managers

(a) Except as otherwise provided in this chapter or in the articles of organization or a written operating agreement, and subject to subsection (b) of this Code section:

(1) If management of the limited liability company is vested in the members, each member shall have one vote with respect to, and the affirmative vote, approval, or consent of a majority of the members shall be required to decide, any matter arising in connection with the business and affairs of the limited liability company; and

(2) If management of the limited liability company is vested in a manager or managers, each manager shall have one vote with respect to, and the affirmative vote, approval, or consent of a majority of the managers shall be required to decide, any matter arising in connection with the business and affairs of the limited liability company.

(b) Unless otherwise provided in the articles of organization or a written operating agreement, the unanimous vote or consent of the members shall be required to approve the following matters:

(1) The dissolution of the limited liability company under paragraph (3) of subsection (a) or paragraph (3) of subsection (b) of Code Section 14-11-602;

(2) The merger of the limited liability company under subsection (a) of Code Section 14-11-903;

(3) The sale, exchange, lease, or other transfer of all or substantially all of the assets of the limited liability company. For the purposes of this paragraph, assets shall be deemed to be less than all or substantially all of a limited liability company's assets if the value of the assets does not exceed two-thirds of the value of all of the assets of the limited liability company and the revenues represented or produced by such assets do not exceed two-thirds of the total revenues of the limited liability company; provided, however, that this paragraph shall not create any inference that the sale, exchange, lease, or other transfer of assets exceeding the amounts described in this paragraph is the sale of all or substantially all of the assets of the limited liability company;

(4) The admission of any new member of the limited liability company under subsection (b) of Code Section 14-11-505;

(5) An amendment to the articles of organization under Code Section 14-11-210 or an amendment to a written operating agreement;

(6) Action under subsection (b) of Code Section 14-11-402 to reduce or eliminate an obligation to make a contribution to the capital of a limited liability company;

(7) Action to approve a distribution under Code Section 14-11-404; or

(8) Action to continue a limited liability company under paragraph (4) of subsection (a) or paragraph (4) of subsection (b) of Code Section 14-11-602.

§ 14-11-309. Action without meeting

Except as otherwise provided in the articles of organization or a written operating agreement:

(1) Action required or permitted by this chapter to be taken by members or managers may be taken without a meeting if the action is taken by all the members or managers entitled to vote on the action or, if so provided in the articles of organization or a written operating agreement, by persons who would be entitled to vote not less than the minimum number of votes that would be necessary to authorize or take the action. The action must be evidenced by

one or more written consents describing the action taken, signed by members or managers entitled to take such action, and delivered to the limited liability company for inclusion in its records;

(2) If not otherwise fixed under the articles of organization or a written operating agreement, the record date for determining members or managers entitled to take action without a meeting is the date the first member or manager signs the consent;

(3) A consent signed under this Code section has the effect of a meeting vote and may be described as such in any document; and

(4) If action is taken under this Code section by less than all of the members or managers entitled to vote on the action, all members or managers entitled to vote on the action who did not participate in taking the action shall be given written notice of the action not more than ten days after the taking of the action without a meeting, but the failure to give such notice shall not invalidate the action so taken.

§ 14-11-310. Meetings

(a) Except as otherwise provided in the articles of organization or a written operating agreement, if the limited liability company has more than one manager:

(1) Meetings of managers may be called by any manager;

(2) At least two days' notice of any meeting of managers shall be given by any manager calling the meeting;

(3) Managers may participate in any meeting by, or conduct the meeting through the use of, any means of communication by which all members participating may simultaneously hear each other during the meeting. A manager participating in a meeting by this means is deemed to be present in person at the meeting;

(4) A majority in number of managers shall constitute a quorum for a meeting of managers; and

(5) The act of a majority of managers at a meeting of managers at which a quorum is present shall be required for managers to take action on any matter where a vote of managers is required.

(b) Unless otherwise provided in the articles of organization or a written operating agreement:

(1) Meetings of members may be called by at least 25 percent of the members;

(2) At least two days' notice of all meetings of members shall be given by the members authorized to call meetings;

(3) Members may participate in any meeting by, or conduct the meeting through the use of, any means of communication by which all members participating may simultaneously hear each other during the meeting. A member participating in a meeting by this means is deemed to be present in person at the meeting;

(4) A majority of the members shall constitute a quorum for a meeting of members; and

(5) Except as otherwise provided in this chapter, the act of a majority of members present at a meeting at which a quorum is present shall be required to take action on any matter where a vote of members is required.

§ 14-11-311. Notice

Except as otherwise provided in the articles of organization or a written operating agreement:

(1) Notice shall be in writing unless oral notice is reasonable under the circumstances;

(2) Notice may be communicated in person; by telephone, electronic transmission, or other form of wire or wireless communication; or by mail or private carrier. If these forms of personal notice are impracticable, notice may be communicated by a newspaper of general circulation in the area where published or by radio, television, or other form of public broadcast communication;

(3) Written notice to a person that is required by this title to maintain a registered agent and a registered office in this state may be, but is not required to be, addressed to its registered agent at its registered office;

(4) Written notice, if in a comprehensible form, is effective at the earliest of the following:

(A) When received, or when delivered, properly addressed, as permitted by paragraph (2) of this Code section or to the addressee's last known principal place of business or residence;

(B) Five days, or such other period as shall be provided in the articles of organization or a written operating agreement, after its deposit in the mail, as evidenced by the postmark, if mailed with first-class postage prepaid and correctly addressed to a member or manager at the address shown in the limited liability company's current record of members or managers; or

(C) On the date shown on the return receipt, if sent by registered or certified mail or statutory overnight delivery, return receipt requested, and the receipt is signed by or on behalf of the addressee;

(5) Oral notice is effective when communicated if communicated in a comprehensible manner;

(6) In calculating time periods for notice under this chapter, when a period of time measured in days, weeks, months, years, or other measurement of time is prescribed for the exercise of any privilege or the discharge of any duty, the first day shall not be counted but the last day shall be counted; and

(7) If this chapter prescribes notice requirements for particular circumstances, those requirements govern.

§ 14-11-312. Waiver of notice

Except as otherwise provided in the articles of organization or a written operating agreement:

(1) A member or manager may waive any notice required by this chapter, the articles of organization, or an operating agreement before or after the date and time stated in the notice. The waiver must be in writing, be signed by the member or manager entitled to the notice, and be delivered to the limited liability company for inclusion in its records;

(2) A member or manager's attendance at a meeting:

(A) Waives objection to lack of notice or defective notice of the meeting, unless the member or manager at the beginning of the meeting objects to holding the meeting or transacting business at the meeting; and

(B) Waives objection to consideration of a particular matter at the meeting that is not within the purpose or purposes described in the meeting notice, unless the member or manager objects to considering the matter when it is presented; and

(3) Unless required by a written operating agreement, neither the business transacted nor the purpose of the meeting need be specified in the waiver.

§ 14-11-313. Records and information

Except as otherwise provided in the articles of organization or a written operating agreement:

(1) Each limited liability company shall keep at its principal office the following:

(A) A current list of the name and last known address of each member and manager;

(B) Copies of records that would enable a member to determine the relative voting rights, if any, of the members;

(C) A copy of the articles of organization, together with any amendments thereto;

(D) Copies of the limited liability company's federal, state, and local income tax returns, if any, for the three most recent years;

(E) A copy of any operating agreement that is in writing, together with any amendments thereto; and

(F) Copies of financial statements, if any, of the limited liability company for the three most recent years;

(2) A member may:

(A) At the member's own expense, inspect and copy any limited liability company record upon reasonable request during ordinary business hours;

(B) Obtain from time to time upon reasonable demand:

(i) True and complete information regarding the state of the business and financial condition of the limited liability company;

(ii) Promptly after becoming available, a copy of the limited liability company's federal, state, and local income tax returns, if any, for each year; and

(iii) Other information regarding the affairs of the limited liability company as is just and reasonable; and

(3) If the limited liability company refuses to permit the inspection authorized by paragraph (2) of this Code section, the member demanding inspection may apply to the superior court for the county in which the registered office of the limited liability company is located, upon such notice as the court may require, for an order directing the limited liability company to show cause why an order permitting such inspection by the applicant should not be granted. The court shall hear the parties summarily, by affidavit or otherwise, and if the limited liability company fails to establish that the applicant is not entitled to such inspection, the court shall grant an order permitting such inspection, subject to any limitations which the court may prescribe, and grant such other relief, including costs and reasonable attorneys' fees, as the court may deem just and proper.

§ 14-11-314. Professional relationships

This chapter does not alter any law applicable to the relationship between a person rendering professional services and a person receiving those services, including liability arising out of those professional services. This chapter does not alter any law with respect to disregarding legal entities. The failure of a limited liability company to observe formalities relating to the exercise of its powers or the management of its business and affairs is not a ground for imposing personal liability on a member, manager, agent, or employee of the limited liability company for liabilities of the limited liability company.

ARTICLE 4. FINANCE

§ 14-11-401. Contributions to capital

A contribution to the capital of a limited liability company may be in cash, tangible or intangible property, services rendered, or a promissory note or other obligation to contribute cash or tangible or intangible property, or to perform services.

§ 14-11-402. Liability for contribution

(a) Notwithstanding any other provision of law regarding unwritten contracts, including but not limited to Code Section 13-5-31, a promise to make a contribution to the capital of a limited liability company is not enforceable unless it is set out in the articles of organization or a written operating agreement that is binding on the person to be charged or in another writing signed by that person.

(b) Unless otherwise provided in the articles of organization or a written operating agreement, the obligation of a person to make a contribution to the capital of a limited liability company may be reduced or eliminated only with the unanimous consent of the members.

(c) A written operating agreement may provide that the interest of any member who fails to make any contribution that he or she is obligated to make shall be subject to specified penalties for, or specified consequences of, such failure. Such penalty or consequence may take the form of reducing or eliminating the defaulting member's proportionate interest in a limited liability company, subordinating his or her limited liability company interest to that of nondefaulting members, a forced sale of his or her limited liability company interest, forfeiture of his or her limited liability company interest, the lending by other members of the amounts necessary to meet his or her commitment, a fixing of the value of his or her limited liability company interest by appraisal or by formula and redemption or sale of his or her limited liability company interest at such value, or other penalty or consequence.

§ 14-11-403. Allocation of profits and losses

The profits and losses, and each item thereof, of a limited liability company shall be allocated among the members in the manner provided in the articles of organization or in a written operating agreement. If the articles of organization or a written operating agreement does not so provide, profits and losses, and each item thereof, shall be allocated equally among the members.

§ 14-11-404. Distributions

A member shall be entitled to receive distributions from a limited liability company before the dissolution and winding up of the limited liability company only to the extent, and at the times or upon the happening of the events, specified in the articles of organization or a written operating agreement, or as otherwise approved by all of the members. Subject to Code Section 14-11-405, distributions by a limited liability company to its members, both prior to and after the dissolution of the limited liability company, shall be shared among the members in the manner provided in the articles of organization or a written operating agreement. Subject to Code Section 14-11-405, if the articles of organization or a written operating agreement does not provide the manner in which distributions are to be shared, distributions shall be shared equally among the members.

§ 14-11-405. Distributions upon event of dissociation

(a) Effective for limited liability companies formed prior to July 1, 1999, except as otherwise provided in the articles of organization or a written operating agreement, and subject to Code Section 14-11-407, a member with respect to which an event of dissociation occurs (other than one of the events specified in paragraphs (1), (2), and (4) of subsection (b) of Code Section 14-11-601) is entitled to receive, within a reasonable time after the occurrence of the event, the fair value of the member's interest in the limited liability company as of the date of such occurrence, but only if such event does not result in dissolution of the limited liability company.

(b) Effective for limited liability companies formed on or after July 1, 1999, except as otherwise provided in the articles of organization or a written operating agreement, a member with respect to which an event of dissociation occurs under Code Section 14-11-601.1 is not entitled to receive any payment by reason of such event and will become an assignee as to such limited liability company interest.

§ 14-11-406. Distributions in kind

Except as provided in the articles of organization or a written operating agreement:

(1) A member, regardless of the nature of the member's contribution, has no right to demand and receive any distribution from a limited liability company in any form other than cash; and

(2) No member may be compelled to accept from a limited liability company a distribution of any asset in kind to the extent that the percentage of the asset distributed to the member exceeds a percentage that is equal to the percentage in which the member shares in distributions from the limited liability company.

§ 14-11-407. Restrictions on making distributions

(a) No distribution to a member, to an assignee, or with respect to the interest of a member as to which an event of dissociation has occurred may be made if, after giving effect to the distribution:

(1) The limited liability company would not be able to pay its debts as they become due in the usual course of business; or

(2) The limited liability company's total assets would be less than the sum of its total liabilities plus, unless the articles of organization or a written operating agreement provides otherwise, the amount that would be needed, if the limited liability company were to be dissolved at the time of the distribution, to satisfy the preferential rights, if any, of other members upon dissolution that are superior to the rights of the member receiving the distribution.

(b) The limited liability company may base a determination that a distribution is not prohibited under subsection (a) of this Code section either on:

(1) Financial statements prepared on the basis of accounting practices and principles that are reasonable under the circumstances; or

(2) A fair valuation or other method that is reasonable under the circumstances.

(c) Except as provided in subsection (e) of this Code section, the effect of a distribution under subsection (a) of this Code section is measured:

(1) In the case of distribution by purchase, redemption, or other acquisition of a limited liability company interest, as of the earlier of:

(A) The date money or other property is transferred or debt incurred by the limited liability company; or

(B) The date the member ceases to be a member with respect to the acquired limited liability company interest;

(2) In the case of any other distribution of indebtedness, as of the date the indebtedness is distributed; and

(3) In all other cases, as of:

(A) The date the distribution is authorized if payment occurs within 120 days after the date of authorization; or

(B) The date the payment is made if it occurs more than 120 days after the date of authorization.

(d) A limited liability company's indebtedness incurred by reason of a distribution made in accordance with this Code section is at parity with the limited liability company's indebtedness to its general, unsecured creditors, except to the extent subordinated by agreement or except to the extent secured.

(e) Indebtedness of a limited liability company, including indebtedness issued as a distribution, is not considered a liability for purposes of determinations made under subsection (a) of this Code section if its terms provide that payment of principal and interest is to be made only if, and to the extent that, payment of a distribution to members could then be made under this Code section, and if such indebtedness is issued as a distribution, each payment of principal or interest on the indebtedness is treated as a distribution, the effect of which is measured on the date the payment is actually made.

§ 14-11-408. Liability upon wrongful distribution

(a) A member or manager who votes for or expressly consents to a distribution that is made in violation of Code Section 14-11-407 is personally liable to the limited liability company for the amount of the distribution that exceeds what could have been distributed without violating Code Section 14-11-407, if it is established that such member or manager did not act in compliance with Code Section 14-11-407 and violated a duty owed under Code Section 14-11-305 (without regard to any limitation on such duty permitted by paragraph (4) of Code Section 14-11-305).

(b) Each member or manager held liable under subsection (a) of this Code section for an unlawful distribution is entitled to contribution:

(1) From each other member or manager who could be held liable under subsection (a) of this Code section for the unlawful distribution; and

(2) From each member for the amount the member received knowing that the distribution was made in violation of Code Section 14-11-407.

(c) A proceeding under this Code section is barred unless it is commenced within two years after the date on which the effect of the distribution is measured under Code Section 14-11-407.

§ 14-11-409. Right to distribution

At the time a member becomes entitled to receive a distribution, the member has the status of, and is entitled to all remedies available to, a creditor of the limited liability company with respect to the distribution.

ARTICLE 5. LIMITED LIABILITY COMPANY INTERESTS; ADMISSION OF MEMBERS

§ 14-11-501. Nature of limited liability company interest

(a) A limited liability company interest is personal property. A member has no interest in specific limited liability company property.

(b) An operating agreement or the articles of organization may provide that a limited liability company interest may be evidenced by a certificate issued by the limited liability company.

§ 14-11-502. Assignment of limited liability company interest

Except as otherwise provided in the articles of organization or a written operating agreement:

(1) A limited liability company interest is assignable in whole or in part;

(2) An assignment entitles the assignee to share in the profits and losses and to receive the distributions to which the assignor was entitled, to the extent assigned;

(3) An assignment of a limited liability company interest does not of itself dissolve the limited liability company or entitle the assignee to participate in the management and affairs of the limited liability company or to become or exercise any rights of a member until admitted as a member pursuant to Code Section 14-11-505;

(4) Until the assignee of a limited liability company interest becomes a member, the assignor continues to be a member with respect to the assigned limited liability company interest, subject to the other members' right to remove the assignor pursuant to subparagraph (b)(3)(B) of Code Section 14-11-601 or subparagraph (b)(2)(B) of Code Section 14-11-601.1;

(5) Until the assignee of a limited liability company interest becomes a member, the assignee shall have no liability as a member solely as a result of the assignment;

(6) A member who assigns his or her entire limited liability company interest ceases to be a member or to have the power to exercise any rights of a member when all of the assignees of his or her entire limited liability company interest become members with respect to the assigned limited liability company interest, subject to the other members' right to remove the assignor earlier pursuant to subparagraph (b)(3)(B) of Code Section 14-11-601 or subparagraph (b)(2)(B) of Code Section 14-11-601.1; and

(7) The pledge of, or granting of a security interest, lien, or other encumbrance in or against, any or all of the limited liability company interest of a member is not an assignment and shall

not cause the member to cease to be a member or to cease to have the power to exercise any rights or powers of a member.

§ 14-11-503. Rights of assignee to become member

Except as otherwise provided in the articles of organization or a written operating agreement:

(1) An assignee of a limited liability company interest may become a member only if the other members unanimously consent;

(2) An assignee who has become a member has, to the extent assigned, the rights and powers, and is subject to the restrictions and liabilities, of a member under the articles of organization, any operating agreement, and this chapter;

(3) An assignee who becomes a member is liable for the obligations to make contributions that are enforceable against his or her assignor under Code Section 14-11-402, but he or she is not liable for:

(A) The obligations of his or her assignor under Code Section 14-11-408; or

(B) Other obligations of his or her assignor (including obligations to make contributions) of which the assignee had no knowledge at the time he or she became a member and which could not be ascertained from the articles of organization or a written operating agreement; and

(4) Whether or not an assignee of a limited liability company interest becomes a member, the assignor is not released from his or her liability to the limited liability company under Code Section 14-11-402 or Code Section 14-11-408.

§ 14-11-504. Rights of judgment creditor

(a) On application to a court of competent jurisdiction by any judgment creditor of a member or of any assignee of a member, the court may charge the limited liability company interest of the member or such assignee with payment of the unsatisfied amount of the judgment with interest. To the extent so charged, the judgment creditor has only the rights of an assignee of the limited liability company interest. This chapter does not deprive any member of the benefit of any exemption laws applicable to his or her limited liability company interest.

(b) The remedy conferred by this Code section shall not be deemed exclusive of others which may exist, including, without limitation, the right of a judgment creditor to reach the limited liability company interest of the member by process of garnishment served on the limited liability company, provided that, except as otherwise provided in the articles of organization or a written operating agreement, a judgment creditor shall have no right under this chapter or any other state law to interfere with the management or force dissolution of a limited liability company or to seek an order of the court requiring a foreclosure sale of the limited liability company interest.

§ 14-11-505. Admission of members

(a) In connection with the formation of a limited liability company, a person is admitted as a member of the limited liability company upon the later to occur of:

(1) The formation of the limited liability company; or

(2) The time provided in and upon compliance with the articles of organization or a written operating agreement or, if the articles of organization and any written operating agreement do not so provide, when the person's admission is reflected in the records of the limited liability company.

(b) After the formation of a limited liability company, a person is admitted as a member of the limited liability company at the time provided in and upon compliance with the articles of organization and any written operating agreement or, if the articles of organization or a written operating agreement does not so provide, upon the consent of all members and when the person's admission is reflected in the records of the limited liability company.

(c) An assignee is admitted as a member of the limited liability company upon compliance with paragraph (1) of Code Section 14-11-503 and at the time provided in and upon compliance with the articles of organization and any written operating agreement or, if the articles of organization or a written operating agreement does not so provide, when any such person's permitted admission is reflected in the records of the limited liability company; provided, however, that an assignee shall not be admitted as a member of the limited liability company until such assignee has consented to such admission.

(d) A written operating agreement may provide that a person shall be admitted as a member of a limited liability company, or shall become an assignee of a limited liability company interest or other rights or powers of a member to the extent assigned, and shall become bound by the operating agreement and the provisions of the articles of organization (A) if such person (or a representative authorized by such person) executes the operating agreement or any other writing evidencing the intent of such person to become a member or assignee, or (B) without such execution, if such person (or a representative authorized by such person) complies with the conditions for becoming a member or assignee as set forth in the written operating agreement or any other writing and such person or representative requests in writing that the records of the limited liability company reflect such admission or assignment.

(e) A person may be admitted to a limited liability company as a member of the limited liability company and may receive a limited liability company interest in the limited liability company without making a contribution or being obligated to make a contribution to the limited liability company. Unless otherwise provided in a written operating agreement, a person may be admitted to a limited liability company as a member of the limited liability company without acquiring a limited liability company interest in the limited liability company. Unless otherwise provided in a written operating agreement, a person may be admitted as the sole member of a limited liability company without making a contribution or being obligated to make a contribution to the limited liability company or without acquiring a limited liability company interest in the limited liability company.

(f) In the case of a person being admitted as a member of a surviving limited liability company pursuant to a merger in accordance with Article 9 of this chapter, a person is admitted as a member of the limited liability company as provided in the operating agreement of the surviving limited liability company or in the agreement of merger, and in the event of any inconsistency, the terms of the agreement of merger shall control. In connection with the conversion into a limited liability company in accordance with Code Section 14-11-212, a person is admitted as a member of the limited liability company as provided in the limited liability company agreement.

§ 14-11-506. Powers of estate of a deceased or incompetent member

Except as otherwise provided in the articles of organization or a written operating agreement, if a member who is an individual dies or a court of competent jurisdiction adjudges him or her to be incompetent to manage his or her person or his or her property, the member's executor, administrator, guardian, conservator, or other legal representative has all of the rights of an assignee of all of the member's limited liability company interest. Except as otherwise provided in the articles of organization or a written operating agreement, if the last member of a limited liability company dies or a court of competent jurisdiction adjudges him or her to be incompetent to manage his or her person or his or her property, the member's executor, administrator, guardian, conservator, or other legal representative shall become a member of the limited liability company, unless such executor, administrator, guardian, conservator, or other legal representative elects not to become a member by written notice given to the limited liability company within 90 days of such death or adjudication (or within such other period as is provided for in a written operating agreement).

ARTICLE 6. EVENTS OF DISSOCIATION, WITHDRAWAL, AND DISSOLUTION

§ 14-11-601. Events of dissociation

(a) This Code section is effective for limited liability companies formed prior to July 1, 1999.

(b) A person ceases to be a member of a limited liability company upon the occurrence of any of the following events:

(1) The member withdraws by voluntary act from the limited liability company as provided in subsection (d) of this Code section;

(2) The member ceases to be a member of the limited liability company as provided in paragraph (6) of Code Section 14-11-502;

(3) The member is removed as a member:

(A) In accordance with the articles of organization or a written operating agreement; or

(B) Subject to contrary provision in the articles of organization or in a written operating agreement, when the member assigns all of his or her limited liability company interest, by an affirmative vote of a majority in number of the members who have not assigned all of their limited liability company interests;

(4) The member's entire interest in the limited liability company is purchased or redeemed by the limited liability company;

(5) Subject to contrary provision in the articles of organization or a written operating agreement, or written consent of all other members at the time, the member (A) makes an assignment for the benefit of creditors; (B) files a voluntary petition in bankruptcy; (C) is adjudicated a bankrupt or insolvent; (D) files a petition or answer seeking for the member any reorganization, arrangement, composition, readjustment, liquidation, dissolution, or similar relief under any statute, law, or regulation; (E) files an answer or other pleading admitting or failing to contest the material allegations of a petition filed against the member in any proceeding of this nature; or (F) seeks, consents to, or acquiesces in the appointment of a trustee, receiver, or liquidator of the member or of all or any substantial part of the member's properties;

(6) Subject to contrary provision in the articles of organization or a written operating agreement, or written consent of all other members at the time, if within 120 days after the commencement of any proceeding against the member seeking reorganization, arrangement, composition, readjustment, liquidation, dissolution, or similar relief under any statute, law, or regulation, the proceeding has not been dismissed, or if within 90 days after the appointment without his or her consent or acquiescence of a trustee, receiver, or liquidator of the member or of all or any substantial part of his or her properties, the appointment is not vacated or stayed, or within 90 days after the expiration of any stay, the appointment is not vacated; or

(7) Subject to contrary provision in the articles of organization or a written operating agreement, or written consent of all other members at the time, in the case of a member who is an individual:

(A) On the date of his or her death; or

(B) On the date of the entry of an order by a court of competent jurisdiction adjudicating the member incompetent to manage his or her person or his or her property.

(c) The articles of organization or a written operating agreement may provide for other events the occurrence of which result in a person ceasing to be a member of the limited liability company.

(d) Except as otherwise provided in the articles of organization or a written operating agreement, a member may withdraw from the limited liability company at any time by giving written notice to the other members at least 30 days in advance of his or her withdrawal or such other notice as is provided for in a written operating agreement.

§ 14-11-601.1. Events resulting in cessation of membership

(a) This Code section is effective for limited liability companies formed on or after July 1, 1999.

(b) A person ceases to be a member of a limited liability company upon the occurrence of any of the following events:

(1) The member ceases to be a member of the limited liability company as provided in paragraph (6) of Code Section 14-11-502;

(2) The member is removed as a member:

(A) In accordance with the articles of organization or a written operating agreement; or

(B) Subject to contrary provision in the articles of organization or in a written operating agreement, when the member assigns all of his or her limited liability company interest, by an affirmative vote of a majority in number of the members who have not assigned all of their limited liability company interests;

(3) The member's entire interest in the limited liability company is purchased or redeemed by the limited liability company;

(4) Subject to contrary provision in the articles of organization or a written operating agreement, or written consent of all other members at the time, the member (A) makes an assignment for the benefit of creditors; (B) files a voluntary petition in bankruptcy; (C) is adjudicated a bankrupt or insolvent; (D) files a petition or answer seeking for the member any reorganization, arrangement, composition, readjustment, liquidation, dissolution, or similar relief under any statute, law, or regulation; (E) files an answer or other pleading admitting or failing to contest the material allegations of a petition filed against the member in any proceeding of this nature; or (F) seeks, consents to, or acquiesces in the appointment of a trustee, receiver, or liquidator of the member or of all or any substantial part of the member's properties;

(5) Subject to contrary provision in the articles of organization or a written operating agreement, or written consent of all other members at the time, if within 120 days after the commencement of any proceeding against the member seeking reorganization, arrangement, composition, readjustment, liquidation, dissolution, or similar relief under any statute, law, or regulation, the proceeding has not been dismissed, or if within 90 days after the appointment without his or her consent or acquiescence of a trustee, receiver, or liquidator of the member or of all or any substantial part of his or her properties, the appointment is not vacated or stayed, or within 90 days after the expiration of any stay, the appointment is not vacated; or

(6) Subject to contrary provision in the articles of organization or a written operating agreement, or written consent of all other members at the time, in the case of a member who is an individual:

(A) On the date of his or her death; or

(B) On the date of the entry of an order by a court of competent jurisdiction adjudicating the member incompetent to manage his or her person or his or her property.

(c) The articles of organization or a written operating agreement may provide for other events the occurrence of which result in a person ceasing to be a member of the limited liability company.

(d) Except as otherwise provided in the articles of organization or a written operating agreement, a member may not withdraw from the limited liability company.

§ 14-11-602. Dissolution

(a) Effective for limited liability companies formed prior to July 1, 1999, a limited liability company is dissolved and its affairs shall be wound up upon the first to occur of the following:

(1) At the time specified in the articles of organization or a written operating agreement;

(2) Upon the happening of events specified in the articles of organization or a written operating agreement;

(3) Subject to contrary provision in the articles of organization or a written operating agreement, at a time approved by all the members;

(4) Subject to contrary provision in the articles of organization or a written operating agreement, 90 days after any event of dissociation with respect to any member (other than an event specified in paragraph (1) of subsection (b) of Code Section 14-11-601), unless within such 90 day period the limited liability company is continued by the written consent of all other members or as otherwise provided in the articles of organization or a written operating agreement; or

(5) Entry of a decree of judicial dissolution under subsection (a) of Code Section 14-11-603.

(b) Effective for limited liability companies formed on or after July 1, 1999, a limited liability company is dissolved and its affairs shall be wound up upon the first to occur of the following:

(1) At the time specified in the articles of organization or a written operating agreement;

(2) Upon the happening of events specified in the articles of organization or a written operating agreement;

(3) Subject to contrary provision in the articles of organization or a written operating agreement, at a time approved by all the members;

(4) Subject to contrary provision in the articles of organization or a written operating agreement, 90 days after an event of dissociation with respect to the last remaining member, unless otherwise provided in the articles of organization or a written operating agreement; or

(5) Entry of a decree of judicial dissolution under subsection (a) of Code Section 14-11-603.

(c) Notwithstanding paragraphs (1), (2), (3), and (4) of subsections (a) and (b) of this Code section, the limited liability company shall not be dissolved and its affairs shall not be wound up if, prior to the filing of a certificate of termination in the office of the Secretary of State, either:

(1) The limited liability company's articles of organization or operating agreement, or both, are amended such that, after giving effect to such amendment, such event does not result in dissolution of the limited liability company pursuant to subsection (a) or (b) of this Code section; or

(2) If the limited liability company then has at least one member, a decision to continue the limited liability is taken by all of the members of the limited liability company (and all other persons, if any, with power to require dissolution of the limited liability company under its articles of organization or written operating agreement).

Any amendment or other action contemplated by paragraph (1) or (2) of this subsection shall, to the extent necessary to achieve the purposes of this subsection, be effective as of and from and after the applicable event described in subsection (a) or (b) of this Code section.

§ 14-11-603. Judicial and administrative dissolution; reservation of name

(a) On application by or for a member, the court may decree dissolution of a limited liability company whenever it is not reasonably practicable to carry on the business in conformity with the articles of organization or a written operating agreement. A certified copy of any such decree shall be delivered to the Secretary of State, who shall file it.

(b)(1) The Secretary of State may commence a proceeding under this subsection to dissolve a limited liability company administratively if:

(A) The limited liability company does not deliver its annual registration to the Secretary of State, together with all required fees and penalties, within 60 days after it is due;

(B) The limited liability company is without a registered agent or registered office in this state for 60 days or more;

(C) The limited liability company does not notify the Secretary of State within 60 days that its registered agent or registered office has been changed, that its registered agent has resigned, or that its registered office has been discontinued; or

(D) The limited liability company pays a fee as required to be collected by the Secretary of State by a check or some other form of payment which is dishonored and the limited liability company or its agent does not submit payment for said dishonored payment within 60 days from notice of nonpayment issued by the Secretary of State.

(2) If the Secretary of State determines that one or more grounds exist under this subsection for dissolving a limited liability company, he or she shall provide the limited liability company with written notice of his or her determination by mailing a copy of the notice, first-class mail, to the limited liability company at the last known address of its principal office or to the registered agent. If the limited liability company does not correct each ground for dissolution or demonstrate to the reasonable satisfaction of the Secretary of State that each ground determined by the Secretary of State does not exist within 60 days after notice is provided to the limited liability company, the Secretary of State shall administratively dissolve the limited liability company by signing a certificate of dissolution that recites the ground or grounds for dissolution and its effective date. The Secretary of State shall file the original of the certificate.

(3) A limited liability company administratively dissolved continues its existence but may not carry on any business except that necessary to wind up and liquidate its business and affairs. Winding up the business of a limited liability company administratively dissolved may include, without limitation, the limited liability company proceeding, at any time after the effective date

of the administrative dissolution, in accordance with Code Sections 14-11-607 and 14-11-608. The administrative dissolution of a limited liability company does not terminate the authority of its registered agent.

(4) A limited liability company administratively dissolved under this Code section may apply to the Secretary of State for reinstatement within five years after the effective date of such dissolution. The application shall:

(A) Recite the name of the limited liability company and the effective date of its administrative dissolution;

(B) State that the ground or grounds for dissolution either did not exist or have been eliminated;

(C) Either be executed by the registered agent or a member or manager of the limited liability company, in each case as set forth in the most recent annual registration of the limited liability company filed with the Secretary of State, or be accompanied by a notarized statement, executed by a person who was a member or manager, or an heir, successor, or assign of a person who was a member or manager, of the limited liability company at the time that the limited liability company was administratively dissolved, stating that such person or decedent was a member or manager of the limited liability company at the time of administrative dissolution and such person has knowledge of and assents to the application for reinstatement;

(D) Contain a statement by the limited liability company reciting that all taxes owed by the limited liability company have been paid; and

(E) Be accompanied by the fee required for the application for reinstatement contained in Code Section 14-11-1101.

If the Secretary of State determines that the application contains the information required by this paragraph and that the information is correct, he or she shall prepare a certificate of reinstatement that recites his or her determination and the effective date of reinstatement, file the original of the certificate, and serve a copy on the limited liability company. When the reinstatement is effective, it relates back to and takes effect as of the effective date of the administrative dissolution, and the limited liability company resumes carrying on its business as if the administrative dissolution had never occurred.

(5) If the Secretary of State denies a limited liability company's application for reinstatement following administrative dissolution, he or she shall serve the limited liability company with a written notice that explains the reason or reasons for denial. The limited liability company may appeal the denial of reinstatement to the superior court of the county where the limited liability company's registered office is or was located within 30 days after service of the notice of denial is perfected. The limited liability company appeals by petitioning the court to set aside the dissolution and attaching to the petition copies of the Secretary of State's certificate of dissolution, the limited liability company's application for reinstatement, and the Secretary of State's notice of denial. The court's final decision may be appealed as in other civil proceedings.

(6) The Secretary of State shall reserve the name of a limited liability company administratively dissolved under Code Section 14-2-1421 for such limited liability company's specific use for a period of five years after the effective date of the dissolution or until the limited liability company is reinstated, whichever is sooner.

§ 14-11-604. Winding up

(a) Except as otherwise provided in the articles of organization or a written operating agreement, upon dissolution, the members or managers in whom management of the limited liability company was vested prior to dissolution may wind up a dissolved limited liability company's affairs, or, if there are no such members or managers at the time of or at any time after such dissolution, such persons as may be designated by the persons then entitled to receive a majority of all subsequent distributions, if any, from the limited liability company may wind up the limited liability company's affairs. For cause shown, the court may wind up a dissolved limited liability company's affairs on application of any member as to which an event of dissociation has not occurred, any such member's legal representative, or any such member's assignee, or if there is no such member, legal representative, or assignee, on application of any assignee of an interest in the limited liability company.

(b) Except so far as may be appropriate to wind up the limited liability company's affairs or to complete transactions begun but not then finished, dissolution terminates all authority of every person to act for the limited liability company; provided, however, that, prior to the filing of a statement of commencement of winding up, the limited liability company shall be bound to any person who lacks knowledge of the dissolution with respect to any transaction which would bind the limited liability company if dissolution had not taken place.

§ 14-11-605. Distribution of assets

(a) In connection with its winding up, a limited liability company shall (1) discharge, make provision to discharge, or dispose of pursuant to Code Sections 14-11-607 and 14-11-608, its liabilities, and (2) subject to any applicable provisions in the articles of organization or a written operating agreement, distribute its remaining assets to its members.

(b) To the extent a dissolved limited liability company does not discharge, make provision to discharge, or dispose of pursuant to Code Sections 14-11-607 and 14-11-608 a claim against it, such claim may be enforced:

(1) Against the limited liability company, to the extent of its undistributed assets; or

(2) Against each member receiving a distribution in winding up, to the extent of the assets so distributed to such member; provided that a member's total liability for all such claims shall not exceed the total amount of assets so distributed to him or her.

As respects any such claims, the limited liability company and its members shall have rights of contribution among themselves so as to produce, insofar as practicable, the effects that would have been produced had such claim been discharged by the limited liability company prior to any distribution to members.

§ 14-11-606. Statement of commencement of winding up

Upon dissolution, a statement of commencement of winding up may be delivered for filing to the Secretary of State by any person authorized to wind up the limited liability company's affairs. Such statement shall set forth:

(1) The name of the limited liability company;

(2) The fact that the limited liability company has dissolved and commenced its winding up activities; and

(3) Any other provision, not inconsistent with law, that the persons charged with winding up the limited liability company's affairs elect to include.

§ 14-11-607. Known claims against dissolved limited liability company

(a) A dissolved limited liability company that has filed a statement of commencement of winding up may dispose of the known claims against it by following the procedures described in this Code section.

(b) The dissolved limited liability company may notify its known claimants in writing of the winding up proceedings at any time after the filing of the statement of commencement of winding up. The written notice must:

(1) Describe information that the limited liability company determines must be included in a claim;

(2) Provide a mailing address where a claim may be sent;

(3) State the deadline, which may not be less than six months from the date of mailing of the written notice, by which the dissolved limited liability company must receive the claim;

(4) State that the claim will be barred if not received by the deadline; and

(5) State that the limited liability company will give notice of acceptance or rejection of all claims that are received in timely fashion within six months after the deadline for receipt of claims.

(c) A claim against a dissolved limited liability company is barred:

(1) If a claimant who was given written notice under subsection (b) of this Code section does not deliver the claim to the dissolved limited liability company by the deadline; or

(2) If a claimant whose claim was rejected by the dissolved limited liability company does not commence a proceeding to enforce the claim within one year from the date of mailing of the rejection notice.

(d) For purposes of this Code section, the term "claim" does not include a contingent liability or a claim based on an event occurring after the filing of the statement of commencement of winding up.

§ 14-11-608. Unknown claims against dissolved limited liability company

(a) A dissolved limited liability company that has filed a statement of commencement of winding up may publish, in the manner prescribed by Code Section 14-11-609, a request that persons with claims against the limited liability company present them in accordance with subsection (b) of this Code section.

(b) The request must:

(1) Describe the information that the limited liability company determines must be included in a claim and provide a mailing address where the claim may be sent; and

(2) State that, except for claims that are contingent at the time of the filing of the statement of commencement of winding up or that arise after the filing of the statement of commencement of winding up, a claim against the limited liability company not otherwise barred will be barred unless a proceeding to enforce the claim is commenced within two years after the publication of the request.

(c) If a dissolved limited liability company that has filed a statement of commencement of winding up publishes a request described in subsection (b) of this Code section, all claims not otherwise barred will be barred unless the claimant commences a proceeding to enforce the claim against the dissolved limited liability company within two years after the date of the publication of the request, except:

(1) Claims that are contingent at the time of the filing of the statement of commencement of winding up; and

(2) Claims that arise after the filing of the statement of commencement of winding up.

(d) If a dissolved limited liability company publishes a request described in subsection (b) of this Code section, a claim not otherwise barred of a claimant whose claim is contingent at the time of the filing of the statement of commencement of winding up or based on an event occurring after the filing of the statement of commencement of winding up is barred against the limited liability company, its members, and managers unless the claimant commences a proceeding to enforce the claim against the dissolved limited liability company within two years after the date of filing of a certificate of termination or five years after the date of the second publication of the request in accordance with subsection (b) of this Code section, whichever is later.

§ 14-11-609. Manner of publication of request for claims

A limited liability company seeking to publish a request for claims described in Code Section 14-11-608 shall mail or deliver to the publisher of a newspaper that is the official organ of the county where the registered office of the limited liability company is located, or that is a newspaper of general circulation published within such county whose most recently published annual statement of ownership and circulation reflects a minimum of 60 percent paid circulation, a request to publish the request for claims. The request for publication of the request for claims shall be accompanied by a check, draft, or money order in the amount of $40.00 in payment of the cost of publication. The notice shall be published once a week for two consecutive weeks commencing within ten days after receipt of the notice by the newspaper.

§ 14-11-610. Certificate of termination

A dissolved limited liability company may deliver to the Secretary of State for filing a certificate of termination when the statements required to be included therein can be truthfully made. Such a certificate of termination shall set forth:

(1) The name of the limited liability company;

(2) That all known debts, liabilities, and obligations of the limited liability company have been paid, discharged, or barred or that adequate provision has been made therefor; and

(3) That there are no actions pending against the limited liability company in any court, or that adequate provision has been made for the satisfaction of any judgment, order, or decree that may be entered against it in any pending action.

§ 14-11-611. Execution of deeds or other instruments by signing

Deeds or other instruments requiring execution after the filing of a certificate of termination by a dissolved limited liability company may be signed by any person who had authority to wind up the dissolved limited liability company under the provisions of subsection (a) of Code Section 14-11-604.

ARTICLE 7. FOREIGN LIMITED LIABILITY COMPANIES

§ 14-11-701. Law applicable to foreign limited liability companies

(a) The laws of the jurisdiction under which a foreign limited liability company is organized govern its organization and internal affairs and the liability of its managers, members, and other owners, regardless of whether the foreign limited liability company procured or should have procured a certificate of authority under this chapter.

(b) A foreign limited liability company may not be denied a certificate of authority by reason of any difference between the laws of the jurisdiction under which such company is organized and the laws of this state.

§ 14-11-702. Requirement for certificate of authority; application; activities not considered transacting business in this state

(a) A foreign limited liability company transacting business in this state shall procure a certificate of authority to do so from the Secretary of State. In order to procure a certificate of authority to transact business in this state, a foreign limited liability company shall submit to the Secretary of State an application for a certificate of authority as a foreign limited liability company, signed by a person duly authorized to sign such instruments by the laws of the jurisdiction under which the foreign limited liability company is organized, setting forth:

(1) The name of the foreign limited liability company and, if different, the name under which it proposes to qualify and transact business in this state;

(2) The name of the jurisdiction under whose laws it is organized;

(3) Its date of organization and period of duration;

(4) The street address and county of its registered office in this state and the name of its registered agent at that office;

(5) A statement that the Secretary of State is, pursuant to subsection (h) of Code Section 14-11-703, appointed the agent of the foreign limited liability company for service of process if no agent has been appointed under subsection (a) of Code Section 14-11-703 or, if appointed, the agent's authority has been revoked or the agent cannot be found or served by the exercise of reasonable diligence;

(6) The address of its principal place of business;

(7) The address of the office at which is kept a list of the names and addresses of its members and other owners, together with an undertaking by it to keep those records until its registration in this state is canceled or revoked; and

(8) The name and a business address of a person who, under the laws of the jurisdiction under which it was formed, has substantial responsibility for managing its business activities.

(b) Without excluding other activities which may not constitute transacting business in this state, a foreign limited liability company shall not be considered to be transacting business in this state, for the purpose of qualification under this chapter, solely by reason of carrying on in this state any one or more of the following activities:

(1) Maintaining or defending any action or administrative or arbitration proceeding or effecting the settlement thereof or the settlement of claims or disputes;

(2) Holding meetings of its managers, members, or other owners or carrying on other activities concerning its internal affairs;

(3) Maintaining bank accounts, share accounts in savings and loan associations, custodial or agency arrangements with a bank or trust company, or stock or bond brokerage accounts;

(4) Maintaining offices or agencies for the transfer, exchange, and registration of membership or other ownership interests in it or appointing and maintaining trustees or depositaries with relation to such interests;

(5) Effecting sales through independent contractors;

(6) Soliciting or procuring orders, whether by mail or through employees or agents or otherwise, where such orders require acceptance outside this state before becoming binding contracts and where such contracts do not involve any local performance other than delivery and installation;

(7) Making loans or creating or acquiring evidences of debt, mortgages, or liens on real or personal property or recording the same;

(8) Securing or collecting debts or enforcing any rights in property securing the same;

(9) Owning, without more, real or personal property;

(10) Conducting an isolated transaction not in the course of a number of repeated transactions of a like nature;

(11) Effecting transactions in interstate or foreign commerce;

(12) Serving as trustee, executor, administrator, or guardian, or in like fiduciary capacity, where permitted so to serve by the laws of this state; or

(13) Owning directly or indirectly an interest in or controlling directly or indirectly another person organized under the laws of or transacting business within this state.

(c) The list of activities in subsection (b) of this Code section is not exhaustive.

(d) This Code section shall not be deemed to establish a standard for activities that may subject a foreign limited liability company to taxation or to service of process under any of the laws of this state.

§ 14-11-703. Registered office and registered agent; requirement and qualifications; change of office or agent; resignation of agent; service on Secretary of State; venue

(a) Each foreign limited liability company that is required to procure a certificate of authority to transact business in this state shall continuously maintain in this state:

(1) A registered office that may, but need not, be a place of its business in this state; and

(2) A registered agent for service of process on the foreign limited liability company. The address of the business office of the registered agent shall be the same as the address of the registered office referred to in paragraph (1) of this subsection.

(b) A registered agent must be an individual resident of this state, a corporation, or a foreign corporation having a certificate of authority to transact business in this state.

(c) A foreign limited liability company may change its registered office or its registered agent, or both, by indicating any such change on its annual registration filed pursuant to this chapter or by delivering to the Secretary of State for filing a statement setting forth:

(1) The name of the foreign limited liability company;

(2) The street address and county of its then registered office;

(3) If the address of its registered office is to be changed, the new street address and county of the registered office;

(4) The name of its then registered agent; and

(5) If its registered agent is to be changed, the name of its successor registered agent.

(d) A registered agent of a foreign limited liability company may resign as such agent by signing and delivering to the Secretary of State for filing a statement of resignation, which may include a statement that the registered office is also discontinued. On or before the date of the filing of the statement of resignation, the registered agent shall deliver or mail a written notice of the registered agent's intent to resign to the foreign limited liability company at the most recent mailing address of the foreign limited liability company's principal place of business listed in the records of the Secretary of State. The agency appointment is terminated, and the registered office discontinued if so provided, on the earlier of the filing of the limited liability company's annual registration or a statement designating a new registered agent and registered office if also discontinued or the thirty-first day after the date on which the statement of resignation was filed.

(e) A registered agent of a foreign limited liability company may change the agent's office and the address of the registered office of any foreign limited liability company of which the agent is registered agent to another place within this state by filing a statement, as required in subsection (c) of this Code section, setting forth the required information for all foreign limited liability companies for which he or she is the registered agent, except that it need be signed only by the registered agent and need not be responsive to paragraph (5) of subsection (c) of this Code section and must recite that a copy of the statement has been mailed to the foreign limited liability company at the most recent mailing address of the foreign limited liability company's principal place of business listed on the records of the Secretary of State.

(f) The registered agent of one or more foreign limited liability companies may resign and appoint a successor registered agent by signing and delivering to the Secretary of State for filing a statement stating that the agent resigns and the name and street address and county of the office of the successor registered agent. There shall be attached to such statement a statement executed by each affected foreign limited liability company ratifying and approving such change of registered agent. Upon such filing, the successor registered agent shall become the registered agent of such foreign limited liability companies as have ratified and approved such substitution, and the successor registered agent's office, as stated in such statement, shall become the registered office in this state of each such foreign limited liability company. The Secretary of State shall furnish to the successor registered agent a certified copy of the statement filed pursuant to this subsection.

(g) The registered agent of a foreign limited liability company authorized to transact business in this state is an agent of the foreign limited liability company on whom may be served any process, notice, or demand required or permitted by law to be served on the foreign limited liability company.

(h) Whenever a foreign limited liability company required to procure a certificate of authority to transact business in this state shall fail to appoint or maintain a registered agent in this state, or whenever its registered agent cannot with reasonable diligence be found at the registered office, then the Secretary of State shall be an agent of such foreign limited liability company upon whom any process, notice, or demand may be served. Service on the Secretary of State of any such process, notice, or demand shall be made by delivering to and leaving with him or her or with any other person or persons designated by the Secretary of State to receive such service two copies of such process, notice, or demand. The plaintiff or his or her attorney shall certify in writing to the Secretary of State that the foreign limited liability company failed either to maintain a registered office or appoint a registered agent in this state and that he or she has forwarded by registered or certified mail or statutory overnight delivery such process, notice, or demand to the last registered agent at the most recent registered office listed on the records of the Secretary of State and that service cannot be effected at such office.

(i) The Secretary of State shall keep a record of all processes, notices, and demands served upon him or her under this Code section and shall record therein the time of such service and his or her action with reference thereto.

(j) This Code section does not prescribe the only means, or necessarily the required means, of serving any process, notice, or demand required or permitted by law to be served on a foreign limited liability company.

§ 14-11-704. Issuance of certificate of authority

(a) If the Secretary of State finds that an application for a certificate of authority conforms to the filing requirements of this chapter and all requisite fees and any penalty due pursuant to Code Section 14-11-711 have been paid, he or she shall:

(1) Stamp or otherwise endorse his or her official title and the date and time of receipt on the application;

(2) File the application in his or her office; and

(3) Issue a certificate of authority to transact business in this state.

(b) The certificate of authority must be returned to the person who filed the application or such person's representative.

(c) If the certificate of authority is issued by the Secretary of State, a foreign limited liability company shall be deemed authorized to transact business in this state from the time of filing its application for the certificate of authority.

§ 14-11-705. Name

(a) A foreign limited liability company may apply for a certificate of authority with the Secretary of State under any name, whether or not it is the name under which it is registered in its jurisdiction of organization; provided, however, that such name:

(1) Must contain the words "limited liability company" or "limited company" (it being permitted to abbreviate the word "limited" as "ltd." and the word "company" as "co.") or the abbreviations "L.L.C.," "LLC," "L.C." or "LC"; and

(2) Must be distinguishable on the records of the Secretary of State from the name of any corporation, limited liability company, or limited partnership; any foreign corporation, foreign limited liability company, or foreign limited partnership having a certificate of authority to transact business in this state; any nonprofit corporation, professional corporation, or professional association, domestic or foreign, on file with the Secretary of State pursuant to this title; or any name reserved or registered under this title.

(b) Whenever a foreign limited liability company is unable to procure a certificate of authority to transact business in this state because its name does not comply with paragraph (2) of subsection (a) of this Code section, it may nonetheless apply for authority to transact business in this state by adding in parentheses to its name in such application a word, abbreviation, or other distinctive and distinguishing element such as the name of the jurisdiction where it is organized. If in the judgment of the Secretary of State the name of the foreign limited liability company with such addition would comply with subsection (a) of this Code section, subsection (a) of this Code section shall not be a bar to the issuance to such foreign limited liability company of a certificate of authority to transact business in this state. In such case, any such certificate issued to such foreign limited liability company shall be issued in its name with such additions, and the foreign limited liability company shall use such name with such additions in all its dealings with the Secretary of State.

§ 14-11-706. Amended certificate required for change of name or jurisdiction of organization; foreign limited liability company converting to foreign limited partnership or foreign corporation

(a) A foreign limited liability company authorized to transact business in this state must procure an amended certificate of authority from the Secretary of State if it changes its name or its jurisdiction of organization. The requirements of Code Sections 14-11-702 and 14-11-704 for procuring an original certificate of authority shall apply to procuring an amended certificate under this Code section.

(b) If a foreign limited liability company authorized to transact business in this state converts into a foreign limited partnership:

(1) The foreign limited liability company shall notify the Secretary of State that such conversion has occurred no later than 30 days after the conversion, using such form as the Secretary of State shall specify, which form may require such information and statements as may be required to be submitted by a foreign limited partnership that applies for a certificate of authority to transact business in this state; and

(2) If such notice is timely given:

(A) The authorization of such entity to transact business in this state shall continue without interruption; and

(B) The certificate of authority issued to such foreign limited liability company under this article shall constitute a certificate of authority issued under Code Section 14-11-903 to the foreign limited partnership resulting from the conversion effective as of the date of the conversion.

The Secretary of State shall adjust its records accordingly.

(c) If a foreign limited liability company authorized to transact business in this state converts into a foreign corporation:

(1) The foreign limited liability company shall notify the Secretary of State that such conversion has occurred no later than 30 days after the conversion, using such form as the

Secretary of State shall specify, which form may require such information and statements as may be required to be submitted by a foreign corporation that applies for a certificate of authority to transact business in this state; and

(2) If such notice is timely given:

(A) The authorization of such entity to transact business in this state shall continue without interruption; and

(B) The certificate of authority issued to such foreign limited liability company under this article shall constitute a certificate of authority issued under Code Section 14-2-1501 to the foreign corporation resulting from the conversion effective as of the date of the conversion.

The Secretary of State shall adjust its records accordingly.

§ 14-11-707. Certificate of withdrawal; application; service after withdrawal

(a) A foreign limited liability company authorized to transact business in this state may not withdraw from this state until it obtains a certificate of withdrawal from the Secretary of State.

(b) A foreign limited liability company authorized to transact business in this state may apply for a certificate of withdrawal by delivering to the Secretary of State for filing an application that sets forth:

(1) The name of the foreign limited liability company and the name of the jurisdiction under whose law it is organized;

(2) That it is not transacting business in this state and that it surrenders its authority to transact business in this state;

(3) That it revokes the authority of its registered agent to accept service on its behalf and appoints the Secretary of State as its agent for service of process in any proceeding based on a cause of action arising during the time it was authorized to transact business in this state;

(4) A mailing address to which a copy of any process served on the Secretary of State pursuant to paragraph (3) of this subsection may be mailed under subsection (c) of this Code section; and

(5) A commitment to notify the Secretary of State in the future of any change in the mailing address provided pursuant to paragraph (4) of this subsection.

(c) After the withdrawal of the foreign limited liability company is effective, service of process on the Secretary of State under this Code section is service on the foreign limited liability company. Any party that serves process on the Secretary of State in accordance with this subsection shall also mail a copy of the process to the foreign limited liability company at the mailing address provided pursuant to subsection (b) of this Code section.

§ 14-11-708. Revocation of certificate; grounds

The Secretary of State may commence a proceeding under Code Section 14-11-709 to revoke the certificate of authority of a foreign limited liability company authorized to transact business in this state if:

(1) The foreign limited liability company does not deliver its annual registration to the Secretary of State within 60 days after it is due;

(2) The foreign limited liability company does not pay within 60 days after they are due any fees, taxes, or penalties imposed by this chapter or other law;

(3) The foreign limited liability company is without a registered agent or registered office in this state for 60 days or more;

(4) The foreign limited liability company does not inform the Secretary of State under Code Section 14-11-703 that its registered agent or registered office has changed, that its registered agent has resigned, or that its registered office has been discontinued within 60 days of the change, resignation, or discontinuance;

(5) A member, manager, other owner, or agent of the foreign limited liability company signed a document such person knew was false in a material respect with intent that the document be delivered to the Secretary of State for filing; or

(6) The Secretary of State receives a duly authenticated certificate from the secretary of state or other official having custody of records in the jurisdiction under whose law the foreign limited liability company is organized stating that it has been dissolved, terminated, or disappeared as the result of a merger.

§ 14-11-709. Revocation of certificate; notice to company; issuance and effect of certificate of revocation; service after revocation

(a) If the Secretary of State determines that one or more grounds exist under Code Section 14-11-708 for revocation of a certificate of authority, the Secretary of State shall provide the foreign limited liability company with written notice of such determination by mailing a copy of the notice, first-class mail, to the foreign limited liability company at the address of its principal place of business indicated in its most recently filed annual registration, or if no annual registration has been filed, in its application for a certificate of authority to transact business, or to its registered agent.

(b) If the foreign limited liability company does not correct each ground for revocation or demonstrate to the reasonable satisfaction of the Secretary of State that each ground determined by the Secretary of State does not exist within 60 days after the notice is provided to the foreign limited liability company, the Secretary of State may revoke the foreign limited liability company's certificate of authority by signing a certificate of revocation that recites the ground or grounds for revocation and its effective date.

(c) The authority of a foreign limited liability company to transact business in this state ceases on the date shown on the certificate revoking its certificate of authority.

(d) The Secretary of State's revocation of a foreign limited liability company's certificate of authority appoints the Secretary of State as the foreign limited liability company's agent for service of process in any proceeding based on a cause of action which arose during the time the foreign limited liability company was authorized to transact business in this state. Service of process on the Secretary of State under this subsection is service on the foreign limited liability company. Any party that serves process on the Secretary of State shall also mail a copy of the process to the foreign limited liability company at the most recent address of its principal place of business listed on the records of the Secretary of State or to its registered agent. This subsection does not prescribe the only means, or necessarily the required means, of serving any process, notice, or demand required or permitted by law to be served on a foreign limited liability company.

(e) Revocation of a foreign limited liability company's certificate of authority does not terminate the authority of the registered agent of the foreign limited liability company.

§ 14-11-710. Appeal of revocation of certificate

(a) A foreign limited liability company may appeal the Secretary of State's revocation of its certificate of authority to the Superior Court of Fulton County within 30 days after service of the certificate of revocation is perfected under Code Section 14-11-709. The foreign limited liability company appeals by petitioning the court to set aside the revocation and attaching to the petition copies of its certificate of authority and the Secretary of State's certificate of revocation.

(b) The court may summarily order the Secretary of State to reinstate the certificate of authority or may take any other action the court considers appropriate.

(c) The court's final decision may be appealed as in other civil proceedings.

§ 14-11-711. Failure of company to procure certificate; effect; penalty

(a) A foreign limited liability company transacting business in this state may not maintain an action, suit, or proceeding in a court of this state until it is authorized to transact business in this state.

(b) The failure of a foreign limited liability company to procure a certificate of authority does not impair the validity of any contract or act of the foreign limited liability company or prevent the foreign limited liability company from defending any action, suit, or proceeding in any court of this state.

(c) A foreign limited liability company that transacts business in this state without registering as required by this chapter shall be liable to the state:

(1) For all fees which would have been imposed by this chapter upon such foreign limited liability company had it registered as required by this article; and

(2) If it has not been authorized to transact business in this state within 30 days after the first day on which it transacts business in this state, for a penalty of $500.00.

§ 14-11-712. Action to restrain company in violation of chapter

The Attorney General may maintain an action to restrain a foreign limited liability company from transacting business in this state in violation of this chapter.

ARTICLE 8. DERIVATIVE ACTIONS

§ 14-11-801. Right of member to bring derivative action

A member may commence a derivative action in the right of the limited liability company to recover a judgment in its favor if all of the following conditions are met:

(1) Either management of the limited liability company is vested in a manager or managers who have the sole authority to cause the limited liability company to sue in its own right or management of the limited liability company is vested in the members but the plaintiff does not have the authority to cause the limited liability company to sue in its own right under the provisions of the articles of organization or a written operating agreement;

(2) The plaintiff has made written demand on those managers or those members with such authority requesting that such managers or such members take suitable action;

(3) Ninety days have expired from the date the demand was made unless the member has earlier been notified that the demand has been rejected by the limited liability company or unless irreparable injury to the limited liability company would result by waiting for the expiration of the 90 day period;

(4) The plaintiff (A) is a member of the limited liability company at the time of bringing the action, and (B) was a member of the limited liability company at the time of the transaction of which he or she complains, or his or her status as a member of the limited liability company has devolved upon him or her by operation of law from a person who was a member at the time of the transaction; and

(5) The plaintiff fairly and adequately represents the interests of the limited liability company in enforcing the right of the limited liability company.

§ 14-11-802. Complaint

In a derivative action, the complaint must set forth with particularity the effort of the plaintiff to secure commencement of the action by the managers or the members who would otherwise have the authority to cause the limited liability company to sue in its own right.

§ 14-11-803. Stay of proceedings

If the limited liability company commences an inquiry into the allegations made in the demand or complaint, the court may stay any derivative action for such period as the court deems appropriate.

§ 14-11-804. Discontinuance or settlement

Except as otherwise provided by the articles of organization or written operating agreement, a derivative action may not be discontinued or settled without the court's approval. If the court determines that a proposed discontinuance or settlement will substantially affect the interests of the limited liability company's members, the court shall direct that notice be given to the members affected.

§ 14-11-805. Dismissal

(a) The court may dismiss a derivative proceeding if, on motion by the limited liability company, the court finds that one of the groups specified in subsection (b) of this Code section has made a determination in good faith after conducting a reasonable investigation upon which its conclusions are based that the maintenance of the derivative suit is not in the best interests of the limited liability company. The limited liability company shall have the burden of proving the independence and good faith of the group making the determination and the reasonableness of the investigation.

(b) The determination in subsection (a) of this Code section shall be made by:

(1) A majority vote of the independent managers or members present at a meeting of managers or members, as the case may be, if the independent managers or members constitute a quorum;

(2) A majority vote of a committee consisting of two or more independent managers or members appointed by a majority of independent managers or members present at a meeting of managers or members, as the case may be, whether or not such independent managers or members constitute a quorum; or

(3) A panel of one or more independent persons appointed by the court upon motion of the limited liability company.

(c) None of the following shall by itself cause a manager or member to be considered not independent for purposes of subsection (b) of this Code section:

(1) The nomination or election of the manager or member by managers or members who are not independent;

(2) The naming of the manager or member as a defendant in the derivative proceeding; or

(3) The fact that the manager or member approved the action being challenged in the derivative proceeding so long as the manager or member did not receive a personal benefit as a result of the action.

§ 14-11-806. Expenses

(a) If a derivative action is successful, in whole or in part, or if anything is received by the plaintiff as a result of a judgment, compromise, or settlement of an action or claim, the court may award the plaintiff reasonable expenses, including reasonable attorneys' fees, and shall direct him or her to remit to the limited liability company the remainder of those proceeds received by him or her.

(b) In any derivative action instituted on or after March 1, 1994, in the right of any domestic or foreign limited liability company by a member or members thereof, the court having jurisdiction, upon termination of such action and a finding that the action was commenced or maintained without reasonable cause or for an improper purpose, may order the plaintiff or plaintiffs to pay to the parties named as defendants the reasonable expenses, including reasonable attorneys' fees, incurred by them in the defense of such action.

§ 14-11-807. Applicability to foreign limited liability companies

In any derivative action in the right of a foreign limited liability company, the matters covered by this article shall be governed by the laws of the jurisdiction of organization of the foreign limited liability company except for Code Sections 14-11-803 and 14-11-804 and paragraph (b) of Code Section 14-11-806.

§ 14-11-901. Merger

(a) Pursuant to a written agreement, which, unless otherwise provided therein, will constitute the plan of merger required by Code Section 14-11-902 if it contains the provisions required by that Code section, a limited liability company may merge with or into one or more business entities with such limited liability company or other business entity as the agreement shall provide being the surviving limited liability company or other business entity.

(b) In the case of a merger involving a foreign limited liability company, foreign limited partnership, or foreign corporation, the merger may take place if:

(1) The merger is permitted by the law of the state or jurisdiction under whose laws each foreign constituent entity is organized or formed and each foreign constituent entity complies with that law in effecting the merger;

(2) The foreign constituent entity complies with Code Section 14-11-904 if it is the surviving entity of the merger; and

(3) Each limited liability company complies with the applicable provisions of this Code section, Code Sections 14-11-902 and 14-11-903, and, if it is the surviving entity, with Code Section 14-11-904.

§ 14-11-902. Plan of merger

(a) Each constituent business entity shall adopt a written plan of merger, which shall be approved in accordance with Code Section 14-11-903.

(b) The plan of merger must set forth:

(1) The name of each limited liability company and each other business entity that is a constituent entity planning to merge and the name of the surviving business entity into which each other constituent entity proposes to merge;

(2) The terms and conditions of the merger; and

(3) The manner and basis of converting the interests of the members of each limited liability company and the shares or other interests in each other business entity that is a constituent

entity in the merger into interests, shares, obligations, or other securities, as the case may be, of the surviving or any other business entity or, in whole or in part, into cash or other property.

(c) The plan of merger may set forth:

(1) Amendments to the articles of organization of a limited liability company that is the surviving entity in the merger; and

(2) Other provisions relating to the merger.

§ 14-11-903. Approval of merger

(a) A limited liability company party to a proposed merger shall have the plan of merger authorized and approved by the unanimous consent of the members, unless the articles of organization or a written operating agreement of such limited liability company provides otherwise. A corporation or limited partnership party to a proposed merger shall have the plan of merger authorized and approved in accordance with the applicable chapter of this title.

(b) A plan of merger complying with the requirements of Code Section 14-11-902 shall be approved by each foreign constituent business entity in accordance with the laws of the state or jurisdiction in which it was organized or formed.

(c) After a merger is authorized, unless the plan of merger provides otherwise, and at any time before articles of merger (as provided for in Code Section 14-11-904) are filed by the Secretary of State, the planned merger may be abandoned (subject to any contractual rights) in accordance with the procedure set forth in the plan of merger or, if none is set forth, as follows:

(1) By the unanimous consent of the members of each limited liability company that is a constituent entity, unless the articles of organization or a written operating agreement of any such limited liability company provides otherwise;

(2) By each corporation and limited partnership that is a constituent entity in accordance with the applicable chapter of this title; and

(3) By each foreign constituent business entity in accordance with the laws of the state or jurisdiction in which it was organized or formed.

§ 14-11-904. Articles of merger

After a plan of merger is approved as provided in Code Section 14-11-903, the surviving limited liability company or other business entity shall deliver to the Secretary of State for filing articles of merger setting forth:

(1) The name and jurisdiction of organization or formation of each constituent business entity that is merging and the name of the surviving limited liability company or other business entity into which each other constituent business entity is merging;

(2) Any amendments to the articles of organization of the surviving limited liability company;

(3) The effective date and time of the merger if later than the date and time the articles of merger are filed;

(4) That the executed plan of merger is on file at the principal place of business of the surviving limited liability company or other business entity, stating the address thereof;

(5) That a copy of the plan of merger will be furnished by the surviving limited liability company or other business entity, on request and without cost, to any member of any constituent entity;

(6) A statement that the plan of merger has been duly authorized and approved by each constituent business entity in accordance with Code Section 14-11-903;

(7) If the surviving entity is a foreign limited liability company, foreign limited partnership, or foreign corporation without a certificate of authority to transact business in this state, that the Secretary of State is appointed as agent of the surviving entity on whom process in this state in any action, suit, or proceeding for the enforcement of an obligation of each limited liability company constituent to the merger may be served and the address to which a copy of the process is to be mailed; and

(8) Any other provisions relating to the merger that the constituent business entities determine to include therein.

§ 14-11-905. Effects of merger

(a) If the surviving entity is a limited liability company, when a merger takes effect:

(1) Every other constituent business entity party to the merger merges into the limited liability company designated in the plan of merger as the surviving entity;

(2) The separate existence of each constituent business entity party to the plan of merger except the surviving limited liability company shall cease;

(3) The title to all real estate and other property owned by each constituent business entity is vested in the surviving limited liability company without reversion or impairment;

(4) The surviving limited liability company has all the liabilities of each constituent business entity;

(5) A proceeding pending against any constituent business entity may be continued as if the merger did not occur or the surviving limited liability company may be substituted in the proceeding for the constituent business entity whose existence ceased;

(6) Neither the rights of creditors nor any liens on the property of any constituent business entity shall be impaired by the merger;

(7) The articles of organization of the surviving limited liability company shall be amended to the extent provided in the articles of merger; and

(8) The interests or shares in each merging constituent business entity that are to be converted into interests of the surviving limited liability company, or into cash or other

property under the terms of the plan of merger, or cancelled, are so converted or cancelled, and the former holders thereof are entitled only to the rights provided in the plan of merger or their rights otherwise provided by law.

(b) If the surviving business entity is to be governed by the laws of any jurisdiction other than this state, the effects of merger shall be the same as provided in this Code section, except insofar as the laws of such other jurisdiction provide otherwise.

(c) Nothing in this article shall abridge or impair any dissenters' or appraisal rights that may otherwise be available to the members or shareholders or other holders of an interest in any constituent business entity.

(d) A foreign business entity authorized to transact business in this state that merges with and into a limited liability company pursuant to this chapter and is not the surviving entity in such merger need not obtain a certificate of withdrawal from the Secretary of State.

§ 14-11-906. Election by a limited liability company to become a foreign limited liability company, a foreign limited partnership, or a foreign corporation; certificate of authority; requirements

(a) A limited liability company may elect to become a foreign limited liability company, a foreign limited partnership, or a foreign corporation, if such a conversion is permitted by the law of the state or jurisdiction under whose law the resulting entity would be formed.

(b) To effect a conversion under this Code section, the limited liability company must adopt a plan of conversion that sets forth the manner and basis of converting the interests of the members of the limited liability company into interests, shares, obligations, or other securities, as the case may be, of the resulting entity. The plan of conversion may set forth other provisions relating to the conversion.

(c) The limited liability company shall have the plan of conversion authorized and approved by the unanimous consent of the members, unless the articles of organization or a written operating agreement of such limited liability company provides otherwise.

(d) After a conversion is authorized, unless the plan of conversion provides otherwise, and at any time before the conversion has become effective, the planned conversion may be abandoned, subject to any contractual rights, in accordance with the procedure set forth in the plan of conversion or, if none is set forth, by the unanimous consent of the members of the limited liability company, unless the articles of organization or a written operating agreement of such limited liability company provides otherwise.

(e) The conversion shall be effected as provided in, and shall have the effects provided by, the law of the state or jurisdiction under whose law the resulting entity is formed and by the plan of conversion, to the extent not inconsistent with such law.

(f) If the resulting entity is required to obtain a certificate of authority to transact business in this state by the provisions of this title governing foreign corporations, foreign limited partnerships, or foreign limited liability companies, it shall do so.

(g) After a plan of conversion is approved by the members, the limited liability company shall deliver to the Secretary of State for filing a certificate of conversion setting forth:

(1) The name of the limited liability company;

(2) The name and jurisdiction of the entity to which the limited liability company shall be converted;

(3) The effective date, or the effective date and time, of such conversion if later than the date and time the certificate of conversion is filed;

(4) A statement that the plan of conversion has been approved as required by subsection (c) of this Code section;

(5) A statement that the authority of its registered agent to accept service on its behalf is revoked as of the effective time of such conversion and that the Secretary of State is irrevocably appointed as the agent for service of process on the resulting entity in any proceeding to enforce an obligation of the limited liability company arising prior to the effective time of such conversion, including the rights, if any, of dissenting members;

(6) A mailing address to which a copy of any process served on the Secretary of State under paragraph (5) of this subsection may be mailed; and

(7) A statement that the Secretary of State shall be notified of any change in the resulting entity's mailing address.

(h) Upon the conversion's taking effect, the resulting entity is deemed:

(1) To appoint the Secretary of State as its agent for service of process in a proceeding to enforce any of its obligations arising prior to the effective time of such conversion, including the rights, if any, of dissenting members; and

(2) To agree that it will promptly pay to any dissenting members the amount, if any, to which such member is entitled under Article 10 of this chapter.

(i) A converting limited liability company pursuant to this Code section may file a copy of its certificate of conversion, certified by the Secretary of State, in the office of the clerk of the superior court of the county where any real property owned by such limited liability company is located and record such certified copy of the certificate of conversion in the books kept by such clerk for recordation of deeds in such county with the limited liability company indexed as the grantor and the foreign entity indexed as the grantee. No real estate transfer tax otherwise required by Code Section 48-6-1 shall be due with respect to recordation of such certificate of conversion.

ARTICLE 10. DISSENTERS' RIGHTS

§ 14-11-1001. Definitions

As used in this article, the term:

(1) "Beneficial member" means the person who is a beneficial owner of the membership interest held in a voting trust or by a nominee as the record member.

(2) "Dissenter" means a member who is entitled to dissent from limited liability company action under Code Section 14-11-1002 and who exercises that right when and in the manner required by Code Sections 14-11-1003 through 14-11-1010.

(3) "Fair value" with respect to a membership interest means the value of the membership interest immediately before the effectuation of the limited liability company action to which the dissenter objects, excluding any appreciation or depreciation in anticipation of such action.

(4) "Interest" means interest from the effective date of the limited liability company action until the date of payment, at a rate that is fair and equitable under all the circumstances.

(5) "Limited liability company" means the limited liability company of which the dissenter is a member before the limited liability company action to which the dissenter objects or the surviving entity by merger of that limited liability company.

(6) "Member" means the record member or the beneficial member.

(7) "Membership interest" means a member's rights in the limited liability company, collectively, including the member's share of the profits and losses of the limited liability company, the right to receive distributions of the limited liability company's assets, and any right to vote or participate in management.

(8) "Record member" means the person in whose name the membership interest is registered in the records of a limited liability company.

§ 14-11-1002. Right to dissent

(a) Unless otherwise provided by the articles of organization or a written operating agreement, a record member of the limited liability company is entitled to dissent from, and obtain payment of the fair value of his or her membership interest in the event of, any of the following actions:

(1) Consummation of a plan of merger to which the limited liability company is a party if approval of less than all of the members of the limited liability company is required for the merger by the articles of organization or a written operating agreement and the member is entitled to vote on the merger;

(2) Consummation of a plan of conversion pursuant to Code Section 14-2-1109.2 or 14-11-906;

(3) Consummation of a sale, lease, exchange, or other disposition of all or substantially all of the property of the limited liability company if approval of less than all of the members is required by the articles of organization or a written operating agreement and the member is

entitled to vote on the sale, lease, exchange, or other disposition, but not including a sale pursuant to court order or a sale for cash pursuant to a plan by which all or substantially all of the net proceeds of the sale will be distributed to the members within one year after the date of sale;

(4) An amendment of the articles of organization that materially and adversely affects rights in respect of a dissenter's membership interest in the limited liability company because it:

(A) Alters or abolishes a preferential right of the member's interest;

(B) Creates, alters, or abolishes a right in respect of redemption, including a provision respecting a sinking fund for the redemption or repurchase, of the membership interest;

(C) Alters or abolishes a preemptive right of the holder of the membership interest to acquire additional interest or other securities;

(D) Excludes or limits the right of the member to vote on any matter, other than a limitation by dilution through additional member contributions or other securities with similar voting rights; or

(E) Cancels, redeems, or repurchases all or part of the membership interest of the class; or

(5) Any limited liability company action taken pursuant to a member vote to the extent that the articles of organization or a written operating agreement provides that voting or nonvoting members are entitled to dissent and obtain payment for their membership interests.

(b) A member entitled to dissent and obtain payment for his or her membership interest under this article may not challenge the limited liability company action creating his or her entitlement unless the limited liability company action fails to comply with procedural requirements of this chapter, the articles of organization, or the written operating agreement or if the vote required to obtain approval of the limited liability company action was obtained by fraudulent and deceptive means, regardless of whether the member has exercised dissenters' rights.

§ 14-11-1003. Notice of dissenters' rights

(a) If proposed limited liability company action creating dissenters' rights under Code Section 14-11-1002 is submitted to a vote at a members' meeting, the meeting notice must state that members are or may be entitled to assert dissenters' rights under this article and be accompanied by a copy of this article.

(b) If limited liability company action creating dissenters' rights under Code Section 14-11-1002 is taken without a vote of members, the limited liability company shall notify in writing all members entitled to assert dissenters' rights that the action was taken and send them the dissenters' notice described in Code Section 14-11-1005.

§ 14-11-1004. Notice of intent to demand payment

(a) If proposed limited liability company action creating dissenters' rights under Code Section 14-11-1002 is submitted to a vote at a members' meeting, a record member who wishes to assert dissenters' rights:

(1) Must deliver to the limited liability company before the vote is taken written notice of his or her intent to demand payment for his or her membership interest if the proposed action is effectuated; and

(2) Must not vote his or her membership interest in favor of the proposed action.

(b) A record member who does not satisfy the requirements of subsection (a) of this Code section is not entitled to payment for his or her membership interest under this article.

§ 14-11-1005. Dissenters' notice

(a) If proposed limited liability company action creating dissenters' rights under Code Section 14-11-1002 is authorized at a members' meeting, the limited liability company shall deliver a written dissenters' notice to all members who satisfied the requirements of Code Section 14-11-1004.

(b) The dissenters' notice must be sent no later than ten days after the limited liability company action was taken and must:

(1) State where the payment demand must be sent and where and when certificates for certificated membership interests must be deposited;

(2) Inform holders of uncertificated membership interests to what extent transfer of the membership interests will be restricted after the payment demand is received;

(3) Set a date by which the limited liability company must receive the payment demand, which date may not be fewer than 30 nor more than 60 days after the date the notice required in subsection (a) of this Code section is delivered; and

(4) Be accompanied by a copy of this article.

§ 14-11-1006. Duty to demand payment

(a) A record member sent a dissenters' notice described in Code Section 14-11-1005 must demand payment and deposit his or her certificates for certificated membership interests in accordance with the terms of the notice.

(b) A record member who demands payment and deposits his or her certificates under subsection (a) of this Code section retains all other rights of a member until these rights are canceled or modified by the taking of the proposed limited liability company action.

(c) A record member who does not demand payment or deposit his or her membership interest certificates where required, each by the date set in the dissenters' notice, is not entitled to payment for his or her membership interest under this article.

§ 14-11-1007. Membership interest restrictions

(a) The limited liability company may restrict the transfer of uncertificated membership interests from the date the demand for their payment is received until the proposed limited liability company action is taken or the restrictions are released under Code Section 14-11-1009.

(b) The person for whom dissenters' rights are asserted as to uncertificated membership interests retains all other rights of a member until these rights are canceled or modified by the taking of the proposed limited liability company action.

§ 14-11-1008. Offer of payment

(a) Except as provided in Code Section 14-11-1010, within ten days of the later of the date the proposed limited liability company action is taken or receipt of a payment demand, the limited liability company shall offer to pay each dissenter who complied with Code Section 14-11-1006 the amount the limited liability company estimates to be the fair value of his or her membership interest, plus accrued interest.

(b) The offer of payment must be accompanied by:

(1) The limited liability company's balance sheet as of the end of a fiscal year ending not more than 16 months before the date of payment, an income statement for that year, a statement of changes in members' equity for that year, and the latest available interim financial statements, if any;

(2) A statement of the limited liability company's estimate of the fair value of the membership interest;

(3) An explanation of how the interest was calculated;

(4) A statement of the dissenter's right to demand payment under Code Section 14-11-1010; and

(5) A copy of this article.

(c) If the member accepts the limited liability company's offer by written notice to the limited liability company within 30 days after the limited liability company's offer, payment for his or her membership interest shall be made within 60 days after the making of the offer or the taking of the proposed limited liability company action, whichever is later.

§ 14-11-1009. Failure to take action

(a) If the limited liability company does not take the proposed action within 60 days after the date set for demanding payment and depositing membership interest certificates, the limited liability company shall return the deposited certificates and release the transfer restrictions imposed on uncertificated membership interests.

(b) If, after returning deposited certificates and releasing transfer restrictions, the limited liability company takes the proposed action, it must send a new dissenters' notice under Code Section 14-11-1005 and repeat the payment demand procedure.

§ 14-11-1010. Procedure if member dissatisfied with payment or offer

(a) A dissenter may notify the limited liability company in writing of his or her own estimate of the fair value of his membership interest and amount of interest due, and demand payment of his or her estimate of the fair value of his or her membership interest and interest due, if:

(1) The dissenter believes that the amount offered under Code Section 14-11-1008 is less than the fair value of his or her membership interest or that the interest due is incorrectly calculated; or

(2) The limited liability company, having failed to take the proposed action, does not return the deposited certificates or release the transfer restrictions imposed on uncertificated membership interests within 60 days after the date set for demanding payment.

(b) A dissenter waives his or her right to demand payment under this Code section unless he or she notifies the limited liability company of his or her demand in writing under subsection (a) of this Code section within 30 days after the limited liability company offered payment for his or her membership interest, as provided in Code Section 14-11-1008.

(c) If the limited liability company does not offer payment within the time set forth in subsection (a) of Code Section 14-11-1008:

(1) The member may demand the information required under subsection (b) of Code Section 14-11-1008, and the limited liability company shall provide the information to the member within ten days after receipt of a written demand for the information; and

(2) The member may at any time, subject to the limitations period of Code Section 14-11-1013, notify the limited liability company of his or her own estimate of the fair value of his membership interest and the amount of interest due and demand payment of his or her estimate of the fair value of his or her membership interest and interest due.

§ 14-11-1011. Court action

(a) If a demand for payment under Code Section 14-11-1010 remains unsettled, the limited liability company shall commence a proceeding within 60 days after receiving the payment demand and petition the court to determine the fair value of the membership interest and accrued interest. If the limited liability company does not commence the proceeding within the 60 day period, it shall pay each dissenter whose demand remains unsettled the amount demanded.

(b) The limited liability company shall commence the proceeding, which shall be a nonjury equitable valuation proceeding, in the superior court of the county where a limited liability company's registered office is located. If the surviving entity is a foreign entity without a registered office in this state, it shall commence the proceeding in the county in this state where the registered office of the domestic entity merged with the foreign entity was located.

(c) The limited liability company shall make all dissenters, whether or not residents of this state, whose demands remain unsettled parties to the proceeding, which shall have the effect of an action quasi in rem against their membership interests. The limited liability company shall serve a copy of the petition in the proceeding upon each dissenting member who is a resident of this state in the manner provided by law for the service of a summons and complaint and upon each nonresident dissenting member either by registered or certified mail or statutory overnight delivery and publication or in any other manner permitted by law.

(d) The jurisdiction of the court in which the proceeding is commenced under subsection (b) of this Code section is plenary and exclusive. The court may appoint one or more persons as appraisers to receive evidence and recommend decision on the question of fair value. The appraisers have the powers described in the order appointing them or in any amendment to it. Except as otherwise provided in this chapter, Chapter 11 of Title 9, known as the "Georgia Civil Practice Act," applies to any proceeding with respect to dissenters' rights under this chapter.

(e) Each dissenter made a party to the proceeding is entitled to judgment for the amount which the court finds to be the fair value of his or her membership interest, plus interest to the date of judgment.

§ 14-11-1012. Court costs and counsel fees

(a) The court in an appraisal proceeding commenced under Code Section 14-11-1011 shall determine all costs of the proceeding, including the reasonable compensation and expenses of appraisers appointed by the court, but not including fees and expenses of attorneys and experts for the respective parties. The court shall assess the costs against the limited liability company, except that the court may assess the costs against all or some of the dissenters, in amounts the court finds equitable, to the extent the court finds the dissenters acted arbitrarily, vexatiously, or not in good faith in demanding payment under Code Section 14-11-1010.

(b) The court may also assess the fees and expenses of attorneys and experts for the respective parties, in amounts the court finds equitable:

(1) Against the limited liability company and in favor of any or all dissenters if the court finds the limited liability company did not substantially comply with the requirements of Code Sections 14-11-1103 through 14-11-1109; or

(2) Against either the limited liability company or a dissenter, in favor of any other party, if the court finds that the party against whom the fees and expenses are assessed acted arbitrarily, vexatiously, or not in good faith with respect to the rights provided by this article.

(c) If the court finds that the services of attorneys for any dissenter were of substantial benefit to other dissenters similarly situated and that the fees for those services should not be assessed against the limited liability company, the court may award to these attorneys reasonable fees to be paid out of the amounts awarded the dissenters who were benefited.

§ 14-11-1013. Limitation of actions

No action by any dissenter to enforce dissenters' rights shall be brought more than three years after the limited liability company action was taken, regardless of whether notice of the limited liability company action and of the right of dissent was given by the limited liability company in compliance with the provisions of Code Section 14-11-1003 and Code Section 14-11-1005.

ARTICLE 11. MISCELLANEOUS

§ 14-11-1101. Filing fees and penalties

(a) The Secretary of State shall collect the following fees when the documents described below are delivered to the Secretary of State for filing pursuant to this chapter:

Document	Fee
--------	---
(1) Articles of organization	$ 100.00
(2) Articles of amendment	20.00
(3) Articles of merger	20.00
(4) Certificate of election under Code Section 14-11-212 (together with articles of organization)	95.00
(5) Application for certificate of authority to transact business	225.00
(6) Statement of commencement of winding up	No fee
(7) Certificate of termination	No fee
(8) Application of withdrawal	No fee
(9) Articles of correction	20.00
(10) Application for reservation of a name	25.00

(11) Statement of change of registered office or registered agent...$ 5.00 per limited liability company (foreign or domestic), but not less than   20.00

(12) Registered agent's statement of resignation pursuant to subsection (d) of Code Section 14-11-209 or subsection (d) of Code Section 14-11-703

No fee

(13) Certificate of judicial dissolution

No fee

(14) Annual registration (foreign or domestic)

50.00

(15) Penalty for late filing of annual registration

25.00

(16) Reinstatement fee

250.00

(17) Any other document required or permitted to be filed by this chapter

20.00

(18) Certificate of conversion

95.00

(b) The Secretary of State shall collect the penalty provided for in paragraph (2) of subsection (c) of Code Section 14-11-711.

§ 14-11-1102. Execution by judicial act

(a) If each person required by Code Section 14-11-205 to execute any document fails or refuses to do so, any other person who is adversely affected by the failure or refusal may petition the superior court of the county where the registered office of the limited liability company is located to direct the execution of the document. If the court finds that it is proper for the document to be executed and that every person so designated has failed or refused to execute the document, it shall order the Secretary of State to file the document in appropriate form notwithstanding the lack of required execution.

(b) The court shall assess the costs and expenses of such proceeding against the limited liability company, except that all or any part of such costs and expenses may be apportioned and assessed, as the court may determine, against any or all of the persons required by Code Section 14-2-205 to execute a document who failed or refused to do so if the court finds that such failure or refusal was arbitrary, vexatious, or otherwise not in good faith.

§ 14-11-1103. Annual registration

(a) Each limited liability company and each foreign limited liability company authorized to transact business in this state shall deliver to the Secretary of State for filing an annual registration that sets forth:

(1) The name of the limited liability company or the foreign limited liability company and the jurisdiction under whose law it is organized;

(2) The street address and county of its registered office and the name of its registered agent at that office in this state;

(3) The mailing address of its principal place of business; and

(4) Any additional information that is necessary to enable the Secretary of State to carry out the provisions of this chapter.

(b) Information in the annual registration must be current as of the date the annual registration is executed on behalf of the limited liability company or foreign limited liability company.

(c) The first annual registration must be delivered to the Secretary of State between January 1 and April 1, or such other date as the Secretary of State may specify by rules or regulations, of the year following the calendar year in which the limited liability company was formed or a foreign limited liability company was authorized to transact business. Subsequent annual registrations must be delivered to the Secretary of State between January 1 and April 1, or such other date as the Secretary of State may specify by rules and regulations, of the following calendar years.

(d) If an annual registration does not contain the information required by this Code section, the Secretary of State shall promptly notify the limited liability company or foreign limited liability company in writing and return the registration to it for correction. If the registration is corrected to contain the information required by this Code section and delivered to the Secretary of State within 30 days after the date of notice, it is deemed to be timely filed.

§ 14-11-1104. Taxation

Each limited liability company and foreign limited liability company shall be classified as a partnership for Georgia income tax purposes unless classified otherwise for federal income tax purposes, in which case the limited liability company or foreign limited liability company shall be classified for Georgia income tax purposes in the same manner as it is classified for federal income tax purposes. A member or an assignee of a member of a limited liability company or foreign limited liability company shall be treated for Georgia income tax purposes as either a resident or nonresident partner in the limited liability company or foreign limited liability company unless classified otherwise for federal income tax purposes, in which case the member or assignee of a member shall have the same status for Georgia income tax purposes as such member or assignee of a member has for federal income tax purposes.

§ 14-11-1105. Administrative powers of Secretary of State

The Secretary of State shall have the power and authority reasonably necessary to enable him or her to administer this chapter efficiently and to perform the duties imposed upon him or her pursuant to this chapter, including, without limitation, the power and authority to employ from time to time such additional personnel as in his or her judgment are required for such purposes.

§ 14-11-1106. Rules and regulations

The Secretary of State may promulgate such rules and regulations, not inconsistent with the provisions of this chapter, as are incidental to and necessary for the implementation and enforcement of such provisions of this chapter as are administered by the Secretary of State. Such rules and regulations shall be promulgated in accordance with Chapter 13 of Title 50, the "Georgia Administrative Procedure Act."

§ 14-11-1107. Laws governing chapter; limited liability companies

(a) The rule that statutes in derogation of the common law are to be strictly construed shall have no application to this chapter.

(b) It is the policy of this state with respect to limited liability companies to give maximum effect to the principle of freedom of contract and to the enforceability of operating agreements.

(c) Unless displaced by particular provisions of this chapter, the principles of law and equity supplement this chapter.

(d) If any provision of this chapter or its application to any person or circumstance is held invalid, the invalidity does not affect other provisions or applications of this chapter that can be given effect without the invalid provision or application. To this end, the provisions of this chapter are severable.

(e) A limited liability company may conduct its business, carry on its operations and have and exercise the powers granted by this chapter in any state, territory, district, or possession of the United States or in any foreign country.

(f) The laws of this state relating to establishment and regulation of professional services are amended and superseded to the extent such laws are inconsistent as to form of organization with the provisions of this chapter and are deemed amended to permit the provision of professional services within this state by limited liability companies.

(g) Nothing in this chapter is intended to restrict or limit in any manner the authority and duty of any regulatory or other body licensing professionals within this state to license individuals rendering professional services or to regulate the practice of any profession that is within the jurisdiction of the regulatory or other body licensing such professionals within this state, notwithstanding that the person is a member, manager, or employee of a limited liability company and rendering the professional services or engaging in the practice of the profession through a limited liability company.

(h) The personal liability of a member of a limited liability company to any person or in any action or proceeding for the debts, obligations, or liabilities of the limited liability company, or for the acts or omissions of other members, managers, employees, or agents of the limited liability company, shall be governed solely and exclusively by this chapter and the laws of this state. Whenever a conflict arises between the laws of this state and the laws of any other state with regard to the liability of members of a limited liability company for the debts, obligations, and liabilities of the limited liability company or for the acts or omissions of other members, managers, employees, or agents of the limited liability company, this state's laws shall be deemed to govern in determining such liability.

(i) The provisions of this chapter shall determine the rights and obligations of a limited liability company organized under this chapter in commerce with foreign nations and among the several states to the extent permitted by law.

(j) A member of a limited liability company is not a proper party to a proceeding by or against a limited liability company, solely by reason of being a member of the limited liability company, except:

  (1) Where the object of the proceeding is to enforce a member's right against or liability to the limited liability company; or

  (2) In a derivative action authorized by Article 8 of this chapter.

(k) The General Assembly has power to amend or repeal all or part of this chapter at any time, and all limited liability companies and foreign limited liability companies subject to this chapter are governed by the amendment or repeal.

(l) Any provision that this chapter requires or permits to be set forth in an operating agreement may be set forth in the articles of organization. In the event of any conflict between a provision of the articles of organization and a provision of an operating agreement, the provision of the articles of organization shall govern.

(m) Each provision of this chapter shall have independent legal significance.

(n) Nothing in this chapter shall be construed as establishing that a limited liability company interest is not a "security" within the meaning of paragraph (31) of Code Section 10-5-2 (or any successor statute).

§ 14-11-1108. Service of process; venue

  (a) A limited liability company's registered agent is the limited liability company's agent for service of process, notice, or demand required or permitted by law to be served on the limited liability company. If a limited liability company has no registered agent or the agent cannot with reasonable diligence be served, the limited liability company may be served by registered or certified mail or statutory overnight delivery, return receipt requested, addressed to the limited liability company at its principal office. Service is perfected under the immediately preceding sentence at the earliest of:

  (1) The date the limited liability company receives the mail;

  (2) The date shown on the return receipt, if signed on behalf of the limited liability company; or

(3) Five days after its deposit in the mail, as evidenced by the postmark, if mailed postage prepaid and correctly addressed.

This subsection does not prescribe the only means, or necessarily the required means, of serving a limited liability company.

(b) Venue in proceedings against a limited liability company or foreign limited liability company shall be determined in accordance with the pertinent constitutional and statutory provisions of this state in effect on March 1, 1994, or thereafter. For purposes of determining venue, the residence of a limited liability company or foreign limited liability company shall be determined in accordance with Code Section 14-2-510 as though such limited liability company or foreign limited liability company were a corporation.

§ 14-11-1109. Effective date; repealer

This chapter shall become effective on March 1, 1994. The provisions of law that became effective on July 1, 1992, and that were codified at Code Sections 14-11-1 through 14-11-19 are hereby repealed. A foreign limited liability company that prior to March 1, 1994, obtained a certificate of authority to transact business in this state is not required to obtain a new certificate of authority by reason of the enactment of this chapter.

REVISED UNIFORM LIMITED LIABILITY COMPANY ACT

TABLE OF CONTENTS

[A R T I C L E] 1

GE NE R AL PR OV I SI ONS

[AR T I C L E] 5

T R ANSFER AB L E I NT ER E ST S AND R I GHT S OF T R ANSFER EES AND C R E DI T OR S

[AR T ICL E] 6

ME MBE R 'S DISSOCIAT ION

[AR T ICL E] 7

DISSOL UT ION AND WINDING UP

[A R T I C L E] 10

M E M B E R ' S DI SSOC I AT I ON

[A R T I C L E] 11

M I SC E L L ANE OUS PR OV I SI ONS

REVISED UNIFORM LIMITED LIABILITY COMPANY ACT

PREFATORY NOTE

Background to this Act:
Developments since the Conference Considered and Approved the Original Uniform Limited Liability Company Act
(ULLCA)

The Uniform Limited Liability Company Act ("ULLCA") was conceived in 1992 and first adopted by the Conference in 1994. By that time nearly every state had adopted an LLC statute, and those statutes varied considerably in both form and substance. Many of those early statutes were based on the first version of the ABA Model Prototype LLC Act.

ULLCA's drafting relied substantially on the then recently adopted Revised Uniform Partnership Act ("RUPA"), and this reliance was especially heavy with regard to member- managed LLCs. ULLCA's provisions for manager-managed LLCs comprised an amalgam fashioned from the 1985 Revised Uniform Limited Partnership Act ("RULPA") and the Model Business Corporation Act ("MBCA"). ULLCA's provisions were also significantly influenced by the then-applicable federal tax classification regulations, which classified an unincorporated organization as a corporation if the organization more nearly resembled a corporation than a partnership. Those same regulations also made the tax classification of single-member LLCs problematic.

Much has changed. All states and the District of Columbia have adopted LLC statutes, and many LLC statutes have been substantially amended several times. LLC filings are significant in every U.S. jurisdiction, and in many states new LLC filings approach or even outnumber new corporate filings on an annual basis. Manager-managed LLCs have become a significant factor in non-publicly-traded capital markets, and increasing numbers of states provide for mergers and conversions involving LLCs and other unincorporated entities.

In 1997, the tax classification context changed radically, when the IRS' "check-the-box" regulations became effective. Under these regulations, an "unincorporated" business entity is taxed either as a partnership or disregarded entity (depending upon the number of owners) unless it elects to be taxed as a corporation. Exceptions exist (e.g., entities whose interests are publicly-traded), but, in general, tax classification concerns no longer constrain the structure of LLCs and the content of LLC statutes. Single-member LLCs, once suspect because novel and of uncertain tax status, are now popular both for sole proprietorships and as corporate subsidiaries.

In 1995, the Conference amended RUPA to add "full-shield" LLP provisions, and today every state has some form of LLP legislation (either through a RUPA adoption or shield-related revisions to a UPA-based statute). While some states still provide only a "partial shield" for LLPs, many states have adopted "full shield" LLP provisions. In full-shield jurisdictions, LLPs and member-managed LLCs offer entrepreneurs very similar attributes and, in the case of professional service organizations, LLPs may dominate the field.

ULLCA was revised in 1996 in anticipation of the "check the box" regulations and has been adopted in a number of states. In many non-ULLCA states, the LLC statute includes

RUPA-like provisions. However, state LLC laws are far from uniform.

Eighteen years have passed since the IRS issued its gate-opening Revenue Ruling 88-76, declaring that a Wyoming LLC would be taxed as a partnership despite the entity's corporate- like liability shield. More than eight years have passed since the IRS opened the gate still further with the "check the box" regulations. It is an opportune moment to identify the best elements of the myriad "first generation" LLC statutes and to infuse those elements into a new, "second generation" uniform act.

Noteworthy Provisions of the New Act

The Revised Uniform Limited Company Act is drafted to replace a state's current LLC statute, whether or not that statute is based on ULLCA. The new Act's noteworthy provisions concern:

- the operating agreement
- fiduciary duty
- the ability to "pre-file" a certificate of organization without having a member at the time of the filing
- the power of a member or manager to bind the limited liability company
- default rules on management structure
- charging orders
- a remedy for oppressive conduct
- derivative claims and special litigation committees
- organic transactions – mergers, conversions, and domestications

The Operating Agreement: Like the partnership agreement in a general or limited partnership, an LLC's operating agreement serves as the foundational contract among the entity's owners. RUPA pioneered the notion of centralizing all statutory provisions pertaining to the foundational contract, and – like ULLCA and ULPA (2001) – the new Act continues that approach. However, because an operating agreement raises issues too numerous and complex to include easily in a single section, the new Act uses three related sections to address the operating agreement:

- o Section 110 – scope, function, and limitations;
- o Section 111 – effect on limited liability company and persons becoming members; preformation agreement; and
- o Section 112 – effect on third parties and relationship to records effective on behalf of limited liability company.

The new Act also contains a number of substantive innovations concerning the operating agreement, including:

- o better delineating the extent to which the operating agreement can define, alter, or even eliminate aspects of fiduciary duty;
- o expressly authorizing the operating agreement to relieve members and managers from liability for money damages arising from breach of duty, subject to specific limitations; and
- o stating specific rules for applying the statutory phrase "manifestly unreasonable" and thereby providing clear guidance for courts considering whether to invalidate operating

agreement provisions that address fiduciary duty and other sensitive matters.
liability for money damages arising from breach of duty, subject to specific limitations; and

o   stating specific rules for applying the statutory phrase "manifestly unreasonable" and thereby providing clear guidance for courts considering whether to invalidate operating agreement provisions that address fiduciary duty and other sensitive matters.

Fiduciary Duty: RUPA also pioneered the idea of codifying partners' fiduciary duties in order to protect the partnership agreement from judicial second-guessing. This approach – to "cabin in" (or corral) fiduciary duty – was followed in ULLCA and ULPA (2001). In contrast, the new Act recognizes that, at least in the realm of limited liability companies:

o   the "cabin in" approach creates more problems than it solves (e.g.. by putting inordinate pressure on the concept of "good faith and fair dealing"); and
o   the better way to protect the operating agreement from judicial second-guessing is to:
*   increase and clarify the power of the operating agreement to define or re-shape fiduciary duties (including the power to eliminate aspects of fiduciary duties); and
*   provide some guidance to courts when a person seeks to escape an agreement by claiming its provisions are "manifestly unreasonable."

Accordingly, the new Act codifies major fiduciary duties but does not purport to do so exhaustively. *See* Section 409.

The Ability to "Pre-File" a Certificate of Organization: The Comments to Section 201 explain in detail how the new Act resolves the difficult question of the "shelf LLC" – i.e., an LLC formed without having at least one member upon formation. In short, the Act: (i) permits an organizer to file a certificate of organization without a person "waiting in the wings" to become a member upon formation; but (ii) provides that the LLC is not formed until and unless at least one person becomes a member and the organizer makes a second filing stating that the LLC has at least one member.

The Power of a Member or Manager to Bind the Limited Liability Company: In 1914, the original Uniform Partnership Act codified a particular type of apparent authority by position, providing that "[t]he act of every partner ... for apparently carrying on in the usual way the business of the partnership binds the partnership . . . ." This concept of "statutory apparent authority" applies by linkage in the 1916 Uniform Limited Partnership Act and the 1976/85 Revised Uniform Limited Partnership Act and appears in RUPA, ULLCA, ULPA (2001), and almost every LLC statute in the United States.

The concept makes good sense for general and limited partnerships. A third party dealing with either type of partnership can know by the formal name of the entity and by a person's status as general or limited partner whether the person has the power to bind the entity.

The concept does not make sense for modern LLC law, because: (i) an LLC's status as member-managed or manager-managed is not apparent from the LLC's name (creating traps for unwary third parties); and (ii) although most LLC statutes provide templates for member- management and manager-management, variability of management structure is a key strength of the LLC as a form of business organization.

The new Act recognizes that "statutory apparent authority" is an attribute of partnership formality that does not belong in an LLC statute. Section 301(a) provides that "a member is not an agent of the limited liability company solely by reason of being a member." Other law – most especially the law of agency – will handle power-to-bind questions.

Although conceptually innovative, this approach will not significantly alter the commercial reality that exists between limited liability companies and third parties, because:

1.   The vast majority of interactions between limited liability companies and "third parties" are quotidian and transpire without agency law issues being recognized by the parties, let alone disputed.

2.   When a limited liability company enters into a major transaction with a sophisticated third party, the third party never relies on statutory apparent authority to determine that the person purporting to act for the limited liability company has the authority to do so.

3.   Most LLCs use employees to carry out most of the LLC's dealings with third parties. In that context, the agency power of members and managers is usually irrelevant. (If an employee's authority is contested and the employee "reports to" a member or manager, the member or manager's authority will be relevant to determining the employee's authority. However, in that situation, agency law principles will suffice to delineate the manager or member's supervisory authority.)

4.   Very few current LLC statutes contain rules for attributing to an LLC the wrongful acts of the LLC's members or managers. *Compare* RUPA § 305. In this realm, this Act merely acknowledges pre-existing reality.

5.   As explained in detail in the Comments to section 301 and 407(c), agency law principles are well-suited to the tasks resulting from the "de-codification" of apparent authority by position.

The moment is opportune for this reform. The newly-issued Restatement (Third) of Agency gives substantial attention to the power of an enterprise's participants to bind the enterprise. In addition, the new Act has "souped up" RUPA's statement of authority to permit an LLC to publicly file a statement of authority for a position (not merely a particular person).

Statements of authority will enable LLCs to provide reliable documentation of authority to enter into transactions without having to disclose to third parties the entirety of the operating agreement. (The new Act also has eliminated prolix provisions that sought to restate agency law rules on notice and knowledge.)

Default Rules on Management Structure: The new Act retains the manager-managed and member-managed constructs as options for members to use in configuring their *inter se* relationship, and the operating agreement is the vehicle by which the members make and state their choice of management structure. Given the elimination of statutory apparent authority, it is unnecessary and could be confusing to require the articles of organization to state the members' determination on this point.

Charging Orders: The charging order mechanism: (i) dates back to the 1914 Uniform

Partnership Act and the English Partnership Act of 1890; and (ii) is an essential part of the "pick your partner" approach that is fundamental to the law of unincorporated businesses. The new Act continues the charging order mechanism, but modernizes the statutory language so that the language (and its protections against outside interference in an LLC's activities) can be readily understood.

A Remedy for Oppressive Conduct: Reflecting case law developments around the country, the new Act permits a member (but not a transferee) to seek a court order "dissolving the company on the grounds that the managers or those members in control of the company … have acted or are acting in a manner that is oppressive and was, is, or will be directly harmful to the [member]." Section 701(5)(B). This provision is necessary given the perpetual duration of an LLC formed under this Act, Section 104(c), and this Act's elimination of the "put right" provided by ULLCA, § 701.

Derivative Claims and Special Litigation Committees: The new Act contains modern provisions addressing derivative litigation, including a provision authorizing special litigation committees and subjecting their composition and conduct to judicial review.

Organic Transactions – Mergers, Conversions, and Domestications: The new Act has comprehensive, self-contained provisions for these transactions, including "inter-species" transactions.

No Provision for "Series" LLCs

The new Act also has a very noteworthy omission; it does not authorize "series LLCs." Under a series approach, a single limited liability company may establish and contain within itself separate series. Each series is treated as an enterprise separate from each other and from the LLC itself. Each series has associated with it specified members, assets, and obligations, and – due to what have been called "internal shields" – the obligations of one series are not the obligation of any other series or of the LLC.

Delaware pioneered the series concept, and the concept has apparently been quite useful in structuring certain types of investment funds and in arranging complex financing. Other states have followed Delaware's lead, but a number of difficult and substantial questions remain unanswered, including:

- *conceptual* – How can a series be – and expect to be treated as – a separate legal person for liability and other purposes if the series is defined as part of another legal person?

- *bankruptcy* – Bankruptcy law has not recognized the series as a separate legal person. If a series becomes insolvent, will the entire LLC and the other series become part of the bankruptcy proceedings? Will a bankruptcy court consolidate the assets and liabilities of the separate series?

- *efficacy of the internal shields in the courts of other states* – Will the internal shields be respected in the courts of states whose LLC statutes do not recognize series? Most LLC statutes provide that "foreign law governs" the liability of members of a foreign LLC. However, those provisions do not apply to the series question, because those provisions pertain to the liability of a member for the obligations of the LLC. For a series LLC, the pivotal question is entirely different – namely, whether some assets of an LLC should be immune from some of the creditors of the LLC.

- *tax treatment* – Will the IRS and the states treat each series separately? Will separate returns be filed? May one series "check the box" for corporate tax classification and the others not?

- *securities law* – Given the panoply of unanswered questions, what types of disclosures must be made when a membership interest is subject to securities law?

The Drafting Committee considered a series proposal at its February 2006 meeting, but, after serious discussion, no one was willing to urge adoption of the proposal, even for the limited purposes of further discussion. Given the availability of well-established alternate structures (e.g., multiple single member LLCs, an LLC "holding company" with LLC subsidiaries), it made no sense for the Act to endorse the complexities and risks of a series approach.

REVISED UNIFORM LIMITED LIABILITY COMPANY ACT

[ARTICLE] 1

GENERAL PROVISIONS

SECTION 101. SHORT TITLE. This [act] may be cited as the Revised Uniform Limited Liability Company Act.

Comment

This Act is drafted to replace a state's current LLC statute, whether or not that statute is based on the original Uniform Limited Liability Company Act. Section 1104 contains transition provisions.

SECTION 102. DEFINITIONS. In this [act]:

(1)   "Certificate of organization" means the certificate required by Section 201. The term includes the certificate as amended or restated.

(2)   "Contribution" means any benefit provided by a person to a limited liability company:

(A)   in order to become a member upon formation of the company and in accordance with an agreement between or among the persons that have agreed to become the initial members of the company;

(B)   in order to become a member after formation of the company and in accordance with an agreement between the person and the company; or

(C)   in the person's capacity as a member and in accordance with the operating agreement or an agreement between the member and the company.

(3)   "Debtor in bankruptcy" means a person that is the subject of:

(A)   an order for relief under Title 11 of the United States Code or a successor statute of general application; or

(B)   a comparable order under federal, state, or foreign law governing insolvency.

(4)   "Designated office" means:

(A)   the office that a limited liability company is required to designate and maintain under Section 113; or

(B)   the principal office of a foreign limited liability company.

(5)   "Distribution", except as otherwise provided in Section 405(g), means a transfer of money or other property from a limited liability company to another person on account of a transferable interest.

(6)   "Effective", with respect to a record required or permitted to be delivered to the [Secretary of State] for filing under this [act], means effective under Section 205(c).

(7)   "Foreign limited liability company" means an unincorporated entity formed under the law of a jurisdiction other than this state and denominated by that law as a limited liability company.

(8)   "Limited liability company", except in the phrase "foreign limited liability company", means an entity formed under this [act].

(9)   "Manager" means a person that under the operating agreement of a manager-managed limited liability company is responsible, alone or in concert with others, for performing the management functions stated in Section 407(c).

(10) "Manager-managed limited liability company" means a limited liability company that qualifies under Section 407(a).

(11) "Member" means a person that has become a member of a limited liability company under Section 401 and has not dissociated under Section 602.

(12) "Member-managed limited liability company" means a limited liability company that is not a manager-managed limited liability company.

(13) "Operating agreement" means the agreement, whether or not referred to as an operating agreement and whether oral, in a record, implied, or in any combination thereof, of all the members of a limited liability company, including a sole member, concerning the matters described in Section 110(a). The term includes the agreement as amended or restated.

(14) "Organizer" means a person that acts under Section 201 to form a limited liability company.

(15) "Person" means an individual, corporation, business trust, estate, trust, partnership, limited liability company, association, joint venture, public corporation, government or governmental subdivision, agency, or instrumentality, or any other legal or commercial entity.

(16) "Principal office" means the principal executive office of a limited liability company or foreign limited liability company, whether or not the office is located in this state.

(17) "Record" means information that is inscribed on a tangible medium or that is stored in an electronic or other medium and is retrievable in perceivable form.

(18) "Sign" means, with the present intent to authenticate or adopt a record: (A) to execute or adopt a tangible symbol; or

(B)   to attach to or logically associate with the record an electronic symbol, sound, or process.

(19) "State" means a state of the United States, the District of Columbia, Puerto Rico, the United States Virgin Islands, or any territory or insular possession subject to the jurisdiction of the United States.

(20) "Transfer" includes an assignment, conveyance, deed, bill of sale, lease, mortgage, security interest, encumbrance, gift, and transfer by operation of law.

(21) "Transferable interest" means the right, as originally associated with a person's capacity as a member, to receive distributions from a limited liability company in accordance with the operating agreement, whether or not the person remains a member or continues to own any part of the right.

(22) "Transferee" means a person to which all or part of a transferable interest has been transferred, whether or not the transferor is a member.

Comment

This Section contains definitions for terms used throughout the Act, while Section 1001 contains definitions specific to Article 10's provisions on mergers, conversions and domestications. Section 405(g) contains an exception to the definition of "distribution," which is specific to Section 405.

Paragraph (1) [Certificate of organization] – The original ULLCA and most other LLC statutes use "articles of organization" rather than "certificate of organization." This Act purposely uses the latter term to signal that: (i) the certificate merely reflects the existence of an LLC (rather than being the locus for important governance rules); and (ii) this document is significantly different from articles of *incorporation*, which have a substantially greater power to affect *inter se* rules for the corporate entity and its owners. For the relationship between the certificate of organization and the operating agreement, see Section 112(d).

Paragraph (2) [Contribution] – This definition serves to distinguish capital contributions from other circumstances under which a member or would-be member might provide benefits to a limited liability company (e.g., providing services to the LLC as an employee or independent contractor, leasing property to the LLC). The definition contemplates three typical situations in which contributions are made, and for each situation establishes two "markers" to identify capital contributions – the purpose for which the contributor makes the contribution and the agreement that contemplates the contribution:

circumstance	purpose/cause of providing benefits	the relevant agreement
pre-formation deal among would-be initial members [Paragraph 2(A)]	in order to become initial member(s)	agreement among would-be initial members
deal between an existing LLC and would-be member [Paragraph 2(B)]	in order to become a member	agreement between the LLC and the would-be member
member contribution [Paragraph 2(C)]	in member's capacity as a member	operating agreement or an agreement between the member and the LLC

This definition does not encompass capital raised from transferees, which is sometimes provided for in operating agreements. In such circumstances, the default rules for liquidating distributions should be altered accordingly. See Section 708(b)(1) ("referring to contributions made by a member and not previously returned").

Paragraph (7) [Foreign limited liability company] – Some statutes have elaborate definitions addressing the question of whether a non-U.S. entity is a "foreign limited liability company." The NY statute, for example, defines a "foreign limited liability company" as:

an unincorporated organization formed under the laws of any jurisdiction, including any foreign country, other than the laws of this state (i) that is not authorized to do business in this state under any other law of this state and (ii) of which some or all of the persons who are entitled (A) to receive a distribution of the assets thereof upon the dissolution of the organization or otherwise or (B) to exercise voting rights with respect to an interest in the organization have, or are entitled or authorized to have, under the laws of such other jurisdiction, limited liability for the contractual obligations or other liabilities of the organization.

N.Y. LIMIT LIAB CO. LAW § 102(k) (McKinney 2006). ULLCA § 101(8) takes a similar but less complex approach ("an unincorporated entity organized under laws other than the laws of this State which afford limited liability to its owners comparable to the liability under Section 303 and is not required to obtain a certificate of authority to transact business under any law of this State other than this [Act]"). This Act follows Delaware's still simpler approach. DEL. CODE ANN. tit. 6, § 18-101(4) (2006) ("denominated as such").

Paragraph (8) [Limited liability company] – This definition makes no reference to a limited liability company having members upon formation, but Section 201 does. For a detailed discussion of the "shelf LLC" issue, see the Comment to Section 201.

Paragraph (9) [Manager] – The Act uses the word "manager" as a term of art, whose applicability is confined to manager-managed LLCs. The phrase "manager-managed" is itself a term of art, referring only to an LLC whose operating agreement refers to the LLC as such. Paragraph 10 (defining "manager-managed limited liability company"). Thus, for purposes of this Act, if the members of a *member*-managed LLC delegate plenipotentiary management authority to one person (whether or not a member), this Act's references to "manager" do not apply to that person.

This approach does have the potential for confusion, but confusion around the term "manager" is common to almost all LLC statutes. The confusion stems from the choice to define "manager" as a term of art in a way that can be at odds with other, common usages of the word. For example, a member-managed LLC might well have an "office manager" or a "property manager." Moreover, in a manager-managed LLC, the "property manager" is not likely to be a manager as the term is used in many LLC statutes. *See, e.g., Brown v. MR Group, LLC*, 278 Wis.2d 760, 768-9, 693 N.W.2d 138, 143 (Wis.App. 2005) (rejecting a party's urging to use the dictionary definition of "manager" in determining coverage of a policy applicable to a limited liability company and its "managers" and relying instead on the meaning of the term under the Wisconsin LLC act).

Under this Act, the category of "person" is not limited to individuals. Therefore, a "manager" need not be a natural person. After a person ceases to be a manager, the term "manager" continues to apply to the person's conduct while a manager. See Section 407(c)(7).

Paragraph (10) [Manager-managed] – This Act departs from most LLC statutes (including the original ULLCA) by authorizing a private agreement (the operating agreement) rather than a public document (certificate or articles of organization) to establish an LLC's status as a manager-managed limited liability company. Using the operating agreement makes sense, because under this Act managerial structure creates no statutory power to bind the entity. See Section 301 (eliminating statutory apparent authority). The only direct consequences of manager- managed status are *inter se* – principally the triggering of a set of rules concerning management structure, fiduciary duty, and information rights. Sections 407 – 410. The management structure rules are entirely default provisions – subject to change in whole or in part by the operating agreement. The operating agreement can also significantly affect the duty and rights provisions. Section 110.

For pre-existing limited liability companies that eventually become subject to this Act, Section 1104(c) provides that "language in the limited liability company's articles of organization designating the company's management structure will operate as if that language were in the operating agreement." For limited liability companies formed under this Act, the typical method to select manager-managed status will be an explicit provision of the operating agreement. However, a reference in the certificate of organization to manager-management might be evidence of the contents of the operating agreement. See Comment to Section 112(b).

An LLC that is "manager-managed" under this definition does not cease to be so simply because the members fail to designate anyone to act as a manager. In that situation, absent additional facts, the LLC is manager-managed and the manager position is vacant. Non-manager members who exercise managerial functions during the vacancy (or at any other time) will have duties as determined by other law, most particularly the law of agency.

Paragraph 10(A) and (B) – In these paragraphs, the phrases "manager-managed" and "managed by managers" are "magic words" – i.e., for either subparagraph to apply, the operating agreement must include precisely the required language. However, the word "expressly" does not mean "in writing" or "in a record." This Act permits operating agreements to be oral (in whole or in part), and an oral provision of an operating agreement could contain the magic words. This Act also recognizes that provisions of an operating agreement may be reflected in patterns of conduct.

Oral and implied agreements invite memory problems and "swearing matches." Section 110(a)(4) empowers the operating agreement to determine "the means and conditions for the amending the operating agreement."

Paragraph 10(C) – In contrast to Paragraphs 10(A) and (B), this provision does not contain "magic words" and considers instead all terms of the operating agreement that expressly refer to management by managers.

Paragraph 11 [Member] – After a person has been dissociated as a member, Section 602, the term "member" continues to apply to the person's conduct while a member. See Section 603(b).

Paragraph 12 [Member-managed limited liability company] – A limited liability company that does not effectively designate itself a manager-member limited liability company will operate, subject to any contrary provisions in the operating agreement, under statutory rules providing for management by the members. Section 407(a). For a discussion of potential confusion relating to the term "manager", see the Comment to Paragraph 9 (Manager).

Paragraph (13) [Operating Agreement] – This definition must be read in conjunction with Sections 110 through 112, which further describe the operating agreement. An operating agreement is a contract, and therefore all statutory language pertaining to the operating agreement must be understood in the context of the law of contracts.

The definition in Paragraph 13 is very broad and recognizes a wide scope of authority for the operating agreement: "the matters described in Section 110(a)." Those matters include not only all relations inter se the members and the limited liability company but also all "activities of the company and the conduct of those activities." Section 110(a)(3). Moreover, the definition puts no limits on the form of the operating agreement. To the contrary, the definition contains the phrase "whether oral, in a record, implied, or in any combination thereof".

This Act states no rule as to whether the statute of frauds applies to an oral operating agreement. Case law suggests that an oral agreement to form a partnership or joint venture with a term exceeding one year is within the statute. *E.g. Abbott v. Hurst*, 643 So.2d 589, 592 (Ala. 1994) ("Partnership agreements, like other contracts, are subject to the Statute of Frauds. A contract of partnership for a term exceeding one year is within the Statute of Frauds and is void unless it is in writing; however, a contract establishing a partnership terminable at the will of any partner is generally held to be capable of performance by its terms within one year of its making and, therefore, to be outside the Statute of Frauds.") (citations omitted); Pemberton v. Ladue Realty & Const. Co., 362 Mo. 768, 770-71, 244 S.W.2d 62, 64 (Mo. 1951) (rejecting plaintiff's contention that mere part performance sufficed to take the oral agreement outside the statute and holding that partnership was therefore at will); *Ebker v. Tan Jay Int'l, Ltd.*, 739 F.2d 812, 827-28 (2d Cir.1984) (same analysis with regard to a joint venture). However, it is not possible to form an LLC without someone signing and delivering to the filing officer a certificate of organization in record form, Section 201(a), and the Act itself then establishes the LLC's duration. Subject to the operating agreement, that duration is perpetual. Section 104(c). An oral provision of an operating agreement calling for performance that extends beyond a year might be within the one- year provision – e.g., an oral agreement that a particular member will serve (and be permitted to serve) as manager for three years.

An oral provision of an operating agreement which involves the transfer of land, whether by or to the LLC, might come within the land provision of the statute of frauds. *Froiseth v. Nowlin*, 156 Wash. 314, 316, 287 P. 55. 56 (Wash. 1930) ("[The land provision] applies to an oral contract to transfer or convey partnership real property, and the interest of the other partners therein, to one partner as an individual, as well as to a parol contract by one of the parties to convey certain land owned by him individually to the partnership, or to another partner, or to put it into the partnership stock.") (quoting 27 CORPUS JURIS 220).").

In contrast, the fact that a limited liability company owns or deals in real property does not bring within the land provision agreements pertaining to the LLC's membership interests. Interests in a limited liability company are personal property and reflect no direct interest in the entity's assets. Re-this latter category of circumstances the organizer acts on behalf of the initial member or members is determined under ordinary principles of agency law and depends on the facts of each situation.

Paragraph (20) [Transfer] –The reference to "transfer by operation of law" is significant in connection with Section 502 (Transfer of Transferable Interest). That section severely restricts a transferee's rights (absent the consent of the members), and this definition makes those restrictions applicable, for example, to transfers ordered by a family court as part of a divorce proceeding and transfers resulting from the death of a member. The restrictions also apply to transfers in the context of a member's bankruptcy, except to the extent that bankruptcy law supersedes this Act.

Paragraph (21) [Transferee] – "Transferee" has displaced "assignee" as the Conference's term of art.

SECTION 103. KNOWLEDGE; NOTICE.

(a)   A person knows a fact when the person:

(1)   has actual knowledge of it; or

(2)   is deemed to know it under subsection (d)(1) or law other than this [act].

(b)   A person has notice of a fact when the person:

(1)   has reason to know the fact from all of the facts known to the person at the time in question; or

(2)   is deemed to have notice of the fact under subsection (d)(2).

(c)   A person notifies another of a fact by taking steps reasonably required to inform the other person in ordinary course, whether or not the other person knows the fact.

(d)   A person that is not a member is deemed:

(1)   to know of a limitation on authority to transfer real property as provided in Section 302(g); and

(2)   to have notice of a limited liability company's:

(A)   dissolution, 90 days after a statement of dissolution under Section 702(b)(2)(A) becomes effective;

(B)   termination, 90 days after a statement of termination Section 702(b)(2)(F) becomes effective; and

(C)   merger, conversion, or domestication, 90 days after articles of merger, conversion, or domestication under [Article] 10 become effective.

Comment

This section is substantially slimmer than the corresponding provisions of previous uniform acts pertaining to business organizations (RUPA, ULLCA, and ULPA (2001)). Each of those acts borrowed heavily from the comparable UCC provisions. For the most part, this Act relies instead on generally applicable principles of agency law, and therefore this section is mostly confined to rules specifically tailored to this Act.

Several facets of this section warrant particular note. First, and most fundamentally, because this Act does not provide for "statutory apparent authority," see Section 301, this section contains no special rules for attributing to an LLC information possessed, communicated to, or communicated by a member or manager.

Second, the section contains no generally applicable provisions determining when an organization is charged with knowledge or notice, because those imputation rules: (i) comprise core topics within the law of agency; (ii) are very complicated; (iii) should not have any different content under this Act than in other circumstances; and (iv) are the subject of considerable attention in the new Restatement (Third) of Agency.

Third, this Act does not define "notice" to include "knowledge." Although conceptualizing the latter as giving the former makes logical sense and has a long pedigree, that conceptualization is counter-intuitive for the *non-aficionado*. In ordinary usage, notice has a meaning separate from knowledge. This Act follows ordinary usage and therefore contains some references to "knowledge or notice."

Subsection (a)(2) – In this context, the most important source of "law other than this [act]" is the common law of agency.

Subsection (b)(1) – The "facts known to the person at the time in question" include facts the person is deemed to know under subsection (a)(2).

Subsection (d)(2) – Under this Act, the power to bind a limited liability company to a third party is primarily a matter of agency law. Section 301, Comment. The constructive notice provided under this paragraph will be relevant if a third party makes a claim under agency law that someone who purported to act on behalf of a limited liability company had the apparent authority to do so.

SECTION 104. NATURE, PURPOSE, AND DURATION OF LIMITED LIABILITY COMPANY.

(a)   A limited liability company is an entity distinct from its members.

(b)   A limited liability company may have any lawful purpose, regardless of whether for

profit.

(c)   A limited liability company has perpetual duration.

Legislative Note: *This state should consider whether to amend statutes protecting the public interest in organizations formed for charitable or similar purposes.*

from function or conduct. Contrast Section 301(b) (stating that, although this Act does not make a member as member the agent of a limited liability company, other law may make an LLC liable for the conduct of a member).

This paragraph is stated separately from Paragraph (1), because it can be argued that the liability of members and managers to third parties is not an internal affair. *See, e.g.*, RESTATEMENT (SECOND) OF CONFLICT OF LAWS, § 307 (treating shareholders' liability separately from the internal affairs doctrine). A few cases subsume owner/manager liability into internal affairs, but many do not. *See, e.g., Kalb, Voorhis & Co. v. American Fin. Corp.*, 8 F.3d 130, 132 (2nd Cir. 1993). In any event, the rule stated in this paragraph is correct. All sensible authorities agree that, except in extraordinary circumstances, "shield-related" issues should be determined according to the law of the state of organization.

SECTION 107. SUPPLEMENTAL PRINCIPLES OF LAW. Unless displaced by particular provisions of this [act], the principles of law and equity supplement this [act].

SECTION 108. NAME.

(a)   The name of a limited liability company must contain the words "limited liability company" or "limited company" or the abbreviation "L.L.C.", "LLC", "L.C.", or "LC". "Limited" may be abbreviated as "Ltd.", and "company" may be abbreviated as "Co.".

(b)   Unless authorized by subsection (c), the name of a limited liability company must be distinguishable in the records of the [Secretary of State] from:

(1)   the name of each person that is not an individual and that is incorporated, organized, or authorized to transact business in this state;

(2)   the limited liability company name stated in each certificate of organization that contains the statement as provided in Section 201(b)(3) and that has not lapsed; and

(3)   each name reserved under Section 109 and [cite other state laws allowing the reservation or registration of business names, including fictitious or assumed name statutes].

(c)   A limited liability company may apply to the [Secretary of State] for authorization to use a name that does not comply with subsection (b). The [Secretary of State] shall authorize use of the name applied for if, as to each noncomplying name:

(1)   the present user, registrant, or owner of the noncomplying name consents in a signed record to the use and submits an undertaking in a form satisfactory to the [Secretary of State] to change the noncomplying name to a name that complies with subsection (b) and is distinguishable in the records of the [Secretary of State] from the name applied for; or

(2)   the applicant delivers to the [Secretary of State] a certified copy of the final judgment of a court establishing the applicant's right to use in this state the name applied for.

(d)   Subject to Section 805, this section applies to a foreign limited liability company transacting business in this state which has a certificate of authority to transact business in this state or which has applied for a certificate of authority.

Comment

Subsection (a) is taken verbatim from ULLCA § 105(a). Except for subsection (b)(2), the rest of the section is taken from ULPA (2001) § 108.

Subsection (b)(2) – This language is necessary to protect a name contained in a filed certificate of organization that has not become effective because there are no members. If a statement of membership is not thereafter timely filed, "the certificate lapses and is void," thereby freeing the name. Section 201(e)(1).

SECTION 109. RESERVATION OF NAME.

(a)   A person may reserve the exclusive use of the name of a limited liability company, including a fictitious or assumed name for a foreign limited liability company whose name is not available, by delivering an application to the [Secretary of State] for filing. The application must state the name and address of the applicant and the name proposed to be reserved. If the [Secretary of State] finds that the name applied for is available, it must be reserved for the applicant's exclusive use for a 120-day period.

(b)   The owner of a name reserved for a limited liability company may transfer the reservation to another person by delivering to the [Secretary of State] for filing a signed notice of the transfer which states the name and address of the transferee.

Comment

Source: ULLCA, § 106.

Subsection (a) – Although 120-day reservation period is non-renewable, this subsection does not prevent a person from seeking successive 120-day periods of reservation.

SECTION 110. OPERATING AGREEMENT; SCOPE, FUNCTION, AND LIMITATIONS.

(a)   Except as otherwise provided in subsections (b) and (c), the operating agreement governs:

(1)   relations among the members as members and between the members and the limited liability company;

(2)   the rights and duties under this [act] of a person in the capacity of manager;

(3)   the activities of the company and the conduct of those activities; and

(4)   the means and conditions for amending the operating agreement.

(b)   To the extent the operating agreement does not otherwise provide for a matter described in subsection (a), this [act] governs the matter.

(c)   An operating agreement may not:

(1)   vary a limited liability company's capacity under Section 105 to sue and be sued in its own name;

(2)   vary the law applicable under Section 106;

(3)   vary the power of the court under Section 204;

(4)   subject to subsections (d) through (g), eliminate the duty of loyalty, the duty of care, or any other fiduciary duty;

(5)   subject to subsections (d) through (g), eliminate the contractual obligation of good faith and fair dealing under Section 409(d);

(6)   unreasonably restrict the duties and rights stated in Section 410;

(7)   vary the power of a court to decree dissolution in the circumstances specified in Section 701(a)(4) and (5);

(8)   vary the requirement to wind up a limited liability company's business as specified in Section 702(a) and (b)(1);

(9)   unreasonably restrict the right of a member to maintain an action under

[Article] 9;

(10)   restrict the right to approve a merger, conversion, or domestication under

Section 1014 to a member that will have personal liability with respect to a surviving, converted, or domesticated organization; or

(11)   except as otherwise provided in Section 112(b), restrict the rights under this [act] of a person other than a member or manager.

(d)   If not manifestly unreasonable, the operating agreement may:

(1)   restrict or eliminate the duty:

(A)   as required in Section 409(b)(1) and (g), to account to the limited liability company and to hold as trustee for it any property, profit, or benefit derived by the member in the conduct or winding up of the company's business, from a use by the member of the company's property, or from the appropriation of a limited liability company opportunity;

(B)   as required in Section 409(b)(2) and (g), to refrain from dealing with the company in the conduct or winding up of the company's business as or on behalf of a party having an interest adverse to the company; and

(C)   as required by Section 409(b)(3) and (g), to refrain from competing with the company in the conduct of the company's business before the dissolution of the company;

(2)   identify specific types or categories of activities that do not violate the duty of loyalty;

(3)   alter the duty of care, except to authorize intentional misconduct or knowing violation of law;

(4)   alter any other fiduciary duty, including eliminating particular aspects of that duty; and

(5)   prescribe the standards by which to measure the performance of the contractual obligation of good faith and fair dealing under Section 409(d).

(e)   The operating agreement may specify the method by which a specific act or transaction that would otherwise violate the duty of loyalty may be authorized or ratified by one or more disinterested and independent persons after full disclosure of all material facts.

(f)   To the extent the operating agreement of a member-managed limited liability company expressly relieves a member of a responsibility that the member would otherwise have under this [act] and imposes the responsibility on one or more other members, the operating agreement may, to the benefit of the member that the operating agreement relieves of the responsibility, also eliminate or limit any fiduciary duty that would have pertained to the responsibility.

(g)   The operating agreement may alter or eliminate the indemnification for a member or manager provided by Section 408(a) and may eliminate or limit a member or manager's liability to the limited liability company and members for money damages, except for:

(1)   breach of the duty of loyalty;

(2)   a financial benefit received by the member or manager to which the member or manager is not entitled;

(3)   a breach of a duty under Section 406;

(4)   intentional infliction of harm on the company or a member; or

(5)   an intentional violation of criminal law.

(h)   The court shall decide any claim under subsection (d) that a term of an operating agreement is manifestly unreasonable. The court:

(1)   shall make its determination as of the time the challenged term became part of the operating agreement and by considering only circumstances existing at that time; and

(2)   may invalidate the term only if, in light of the purposes and activities of the

limited liability company, it is readily apparent that:

(A)   the objective of the term is unreasonable; or

(B)   the term is an unreasonable means to achieve the provision's objective.

Comment

The operating agreement is pivotal to a limited liability company, and Sections 110 through 112 are pivotal to this Act. They must be read together, along with Section 102(13) (defining the operating agreement).

One of the most complex questions in the law of unincorporated business organizations is the extent to which an agreement among the organization's owners can affect the law of fiduciary duty. This section gives special attention to that question and is organized as follows:

Subsection (a)	grants broad, *general* authority to the operating agreement
Subsection (b)	establishes this Act as comprising the "default rules" ("gap fillers") for matters within the purview of the operating agreement but not addressed by the operating agreement
Subsection (c)	states restrictions on the power of the operating agreement, especially but not exclusively with regard to fiduciary duties and the contractual obligation of good faith
Subsection (d)	contains *specific* grants of authority for the operating agreement with regard to fiduciary duty and the contractual obligation of good faith; expressed so as to state restrictions on those specific grants – including the "if not manifestly unreasonable" standard
Subsection (e)	specifically grants the operating agreement the power to provide mechanisms for approving or ratifying conduct that would otherwise violate the duty of loyalty; expressed so as to state restrictions on those mechanism – full disclosure and disinterested and independent decision makers
Subsection (f)	specifically authorizes the operating agreement to divest a member of fiduciary duty with regard to a matter if the operating agreement is also divesting the person of responsibility for the matter (and imposing that responsibility on one or more other members)
Subsection (g)	contains *specific* grants of authority for the operating agreement with regard to indemnification and exculpatory provisions; expressed so as to state restrictions on those specific grants
Subsection (h)	provides rules for applying the "not manifestly unreasonable" standard established by subsection (d)

A limited liability company is as much a creature of contract as of statute, and Section 102(13) delineates a very broad scope for "operating agreement." As a result, once an LLC comes into existence and has a member, the LLC necessarily has an operating agreement. See Comment to Section 102(13). Accordingly, this Act refers to "the operating agreement" rather than "an operating agreement."

This phrasing should not, however, be read to require a limited liability company or its members to take any formal action to adopt an operating agreement. Compare CAL. CORP. CODE § 17050(a) (West 2006) ("In order to form a limited liability company, one or more persons shall execute and file articles of organization with, and on a form prescribed by, the Secretary of State and, either before or after the filing of articles of organization, the members shall have entered into an operating agreement.")

The operating agreement is the exclusive consensual process for modifying this Act's various default rules pertaining to relationships inter se the members and between the members and the limited liability company. Section 110(b). The operating agreement also has power over "the rights and duties under this [act] of a person in the capacity of manager," subsection (a)(2), and "the obligations of a limited liability company and its members to a person in the person's capacity as a transferee or dissociated member." Section 112(b).

Subsection (a) – This section describes the very broad scope of a limited liability company's operating agreement, which includes all matters constituting "internal affairs." Compare Section 106(1) (using the phrase "internal affairs" in stating a choice of law rule). This broad grant of authority is subject to the restrictions stated in subsection (c), including the broad restriction stated in paragraph (c)(11) (concerning the rights under this Act of third parties).

Subsection (a)(2) – Under this paragraph, the operating agreement has the power to affect the rights and duties of managers (including non-member managers). Because the term "[o]perating agreement . . . . includes the agreement as amended or restated," Section 102(13), this paragraph gives the members the ongoing power to define the role of an LLC's managers. Power is not the same as right, however, and exercising the power provided by this paragraph might constitute a breach of a separate contract between the LLC and the manager. A non- member manager might also have rights under Section 112(a).

Subsection (a)(4) – If the operating agreement does not address this matter, under subsection (b) this Act provides the rule. The rule appears in Section 407(b)(5) and 407(c)(4)(D) (unanimous consent).

This Act does not specially authorize the operating agreement to limit the sources in which terms of the operating agreement might be found or limit amendments to specified modes (e.g., prohibiting modifications except when consented to in writing). Compare UCC § 2-209(2) (authorizing such prohibitions in a "signed agreement" for the sale of goods). However, this Paragraph (a)(4) could be read to encompass such authorization. Also, under Section 107 the parol evidence rule will apply to a written operating agreement containing an appropriate merger provision.

Subsection (c) – If a person claims that a term of the operating agreement violates this subsection, as a matter of ordinary procedural law the burden is on the person making the claim.

Subsection (c)(1) – Under this Act, a limited liability company is emphatically an entity, and the members lack the power to alter that characteristic.

Subsection (c)(4) – This limitation is less powerful than might first appear, because subsections (d) through (g) specifically authorize significantly alterations to fiduciary duty. The reference to "or any other fiduciary duty" is necessary because the Act has "un-cabined" fiduciary duty. See Comment to Section 409.

Subsection (c)(9) – Arbitration and forum selection provisions are commonplace in business agreements, and this paragraph's restrictions do not reflect any special hostility to or skepticism of such provisions.

Subsection (c)(10) – Under Section 1014:

- each member is protected from being merged, converted, or domesticated "into" the status of an unshielded general partner (or comparable position) without the member having *directly* consented to either:
  - the merger, conversion, or domestication; or
  - an operating agreement provision that permits such transactions to occur with less than unanimous consent of the members; and
- merely consenting to an operating agreement provision that permits amendment of the operating agreement with less than unanimous consent of the members does not qualify as the requisite direct consent.

The sole function of subsection (c)(10) is to protect Section 1014 by denying the operating agreement the power to restrict or otherwise undercut the protections of Section 1014.

Subsection (c)(11) – This limitation pertains only to "the rights under this[act] of" third parties. The extent to which an operating agreement can affect other rights of third parties is a question for other law, particularly the law of contracts.

Subsection (d) – Delaware recently amended its LLC statute to permit an operating agreement to fully "eliminate" fiduciary duty within an LLC. This Act rejects the ultra- contractarian notion that fiduciary duty within a business organization is merely a set of default rule and seeks instead to balance the virtues of "freedom of contract" against the dangers that inescapably exist when some have power over the interests of others. As one source has explained:

The open-ended nature of fiduciary duty reflects the law's long-standing recognition that devious people can smell a loophole a mile away. For centuries, the law has assumed that

(1) power creates opportunities for abuse and (2) the devious creativity of those in power may outstrip the prescience of those trying, through ex ante contract drafting, to constrain that combination of power and creativity.

CARTER G. BISHOP AND DANIEL S. KLEINBERGER, LIMITED LIABILITY COMPANIES: TAX AND BUSINESS LAW, ¶ 14.05[4][a][ii]

Subsection (h) contains rules for applying the "not manifestly unreasonable" standard.

Subsection (d)(1) – Subject to the "not manifestly unreasonable" standard, this paragraph empowers the operating agreement to eliminate all aspects of the duty of loyalty listed in Section

409. The contractual obligation of good faith would remain, see subsections(c)(5) and (d)(5), as would any other, uncodified aspects of the duty of loyalty. See Comment to Section 409 (explaining the decision to "un-cabin" fiduciary duty). See also subsection (d)(4) (empowering the operating agreement to "alter any other fiduciary duty, including eliminating particular aspects of that duty").

Subsection (d)(3) – The operating agreement's power to affect this Act's duty of care both parallels and differs from the agreement's power to affect this Act's duty of loyalty as well as any other fiduciary duties not codified in the statute. With regard to all fiduciary duties, the operating agreement is subject to the "manifestly unreasonable" standard. The differences concern: (i) the extent of the operating agreement's power to restrict the duty; and (ii) the power of the operating agreement to provide indemnity or exculpation for persons subject to the duty.

duty	extent of operating agreement's power to restrict the duty (subject to the "manifestly unreasonable" standard) Section 110(d)(1), (3) and (4)	power of the operating agreement to provide indemnity or exculpation w/r/t breach of the duty Section 110(g)
loyalty	restrict or completely eliminate	none
care	alter, but not eliminate; specifically may not authorize intentional misconduct or knowing violation of law	complete
other fiduciary duties, not codified in the statute	restrict or completely eliminate Section 110(4)	complete

Subsection (e) – Section 409(f) states the Act's default rule for authorization or ratification – unanimous consent. This subsection specifically empowers the operating agreement to provide alternate mechanisms but, in doing so, imposes significant restrictions – namely, any alternate mechanism must involve full disclosure to, and the disinterestedness and independence of, the decision makers. These restrictions are consonant with ordinary notions of authorization and ratification.

This Act provides four separate methods through which those with management power in a limited liability company can proceed with conduct that would otherwise violate the duty of loyalty:

Method	Statutory Authority
The operating agreement might eliminate the duty or otherwise permit the conduct, without need for further authorization or ratification.	Section 110(d)(1) and (2)
The conduct might be authorized or ratified by all the members after full disclosure.	Section 409(f)
The operating agreement might establish a mechanism other than the informed consent for authorizing or ratifying the conduct.	Section 110(e)
In the case of self-dealing the conduct might be successfully defended as being or having been fair to the limited liability company.	Section 409(e)

Subsection (f) – This subsection is intended to make clear that – regardless of the strictures stated elsewhere in this section – in the specified circumstances the operating agreement can entirely strip away the pertinent fiduciary duties.

Subsection (g) – This subsection specifically empowers the operating agreement to address matters of indemnification and exculpation but subjects that power to stated limitations.

Those limitations are drawn from the raft of exculpatory provisions that sprung up in corporate statutes in response to Smith v. Van Gorkum, 488 A.2d 858 (Del. 1985). Delaware led the response with DEL. CODE ANN. tit. 8, § 102(b)(7) (2006), and a number of LLC statutes have similar provisions. E.g. GA. CODE ANN. § 14-11-305(4)(A) (West 2006); IDAHO CODE ANN. § 53-624(1) (2006). For an extreme example, see VA. CODE ANN. § 13.1-1025 (West 2006) (establishing limits of monetary liability as the default rule).

The restrictions stated in paragraphs (1) through (5) apply both to indemnification and exculpation. The power to "alter or eliminate the indemnification provided by Section 408(a)" includes the power to expand or reduce that indemnification.

Subsection (g)(4) – Due to this paragraph, an exculpatory provision cannot shield against a member's claim of oppression. See Section 701(a)(5)(B) and (b).

Subsection (h) – The "not manifestly unreasonable standard" became part of uniform business entity statutes when RUPA imported the concept from the Uniform Commercial Code. This subsection provides rules for applying that standard, which are necessary because:

- Determining unreasonableness *inter se* owners of an organization is a different task than doing so in a commercial context, where concepts like "usages of trade" are available to inform the analysis. Each business organization must be understood in its own terms and context.
- If loosely applied, the standard would permit a court to rewrite the members' agreement, which would destroy the balance this Act seeks to establish between freedom of contract and fiduciary duty.
- Case law research indicates that courts have tended to disregard the significance of the word "manifestly."
- Some decisions have considered reasonableness as of the time of the complaint, which means that a prospectively reasonable allocation of risk could be overturned because it functioned as agreed.

If a person claims that a term of the operating agreement in manifestly unreasonable under subsections (d) and (h), as a matter of ordinary procedural law the burden is on the person making the claim.

Subsection (h)(1) – The significance of the phrase "as of the time the term as challenged became part of the operating agreement" is best shown by example.

EXAMPLE: An LLC's operating agreement as initially adopted includes a provision subjecting a matter to "the manager's sole, reasonable discretion." A year later, the agreement is amended to delete the word "reasonable." Later, a member claims that, without the word "reasonable," the provision is manifestly unreasonable. The relevant time under subsection (h)(1) is when the agreement was amended, not when the agreement was initially adopted.

EXAMPLE: When a particular manager-managed LLC comes into existence, its business plan is quite unusual and its success depends on the willingness of a particular individual to serve as the LLC's sole manager. This individual has a rare combination of skills, experiences, and contacts, which are particularly appropriate for the LLC's start- up. In order to induce the individual to accept the position of sole manager, the members are willing to have the operating agreement significantly limit the manager's fiduciary duties. Several years later, when the LLC's operations have turned prosaic and the manager's talents and background are not nearly so crucial, a member challenges the fiduciary duty limitations as manifestly unreasonable. The relevant time under subsection (h)(1) is when the LLC began. Subsequent developments are not relevant, except as they might inferentially bear on the circumstances in existence at the relevant time.

SECTION 111. OPERATING AGREEMENT; EFFECT ON LIMITED LIABILITY COMPANY AND PERSONS BECOMING MEMBERS; PREFORMATION AGREEMENT.

(a)   A limited liability company is bound by and may enforce the operating agreement, whether or not the company has itself manifested assent to the operating agreement.

(b)   A person that becomes a member of a limited liability company is deemed to assent to the operating agreement.

(c)   Two or more persons intending to become the initial members of a limited liability company may make an agreement providing that upon the formation of the company the agreement will become the operating agreement. One person intending to become the initial member of a limited liability company may assent to terms providing that upon the formation of the company the terms will become the operating agreement.

Comment

Subsection (a) – This subsection does not consider whether a limited liability company is an indispensable party to a suit concerning the operating agreement. That is a question of procedural law, which can determine whether federal diversity jurisdiction exists.

Subsection (b) – Given the possibility of oral and implied-in-fact components to the operating agreement, see Comment to Section 110(a)(4), a person becoming a member of an existing limited liability company should take precautions to ascertain fully the contents of the operating agreement.

Subsection (c) – The second sentence refers to "assent to terms" rather than "make an agreement" because, under venerable principles of contract law, an agreement presupposes at least two parties. This Act specifically defines the operating agreement to include a sole member, Section 102(13), but a preformation arrangement is not an operating agreement. An operating agreement is among "members," and, under this Act, the earliest a person can become a member is upon the formation of the limited liability company. Section 401.

SECTION 112. OPERATING AGREEMENT; EFFECT ON THIRD PARTIES AND RELATIONSHIP TO RECORDS EFFECTIVE ON BEHALF OF LIMITED LIABILITY COMPANY.

(a) An operating agreement may specify that its amendment requires the approval of a person that is not a party to the operating agreement or the satisfaction of a condition. An amendment is ineffective if its adoption does not include the required approval or satisfy the specified condition.

(b) The obligations of a limited liability company and its members to a person in the person's capacity as a transferee or dissociated member are governed by the operating agreement. Subject only to any court order issued under Section 503(b)(2) to effectuate a charging order, an amendment to the operating agreement made after a person becomes a transferee or dissociated member is effective with regard to any debt, obligation, or other liability of the limited liability company or its members to the person in the person's capacity as a transferee or dissociated member.

(c) If a record that has been delivered by a limited liability company to the [Secretary of State] for filing and has become effective under this [act] contains a provision that would be ineffective under Section 110(c) if contained in the operating agreement, the provision is likewise ineffective in the record.

(d) Subject to subsection (c), if a record that has been delivered by a limited liability company to the [Secretary of State] for filing and has become effective under this [act] conflicts with a provision of the operating agreement:

(1) the operating agreement prevails as to members, dissociated members, transferees, and managers; and

(2) the record prevails as to other persons to the extent they reasonably rely on the record.

Comment

Subsection (a) – This subsection, derived from DEL. CODE ANN. tit. 6, § 18-302(e), permits a non-member to have veto rights over amendments to the operating agreement. Such veto rights are likely to be sought by lenders but may also be attractive to non-member managers.

EXAMPLE: A non-member manager enters into a management contract with the LLC, and that agreement provides in part that the LLC may remove the manager without cause only with the consent of members holding 2/3 of the profits interests. The operating agreement contains a parallel provision, but the non-member manager is not a party to the operating agreement. Later the LLC members amend the operating agreement to change the quantum to a simple majority and thereafter purport to remove the manager without cause. Although the LLC has undoubtedly breached its contract with the manager and subjected itself to a damage claim, the LLC has the power under Section 110(a)(2) to effect the removal – unless the operating agreement provided the non-member manager a veto right over changes in the quantum provision.

The subsection does not refer to member veto rights because, unless otherwise provided in the operating agreement, the consent of each member is necessary to effect an amendment. Section 407(b)(5) and (c)(4)(D).

Subsection (b) – The law of unincorporated business organizations is only beginning to grapple in a modern way with the tension between the rights of an organization's owners to carry on their activities as they see fit (or have agreed) and the rights of transferees of the organization's economic interests. (Such transferees can include the heirs of business founders as well as former owners who are "locked in" as transferees of their own interests. See Section 603(a)(3).).

If the law categorically favors the owners, there is a serious risk of expropriation and other abuse. On the other hand, if the law grants former owners and other transferees the right to seek judicial protection, that specter can "freeze the deal" as of the moment an owner leaves the enterprise or a third party obtains an economic interest.

Bauer v. Blomfield Co./Holden Joint Venture, 849 P2d 1365 (Alaska 1993) illustrates this point nicely. The case arose after all the partners had approved a commission arrangement with a third party and the arrangement dried up all the partnership profits. When an assignee of a partnership interest objected, the court majority flatly rejected not only the claim but also the assignee's right to assert the claim. A mere assignee "was not entitled to complain about a decision made with the consent of all the partners." Id. at 1367. A footnote explained, "We are unwilling to hold that partners owe a duty of good faith and fair dealing to assignees of a partner's interest." *Id.* at 1367, n. 2.

The dissent, invoking the law of contracts, asserted that the majority had turned the statutory protection of the partners' management prerogatives into an instrument for abuse of assignees:

It is a well-settled principle of contract law that an assignee steps into the shoes of an assignor as to the rights assigned. Today, the court summarily dismisses this principle in a footnote and leaves the assignee barefoot....

As interpreted by the court, the [partnership] statute now allows partners to deprive an assignee of profits to which he is entitled by law for whatever outrageous motive or reason. The court's opinion essentially leaves the assignee of a partnership interest without remedy to enforce his right.

Id. at 1367-8 (Matthews, J., dissenting).

The *Bauer* majority is consistent with the limited but long-standing case law in this area (all of it pertaining to partnerships rather than LLCs). This subsection follows the *Bauer* majority and other cases by expressly subjecting transferees and dissociated members to operating agreement amendments made after the transfer or dissociation. *Compare* UPA § 32(2) (permitting an assignee to seek judicial dissolution of an at-will general partnership at any time and of a partnership for a term or undertaking if partnership continues in existence after the completion of the term or undertaking); RUPA § 801(6) (same except adding the requirement that the court determine that dissolution is equitable); ULLCA, § 801(5) (same as RUPA); ULLCA, § 801(4) (permitting a dissociated member to seek dissolution on the grounds *inter alia* of oppressive conduct). *See also* UCC §§ 9-405(a) and (b) and RESTATEMENT (SECOND) OF CONTRACTS § 338 (1981) (recognizing a duty of good faith applicable to the modification of a contract when an assignment of contract is in effect).

The issue of whether, in extreme and sufficiently harsh circumstances, transferees might be able to claim some type of duty or obligation to protect against expropriation, is a question for other law.

Subsection (d) – A limited liability company is a creature of contract as well as a creature of statute. It will be possible, albeit improvident, for the operating agreement to be inconsistent with the certificate of organization or other public filings pertaining to the limited liability company. For those circumstances, this subsection provides rules for determining which source of information prevails.

For members, managers and transferees, the operating agreement is paramount. For third parties seeking to invoke the public record, actual knowledge of that record is necessary and notice, deemed notice, and deemed knowledge under Section 103 are irrelevant. A third party wishing to enforce the public record over the operating agreement must show reasonable reliance on the public record, and reliance presupposes knowledge.

The mere fact that a term is present in a publicly-filed record and not in the operating agreement, or vice versa, does not automatically establish a conflict. This subsection does not expressly cover a situation in which (i) one of the specified filed records contains information in addition to, but not inconsistent with, the operating agreement, and (ii) a person, other than a member or transferee, reasonably relies on the additional information. However, the policy reflected in this subsection seems equally applicable to that situation.

Section 110(a)(4) might also be relevant to the subject matter of this subsection. Absent a contrary provision in the operating agreement, language in an LLC's certificate of organization might be evidence of the members' agreement and might thereby constitute or at least imply a term of the operating agreement.

This subsection does not apply to records delivered to the [Secretary of State] for filing on behalf of persons other than a limited liability company.

SECTION 113. OFFICE AND AGENT FOR SERVICE OF PROCESS.

(a) A limited liability company shall designate and continuously maintain in this state:

    (1) an office, which need not be a place of its activity in this state; and

    (2) an agent for service of process.

(b) A foreign limited liability company that has a certificate of authority under Section 802 shall designate and continuously maintain in this state an agent for service of process.

(c) An agent for service of process of a limited liability company or foreign limited liability company must be an individual who is a resident of this state or other person with authority to transact business in this state.

Comment

Source: ULPA (2001), § 114.

SECTION 114. CHANGE OF DESIGNATED OFFICE OR AGENT FOR SERVICE OF PROCESS.

(a)   A limited liability company or foreign limited liability company may change its designated office, its agent for service of process, or the address of its agent for service of process by delivering to the [Secretary of State] for filing a statement of change containing:

(1)   the name of the company;

(2)   the street and mailing addresses of its current designated office;

(3)   if the current designated office is to be changed, the street and mailing addresses of the new designated office;

(4)   the name and street and mailing addresses of its current agent for service of

process; and

(5)   if the current agent for service of process or an address of the agent is to be

changed, the new information.

(b)   Subject to Section 205(c), a statement of change is effective when filed by the [Secretary of State].

Comment

Source – ULPA (2001) § 115, which is based on ULLCA § 109.

Subsection (a) – This subsection uses "may" rather than "shall" because other avenues exist. A limited liability company may also change the information by amending its certificate of organization, Section 202, or through its annual report. Section 209(e). A foreign limited liability company may use its annual report. Section 209(e). However, neither a limited liability company nor a foreign limited liability company may wait for the annual report if the information described in the public record becomes inaccurate. See Sections 207 (imposing liability for false information in record) and 116(b) (providing for substitute service).

SECTION 115. RESIGNATION OF AGENT FOR SERVICE OF PROCESS.

(a)   To resign as an agent for service of process of a limited liability company or foreign limited liability company, the agent must deliver to the [Secretary of State] for filing a statement of resignation containing the company name and stating that the agent is resigning.

(b)   The [Secretary of State] shall file a statement of resignation delivered under subsection (a) and mail or otherwise provide or deliver a copy to the designated office of the limited liability company or foreign limited liability company and another copy to the principal office of the company if the mailing addresses of the principal office appears in the records of the [Secretary of State] and is different from the mailing address of the designated office.

(c)   An agency for service of process terminates on the earlier of:

(1)   the 31st day after the [Secretary of State] files the statement of resignation;

(2)   when a record designating a new agent for service of process is delivered to the [Secretary of State] for filing on behalf of the limited liability company and becomes effective.

Comment

Source – ULPA (2001) § 116, which is based on ULLCA §110.

SECTION 116. SERVICE OF PROCESS.

(a)   An agent for service of process appointed by a limited liability company or foreign limited liability company is an agent of the company for service of any process, notice, or demand required or permitted by law to be served on the company.

(b)   If a limited liability company or foreign limited liability company does not appoint or maintain an agent for service of process in this state or the agent for service of process cannot with reasonable diligence be found at the agent's street address, the [Secretary of State] is an agent of the company upon whom process, notice, or demand may be served.

(c)   Service of any process, notice, or demand on the [Secretary of State] as agent for a

limited liability company or foreign limited liability company may be made by delivering to the [Secretary of State] duplicate copies of the process, notice, or demand. If a process, notice, or demand is served on the [Secretary of State], the [Secretary of State] shall forward one of the copies by registered or certified mail, return receipt requested, to the company at its designated office.

(d)   Service is effected under subsection (c) at the earliest of:

(1)   the date the limited liability company or foreign limited liability company receives the process, notice, or demand;

(2)   the date shown on the return receipt, if signed on behalf of the company; or

(3)   five days after the process, notice, or demand is deposited with the United States Postal Service, if correctly addressed and with sufficient postage.

(e)   The [Secretary of State] shall keep a record of each process, notice, and demand served pursuant to this section and record the time of, and the action taken regarding, the service.

(f)   This section does not affect the right to serve process, notice, or demand in any other manner provided by law.

Comment

Source – ULPA (2001) § 117, which is based on ULLCA §111.

[ARTICLE] 2

FORMATION; CERTIFICATE OF ORGANIZATION AND OTHER FILINGS
SECTION 201. FORMATION OF LIMITED LIABILITY COMPANY;

CERTIFICATE OF ORGANIZATION.

(a)   One or more persons may act as organizers to form a limited liability company by signing and delivering to the [Secretary of State] for filing a certificate of organization.

(b)   A certificate of organization must state:

(1)   the name of the limited liability company, which must comply with Section 108;

(2)   the street and mailing addresses of the initial designated office and the name

and street and mailing addresses of the initial agent for service of process of the company; and

(3)   if the company will have no members when the [Secretary of State] files the certificate, a statement to that effect.

(c)   Subject to Section 112(c), a certificate of organization may also contain statements as to matters other than those required by subsection (b). However, a statement in a certificate of organization is not effective as a statement of authority.

(d)   Unless the filed certificate of organization contains the statement as provided in subsection (b)(3), the following rules apply:

(1)   A limited liability company is formed when the [Secretary of State] has filed the certificate of organization and the company has at least one member, unless the certificate states a delayed effective date pursuant to Section 205(c).

(2)   If the certificate states a delayed effective date, a limited liability company is not formed if, before the certificate takes effect, a statement of cancellation is signed and delivered to the [Secretary of State] for filing and the [Secretary of State] files the certificate.

(3)   Subject to any delayed effective date and except in a proceeding by this state to dissolve a limited liability company, the filing of the certificate of organization by the [Secretary of State] is conclusive proof that the organizer satisfied all conditions to the formation of a limited liability company.

(e)   If a filed certificate of organization contains a statement as provided in subsection (b)(3), the following rules apply:

(1)   The certificate lapses and is void unless, within [90] days from the date the

[Secretary of State] files the certificate, an organizer signs and delivers to the [Secretary of State] for filing a notice stating:

  (A) that the limited liability company has at least one member; and

  (B) the date on which a person or persons became the company's initial

member or members.

  (2) If an organizer complies with paragraph (1), a limited liability company is deemed formed as of the date of initial membership stated in the notice delivered pursuant to paragraph (1).

  (3) Except in a proceeding by this state to dissolve a limited liability company, the filing of the notice described in paragraph (1) by the [Secretary of State] is conclusive proof that the organizer satisfied all conditions to the formation of a limited liability company.

  Legislative Note: Enacting jurisdictions should consider revising their "name statutes" generally, to protect "the limited liability company name stated in each certificate of organization that contains the statement as provided in Section 201(b)(3)". Section 108(b)(2).

Comment

  No topic received more attention or generated more debate in the drafting process for this Act than the question of the "shelf LLC" – i.e., an LLC formed without having at least one member upon formation. Reasonable minds differed (occasionally intensely) as to whether the "shelf" approach (i) is necessary to accommodate current business practices; and (ii) somehow does conceptual violence to the partnership antecedents of the limited liability company.

  The 2006 Annual Meeting Draft provided for a "limited shelf" – a shelf that lacked capacity to conduct any substantive activities:

  a) Except as otherwise provided in subsection (b), a limited liability company has the capacity to sue and be sued in its own name and the power to do all things necessary or convenient to carry on its activities.

  (b) Until a limited liability company has or has had at least one member, the company lacks the capacity to do any act or carry on any activity except:

    (1) delivering to the [Secretary of State] for filing a statement of change under Sections 114, an amendment to the certificate under Section 202, a statement of correction under Section 206, an annual report under section 209, and a statement of termination under Section 702(b)(2)(F);

    (2) admitting a member under section 401; and

    (3) dissolving under Section 701.

  (c) A limited liability company that has or has had at least one member may ratify an act or activity that occurred when the company lacked capacity under subsection (b).

However, when the Conference considered the 2006 Annual Meeting Draft, the Drafting Committee itself proposed an amendment, and the Conference agreed. A product of intense discussion and compromise with several ABA Advisors, the amendment substituted a double filing and "embryonic certificate" approach. An organizer may deliver for filing a certificate of organization without the company having any members and the filing officer will file the certificate, but:

- the certificate as delivered to the filing officer must acknowledge that situation, Subsection (a)(3);

- the limited liability company is not formed until and unless the organizer timely delivers to the filing officer a notice that the company has at least one member, Subsection (e)(1); and

- if the organizer does not timely deliver the required notice, the certificate lapses and is void. *Id.*

The Conference recommends a 90-day "window" for filing the notice, which must state "the date on which a person or persons became the company's initial member or members." When the filing officer files that notice, the company is deemed formed as of the date stated in the notice. Subsection (e)(2).

Thus under this Act, the delivery to the filing officer of a certificate of organization has different consequences, depending on whether the certificate contains the "no members" statement as provided by subsection (b)(3).

does the certificate contain the "no members" statement under subsection (b)(3)	by delivering the certificate for filing, what is the organizer affirming, per Section 207(c), about members	effect of the filing officer filing the certificate	logical relationship of the filed certificate to the formation of the LLC
no	that the LLC will have at least one member upon formation	LLC is formed, subject to any delayed effective date	necessary and sufficient
yes	that the LLC will have no members when the filing officer files the certificate	the document is part of the public record, protects the name, and starts the 90-day clock ticking	necessary but not sufficient

Subsection (b) – This Act does not require the certificate of organization to designate whether the limited liability company is manager-managed or member-managed. Under this Act, those characterizations pertain principally to *inter se* relations, and the Act therefore looks to the operating agreement to make the characterization. *See* Sections 102(10) and (12); 407(a).

Subsection (d) – This subsection states the "pathway" through which a limited liability company is formed if the certificate of organization does not contain a statement as provided in subsection (b)(3) – i.e., if the limited liability company will have at least one member when the filing officer files the certificate.

Subsection (e) – This subsection states the "pathway" through which a limited liability company is formed if the certificate of organization contains a statement as provided in subsection (b)(3) – i.e., if the limited liability company will not have at least one member when the filing officer files the certificate.

This pathway requires a second filing in order to form the limited liability company: "a notice stating (A) that the limited liability company has at least one member; and (B) the date on which a person or persons became the company's initial member or members." Subsection (e)(1).

In this pathway, a certificate of organization may not itself state a delayed effective date, Section 205(c), because:

- the reason to state a delayed effective date in a certificate of organization is to set the date on which the limited liability company is formed, Section 205(c); and

- when a certificate contains a statement as provided in subsection (b)(3), this Act mandates when (if at all) the limited liability company is deemed formed – i.e., "as of the date of initial membership stated in the notice delivered" to the filing officer as the second filing. Subsection (e)(2).

SECTION 202. AMENDMENT OR RESTATEMENT OF CERTIFICATE OF ORGANIZATION.

(a)   A certificate of organization may be amended or restated at any time.

(b)   To amend its certificate of organization, a limited liability company must deliver to the [Secretary of State] for filing an amendment stating:

> (1)   the name of the company;

> (2)   the date of filing of its certificate of organization; and

> (3)   the changes the amendment makes to the certificate as most recently amended

or restated.

(c)   To restate its certificate of organization, a limited liability company must deliver to the [Secretary of State] for filing a restatement, designated as such in its heading, stating:

> (1)   in the heading or an introductory paragraph, the company's present name and the date of the filing of the company's initial certificate of organization;

> (2)   if the company's name has been changed at any time since the company's formation, each of the company's former names; and

(3)   the changes the restatement makes to the certificate as most recently amended or restated.

(d)   Subject to Sections 112(c) and 205(c), an amendment to or restatement of a certificate of organization is effective when filed by the [Secretary of State].

(e)   If a member of a member-managed limited liability company, or a manager of a manager-managed limited liability company, knows that any information in a filed certificate of organization was inaccurate when the certificate was filed or has become inaccurate owing to changed circumstances, the member or manager shall promptly:

(1)   cause the certificate to be amended; or

(2)   if appropriate, deliver to the [Secretary of State] for filing a statement of change under Section 114 or a statement of correction under Section 206.

Comment

Subsection (e) – This subsection is taken from ULPA (2001) § 202(c), which imposes the responsibility on general partners. The original ULLCA had no comparable provision.

This subsection imposes an obligation directly on the members and managers rather than on the limited liability company. A member or manager's failure to meet the obligation exposes the member or manager to liability to third parties under Section 207(a)(2) and might constitute a breach of the member or manager's duties under Section 409(c) and (g)(1). In addition, an aggrieved person may seek a remedy under Section 204 (Signing and Filing Pursuant to Judicial Order).

Like other provisions of the Act requiring records to be delivered to the filing officer for filing, this section is not subject to change by the operating agreement. See Section 110(c)(11) (precluding the operating agreement from "restrict[ing] the rights under this [act] of a person other than a member or manager").

SECTION 203. SIGNING OF RECORDS TO BE DELIVERED FOR FILING TO [SECRETARY OF STATE].

(a)   A record delivered to the [Secretary of State] for filing pursuant to this [act] must be signed as follows:

(1)   Except as otherwise provided in paragraphs (2) through (4), a record signed on behalf of a limited liability company must be signed by a person authorized by the company.

(2)   A limited liability company's initial certificate of organization must be signed by at least one person acting as an organizer.

(3)   A notice under Section 201(e)(1) must be signed by an organizer.

(4)   A record filed on behalf of a dissolved limited liability company that has no members must be signed by the person winding up the company's activities under Section 702(c) or a person appointed under Section 702(d) to wind up those activities.

(5)   A statement of cancellation under Section 201(d)(2) must be signed by each organizer that signed the initial certificate of organization, but a personal representative of a deceased or incompetent organizer may sign in the place of the decedent or incompetent.

(6)   A statement of denial by a person under Section 303 must be signed by that person.

(7)   Any other record must be signed by the person on whose behalf the record is delivered to the [Secretary of State].

(b)   Any record filed under this [act] may be signed by an agent.

Comment

Subsection (b) – This subsection does not require that the agent's authority be memorialized in a writing or other record. However, a person signing as an agent "thereby affirms under penalties of perjury that [the assertion of agent status is] . . . accurate." Section 207(c).

SECTION 204. SIGNING AND FILING PURSUANT TO JUDICIAL ORDER.

(a)   If a person required by this [act] to sign a record or deliver a record to the [Secretary of State] for filing under [this act] does not do so, any other person that is aggrieved may petition the [appropriate court] to order:

(1)   the person to sign the record;

(2)   the person to deliver the record to the [Secretary of State] for filing; or

(3)   the [Secretary of State] to file the record unsigned.

(b)   If a petitioner under subsection (a) is not the limited liability company or foreign limited liability company to which the record pertains, the petitioner shall make the company a party to the action.

Comment

Source – ULPA (2001) § 205, which is based on RULPA § 205, which was the source of ULLCA § 210.

Subsection (a)(3) – A record filed under this paragraph is effective without being signed.

SECTION 205. DELIVERY TO AND FILING OF RECORDS BY [SECRETARY OF STATE]; EFFECTIVE TIME AND DATE.

(a)   A record authorized or required to be delivered to the [Secretary of State] for filing under this [act] must be captioned to describe the record's purpose, be in a medium permitted by the [Secretary of State], and be delivered to the [Secretary of State]. If the filing fees have been paid, unless the [Secretary of State] determines that a record does not comply with the filing requirements of this [act], the [Secretary of State] shall file the record and:

(1)   for a statement of denial under Section 303, send a copy of the filed statement and a receipt for the fees to the person on whose behalf the statement was delivered for filing and to the limited liability company; and

(2)   for all other records, send a copy of the filed record and a receipt for the fees to the person on whose behalf the record was filed.

(b)   Upon request and payment of the requisite fee, the [Secretary of State] shall send to the requester a certified copy of a requested record.

(c)   Except as otherwise provided in Sections 115 and 206 and except for a certificate of organization that contains a statement as provided in Section 201(b)(3), a record delivered to the [Secretary of State] for filing under this [act] may specify an effective time and a delayed effective date. Subject to Sections 115, 201(d)(1), and 206, a record filed by the [Secretary of State] is effective:

(1)   if the record does not specify either an effective time or a delayed effective date, on the date and at the time the record is filed as evidenced by the [Secretary of State's] endorsement of the date and time on the record;

(2)   if the record specifies an effective time but not a delayed effective date, on the date the record is filed at the time specified in the record;

(3)   if the record specifies a delayed effective date but not an effective time, at 12:01 a.m. on the earlier of:

(A)   the specified date; or

(B)   the 90th day after the record is filed; or

(4)   if the record specifies an effective time and a delayed effective date, at the specified time on the earlier of:

(A)   the specified date; or

(B)   the 90th day after the record is filed.

Comment

Source – ULPA (2001) § 206, which was based on ULLCA §206.

This Act uses the concept of "filing" to refer to the official act of the [Secretary of State], which is typically preceded by a person "delivering" some record "to the [Secretary of State] for filing."

Subsection (c)(3)(B) and 4(B) – If a person delivers to the Secretary of State for filing a record that contains an over-long delay in the effective date, the Secretary of State: (i) will not reject the record; and (ii) is neither required nor authorized to inform the person that this Act will truncate the period of delay specified in the record.

SECTION 206. CORRECTING FILED RECORD.

(a) A limited liability company or foreign limited liability company may deliver to the [Secretary of State] for filing a statement of correction to correct a record previously delivered by the company to the [Secretary of State] and filed by the [Secretary of State], if at the time of filing the record contained inaccurate information or was defectively signed.

(b) A statement of correction under subsection (a) may not state a delayed effective date and must:

(1) describe the record to be corrected, including its filing date, or attach a copy of the record as filed;

(2) specify the inaccurate information and the reason it is inaccurate or the manner in which the signing was defective; and

(3) correct the defective signature or inaccurate information.

(c) When filed by the [Secretary of State], a statement of correction under subsection (a) is effective retroactively as of the effective date of the record the statement corrects, but the statement is effective when filed:

(1) for the purposes of Section 103(d); and

(2) as to persons that previously relied on the uncorrected record and would be adversely affected by the retroactive effect.

Comment

Source – ULPA (2001) § 207, which was based on ULLCA §207.

SECTION 207. LIABILITY FOR INACCURATE INFORMATION IN FILED RECORD.

(a) If a record delivered to the [Secretary of State] for filing under this [act] and filed by the [Secretary of State] contains inaccurate information, a person that suffers a loss by reliance on the information may recover damages for the loss from:

(1) a person that signed the record, or caused another to sign it on the person's behalf, and knew the information to be inaccurate at the time the record was signed; and

(2) subject to subsection (b), a member of a member-managed limited liability company or the manager of a manager-managed limited liability company, if:

(A)   the record was delivered for filing on behalf of the company; and

(B)   the member or manager had notice of the inaccuracy for a reasonably sufficient time before the information was relied upon so that, before the reliance, the member or manager reasonably could have:

(i)   effected an amendment under Section 202;

(ii)   filed a petition under Section 204; or

(iii)   delivered to the [Secretary of State] for filing a statement of change under Section 114 or a statement of correction under Section 206.

(b)   To the extent that the operating agreement of a member-managed limited liability company expressly relieves a member of responsibility for maintaining the accuracy of information contained in records delivered on behalf of the company to the [Secretary of State] for filing under this [act] and imposes that responsibility on one or more other members, the liability stated in subsection (a)(2) applies to those other members and not to the member that the operating agreement relieves of the responsibility.

(c)   An individual who signs a record authorized or required to be filed under this [act] affirms under penalty of perjury that the information stated in the record is accurate.

Comment

Source: ULPA (2001) § 208, which expanded on ULLCA § 209.

Section (a)(2)(B) – This subparagraph implies that doing any of the acts listed in clauses

(i)   through (iii) will preclude liability arising from subsequent reliance. In this connection, Clause (a)(2)(B)(ii) warrants special attention, because that act (filing a petition in court) can occur without any immediate effect on the records relevant to a limited liability company maintained by the filing officer. The other clauses refer to acts that (assuming no filing backlog) affect that public record immediately.

SECTION 208. CERTIFICATE OF EXISTENCE OR AUTHORIZATION.

(a)   The [Secretary of State], upon request and payment of the requisite fee, shall furnish to any person a certificate of existence for a limited liability company if the records filed in the [office of the Secretary of State] show that the company has been formed under Section 201 and the [Secretary of State] has not filed a statement of termination pertaining to the company. A certificate of existence must state:

(1)   the company's name;

(2)   that the company was duly formed under the laws of this state and the date of formation;

(3)   whether all fees, taxes, and penalties due under this [act] or other law to the

[Secretary of State] have been paid;

(4)   whether the company's most recent annual report required by Section 209 has been filed by the [Secretary of State];

(5)   whether the [Secretary of State] has administratively dissolved the company;

(6)   whether the company has delivered to the [Secretary of State] for filing a statement of dissolution;

(7)   that a statement of termination has not been filed by the [Secretary of State];

and

(8)   other facts of record in the [office of the Secretary of State] which are

specified by the person requesting the certificate.

(b)   The [Secretary of State], upon request and payment of the requisite fee, shall furnish to any person a certificate of authorization for a foreign limited liability company if the records filed in the [office of the Secretary of State] show that the [Secretary of State] has filed a certificate of authority, has not revoked the certificate of authority, and has not filed a notice of cancellation. A certificate of authorization must state:

(1)   the company's name and any alternate name adopted under Section 805(a) for use in this state;

(2)   that the company is authorized to transact business in this state;

(3)   whether all fees, taxes, and penalties due under this [act] or other law to the [Secretary of State] have been paid;

(4)   whether the company's most recent annual report required by Section 209 has been filed by the [Secretary of State];

(5)   that the [Secretary of State] has not revoked the company's certificate of authority and has not filed a notice of cancellation; and

(6)   other facts of record in the [office of the Secretary of State] which are specified by the person requesting the certificate.

(c)   Subject to any qualification stated in the certificate, a certificate of existence or certificate of authorization issued by the [Secretary of State] is conclusive evidence that the limited liability company is in existence or the foreign limited liability company is authorized to transact business in this state.

Comment

Source – ULPA (2001), § 209, which was based on ULLCA, § 208.

The information provided in a certificate of existence or authorization is, of course, current only as of the date of the certificate.

SECTION 209. ANNUAL REPORT FOR [SECRETARY OF STATE].

(a)   Each year, a limited liability company or a foreign limited liability company authorized to transact business in this state shall deliver to the [Secretary of State] for filing a report that states:

(1)   the name of the company;

(2)   the street and mailing addresses of the company's designated office and the name and street and mailing addresses of its agent for service of process in this state;

(3)   the street and mailing addresses of its principal office; and

(4)   in the case of a foreign limited liability company, the state or other jurisdiction under whose law the company is formed and any alternate name adopted under Section 805(a).

(b)   Information in an annual report under this section must be current as of the date the report is delivered to the [Secretary of State] for filing.

(c)   The first annual report under this section must be delivered to the [Secretary of State] between [January 1 and April 1] of the year following the calendar year in which a limited liability company was formed or a foreign limited liability company was authorized to transact business. A report must be delivered to the [Secretary of State] between [January 1 and April 1] of each subsequent calendar year.

(d)   If an annual report under this section does not contain the information required in subsection (a), the [Secretary of State] shall promptly notify the reporting limited liability company or foreign limited liability company and return the report to it for correction. If the report is corrected to contain the information required in subsection (a) and delivered to the [Secretary of State] within 30 days after the effective date of the notice, it is timely delivered.

(e)   If an annual report under this section contains an address of a designated office or the name or address of an agent for service of process which differs from the information shown in the records of the [Secretary of State] immediately before the annual report becomes effective, the differing information in the annual report is considered a statement of change under Section 114.

Comment

Source – ULPA (2001) § 210, which was based on ULLCA § 211.

A limited liability company that fails to comply with this section is subject to administrative dissolution. Section 705(a)(2). A foreign limited liability company that fails to comply with this section is subject to having its certificate of authority revoked. Section 806(a)(2).

[ARTICLE] 3

RELATIONS OF MEMBERS AND MANAGERS

TO PERSONS DEALING WITH LIMITED LIABILITY COMPANY

SECTION 301. NO AGENCY POWER OF MEMBER AS MEMBER.

(a)   A member is not an agent of a limited liability company solely by reason of being a member.

(b)   A person's status as a member does not prevent or restrict law other than this [act] from imposing liability on a limited liability company because of the person's conduct.

Comment

Subsection (a) – Most LLC statutes, including the original ULLCA, provide for what might be termed "statutory apparent authority" for members in a member-managed limited liability company and managers in a manager-managed limited liability company. This approach codifies the common law notion of apparent authority by position and dates back at least to the original, 1914 Uniform Partnership Act. UPA, § 9 provided that "the act of every partner … for apparently carrying on in the usual way the business of the partnership … binds the partnership," and that formulation has been essentially followed by RUPA, § 301, ULLCA, § 301, ULPA (2001), § 402, and myriad state LLC statutes.

This Act rejects the statutory apparent authority approach, for reasons summarized in a "Progress Report on the Revised Uniform Limited Liability Company Act," published in the March 2006 issue of the newsletter of the ABA Committee on Partnerships and Unincorporated Business Organizations:

The concept [of statutory apparent authority] still makes sense both for general and limited partnerships. A third party dealing with either type of partnership can know by the formal name of the entity and by a person's status as general or limited partner whether the person has the power to bind the entity.

Most LLC statutes have attempted to use the same approach but with a fundamentally important (and problematic) distinction. An LLC's status as member-managed or manager-managed determines whether members or managers have the statutory power to bind. But an LLC's status as member- or manager-managed is not apparent from the LLC's name. A third party must check the public record, which may reveal that the LLC is manager-managed, which in turn means a member as member has no power to bind the LLC. As a result, a provision that originated in 1914 as a protection for third parties can, in the LLC context, easily function as a trap for the unwary. The problem is exacerbated by the almost infinite variety of management structures permissible in and used by LLCs.

The new Act cuts through this problem by simply eliminating statutory apparent authority.

PUBOGRAM, Vol. XXIII, no. 2 at 9-10.

Codifying power to bind according to position makes sense only for organizations that have well-defined, well-known, and almost paradigmatic management structures. Because:

- flexibility of management structure is a hallmark of the limited liability company; and

- an LLC's name gives no signal as to the organization's structure, it makes no sense to:

- require each LLC to publicly select between two statutorily preordained structures (i.e., manager-managed/member-managed); and then

- link a "statutory power to bind" to each of those two structures.

Under this Act, other law – most especially the law of agency – will handle power-to-bind questions. See the Comment to subsection (b).

This subsection does not address the power to bind of a manager in a manager-managed LLC, although this Act does consider a manager's management responsibilities. See Section 407(c) (allocating management authority, subject to the operating agreement). For a discussion of how agency law will approach the actual and apparent authority of managers, see Section 407(c), cmt.

Subsection (b) – As the "flip side" to subsection (a), this subsection expressly preserves the power of other law to hold an LLC directly or vicariously liable on account of conduct by a person who happens to be a member. For example, given the proper set of circumstances: (i) a member might have actual or apparent authority to bind an LLC to a contract; (ii) the doctrine of *respondeat superior* might make an LLC liable for the tortious conduct of a member (i.e., in some circumstances a member acts as a "servant" of the LLC); and (iii) an LLC might be liable for negligently supervising a member who is acting on behalf of the LLC. A person's status as a member does not weigh against these or any other relevant theories of law.

Moreover, subsection (a) does not prevent member status from being relevant to one or more elements of an "other law" theory. The most categorical example concerns the authority of a non-manager member of a manager-managed LLC.

EXAMPLE: A vendor knows that an LLC is manager-managed but chooses to accept the signature of a person whom the vendor knows is merely a member of the LLC. Assuring the vendor that the LLC will stand by the member's commitment, the member states, "It's such a simple matter; no one will mind." The member genuinely believes the statement, and the vendor accepts the assurance.

 The person's status as a mere member will undermine a claim of apparent authority. RESTATEMENT (THIRD) OF AGENCY § 2.03, cmt. d (2006) (explaining the "reasonable belief" element of a claim of apparent authority, and role played by context, custom, and the supposed agent's position in an organization). Likewise, the member will have no actual authority. Absent additional facts, section 407(c)(1) (vesting all management authority in the managers) renders the member's belief unreasonable. RESTATEMENT (THIRD) OF AGENCY § 2.01, cmt. c (2006) (explaining the "reasonable belief" element of a claim of actual authority).

In general, a member's actual authority to act for an LLC will depend fundamentally on the operating agreement.

EXAMPLE: Rachael and Sam, who have known each other for years, decide to go into business arranging musical tours. They fill out and electronically sign a one page form available on the website of the Secretary of State and become the organizers of MMT, LLC. They are the only members of the LLC, and their understanding of who will do what in managing the enterprise is based on several lengthy, late-night conversations that preceded the LLC's formation. Sam is to "get the acts," and Rachael is to manage the tour logistics. There is no written operating agreement.

In the terminology of this Act, MMT, LLC is member-managed, Section 407(a), and the understanding reached in the late night conversations has become part of the LLC's operating agreement. Section 111(c). In agency law terms, the operating agreement constitutes a manifestation by the LLC to Rachael and Sam concerning the scope of their respective authority to act on behalf of the LLC. RESTATEMENT (THIRD) OF AGENCY § 2.01, cmt. c (2006) (explaining that a person's actual authority depends first on some manifestation attributable to the principal and stating: "Actual authority is a consequence of a principal's expressive conduct toward an agent, through which the principal manifests assent to be affected by the agent's action, and the agent's reasonable understanding of the principal's manifestation."

Circumstances outside the operating agreement can also be relevant to determining the scope of a member's actual authority.

EXAMPLE: Homeworks, LLC is a manager-managed LLC with three members. The LLC's written operating agreement:

- specifies in considerable detail the management responsibilities of Margaret, the LLC's manager-member, and also states that Margaret is responsible for "the day-to-day operations" of the company;
- puts Garrett, a non-manager member, in charge of the LLC's transportation department; and
- specifies no management role for Brooksley, the third member.

When the LLC's chief financial officer quits suddenly, Margaret asks Brooksley, a CPA, to "step in until we can hire a replacement." Under the operating agreement, Margaret's request to Brooksley is within Margaret's actual authority and is a manifestation attributable to the LLC. If Brooksley manifests assent to Margaret's request, Brooksley will have the actual authority to act as the LLC's CFO.

In the unlikely event that two or more people form a member-managed LLC without any understanding of how to allocate management responsibility between or among them, agency law, operating in the context the Act's "gap fillers" on management responsibility, will produce the following result:

A single member of a multi-member, member-managed LLC:

- has no actual authority to commit the LLC to any matter "outside the ordinary course of the activities of the company," section 407(b)(3); and
- has the actual authority to commit the LLC to any matter "in the ordinary course of the activities of the company," section 407(b)(2), unless the member has reason to know that other members might disagree or the member has some other reason to know that consultation with fellow members is appropriate.

For an explanation of this result, see Section 407(c), cmt., which provides a detailed agency law analysis in the context of a multi-manager, manager-managed LLC whose operating agreement is silent on the analogous question.

The common law of agency will also determine the apparent authority of a member of a member-managed LLC, and in that analysis what the particular third party knows or has reason to know about the management structure and business practices of the particular LLC will always be relevant. RESTATEMENT (THIRD) OF AGENCY § 3.03, cmt. b (2006) ("A principal may also make a manifestation by placing an agent in a defined position in an organization …. Third parties who interact with the principal through the agent will naturally and reasonably assume that the agent has authority to do acts consistent with the agent's position … unless they have notice of facts suggesting that this may not be so.")

Under section 301(a), however, the mere fact that a person is a member of a member- managed limited liability company cannot by itself establish apparent authority by position. A course of dealing, however, may easily change the analysis:

EXAMPLE: David is a one of two members of DS, LLC, a member-managed LLC. David orders paper clips on behalf of the LLC, signing the purchase agreement, "David, as a member of DS, LLC." The vendor accepts the order, sends an invoice to the LLC's address, and in due course receives a check drawn on the LLC's bank account. When David next places an order with the vendor, the LLC's payment of the first order is a manifestation that the vendor may use in establishing David's apparent authority to place the second order.

SECTION 302. STATEMENT OF AUTHORITY.

(a)   A limited liability company may deliver to the [Secretary of State] for filing a statement of authority. The statement:

      (1)   must include the name of the company and the street and mailing addresses of its designated office;

      (2)   with respect to any position that exists in or with respect to the company, may state the authority, or limitations on the authority, of all persons holding the position to:

            (A)   execute an instrument transferring real property held in the name of the company; or

            (B)   enter into other transactions on behalf of, or otherwise act for or bind, the company; and

      (3)   may state the authority, or limitations on the authority, of a specific person to:

            (A)   execute an instrument transferring real property held in the name of the company; or

            (B)   enter into other transactions on behalf of, or otherwise act for or bind, the company.

(b) To amend or cancel a statement of authority filed by the [Secretary of State] under Section 205(a), a limited liability company must deliver to the [Secretary of State] for filing an amendment or cancellation stating:

   (1)   the name of the company;

   (2)   the street and mailing addresses of the company's designated office;

   (3)   the caption of the statement being amended or canceled and the date the statement being affected became effective; and

   (4)   the contents of the amendment or a declaration that the statement being affected is canceled.

(c) A statement of authority affects only the power of a person to bind a limited liability company to persons that are not members.

(d) Subject to subsection (c) and Section 103(d) and except as otherwise provided in subsections (f), (g), and (h), a limitation on the authority of a person or a position contained in an effective statement of authority is not by itself evidence of knowledge or notice of the limitation by any person.

(e) Subject to subsection (c), a grant of authority not pertaining to transfers of real property and contained in an effective statement of authority is conclusive in favor of a person that gives value in reliance on the grant, except to the extent that when the person gives value:

   (1)   the person has knowledge to the contrary;

   (2)   the statement has been canceled or restrictively amended under subsection (b);

   or

   (3)   a limitation on the grant is contained in another statement of authority that

became effective after the statement containing the grant became effective.

(f) Subject to subsection (c), an effective statement of authority that grants authority to transfer real property held in the name of the limited liability company and that is recorded by certified copy in the office for recording transfers of the real property is conclusive in favor of a person that gives value in reliance on the grant without knowledge to the contrary, except to the extent that when the person gives value:

   (1)   the statement has been canceled or restrictively amended under subsection (b) and a certified copy of the cancellation or restrictive amendment has been recorded in the office for recording transfers of the real property; or

   (2)   a limitation on the grant is contained in another statement of authority that became effective after the statement containing the grant became effective and a certified copy of the later-effective statement is recorded in the office for recording transfers of the real property.

(g)   Subject to subsection (c), if a certified copy of an effective statement containing a limitation on the authority to transfer real property held in the name of a limited liability company is recorded in the office for recording transfers of that real property, all persons are deemed to know of the limitation.

(h)   Subject to subsection (i), an effective statement of dissolution or termination is a cancellation of any filed statement of authority for the purposes of subsection (f) and is a limitation on authority for the purposes of subsection (g).

(i)   After a statement of dissolution becomes effective, a limited liability company may deliver to the [Secretary of State] for filing and, if appropriate, may record a statement of authority that is designated as a post-dissolution statement of authority. The statement operates as provided in subsections (f) and (g).

(j)   Unless earlier canceled, an effective statement of authority is canceled by operation of

law five years after the date on which the statement, or its most recent amendment, becomes effective. This cancellation operates without need for any recording under subsection (f) or (g).

(k)   An effective statement of denial operates as a restrictive amendment under this section and may be recorded by certified copy for the purposes of subsection (f)(1).

Comment

This section is derived from and builds on RUPA, § 303, and, like that provision is conceptually divided into two realms: statements pertaining to the power to transfer interests in the LLC's real property and statements pertaining to other matters. In the latter realm, statements are filed only in the records of the [Secretary of State], operate only to the extent the statements are actually known. Section 302(d) and (e).

As to interests in real property, in contrast, this section: (i) requires double-filing – with the [Secretary of State] and in the appropriate land records; and (ii) provides for constructive knowledge of statements limiting authority. Thus, a properly filed and recorded statement can protect the limited liability company, Section 302(g), and, in order for a statement pertaining to real property to be a sword in the hands of a third party, the statement must have been both filed and properly recorded. Section 302(f).

Subsection (a)(2) – This paragraph permits a statement to designate authority by position (or office) rather than by specific person. This type of a statement will enable LLCs to provide evidence of ongoing authority to enter into transactions without having to disclose to third parties the entirety of the operating agreement.

Here and elsewhere in the section, the phrase "real property" includes interests in real property, such as mortgages, easements, etc.

Subsection (b) – For the requirement that the original statement, like any other record, be appropriately captioned, see Section 205(a).

Subsection (c) – This subsection contains a very important limitation – i.e., that this section's rules do not operate viz a viz members. The text of RUPA, § 303 makes this very important point only obliquely, but the Comment to that section is unequivocal:

It should be emphasized that Section 303 concerns the authority of partners to bind the partnership to third persons. As among the partners, the authority of a partner to take any action is governed by the partnership agreement, or by the provisions of RUPA governing the relations among partners, and is not affected by the filing or recording of a statement of partnership authority.

RUPA § 303, comment 4.

However, like any other record delivered for filing on behalf of an LLC, a statement of authority might be some evidence of the contents of the operating agreement. See Comment to

Section 112(d).

Subsection (d) - The phrase "by itself" is important, because the existence of a limitation could be evidence if, for example, the person in question reviewed the public record at a time when the limitation was of record.

Subsection (e)(1) – What happens if a statement of authority conflicts with the contents of an LLC's certificate of organization? The contents of the certificate are not statements of authority, Section 201(c), so the information in the certificate does not directly figure into the operation of this section. However, if the person claiming to rely on a statement of authority had read the certificate's conflicting information before giving value, that fact might be evidence that person gave value with "knowledge to the contrary" of the statement.

SECTION 303. STATEMENT OF DENIAL. A person named in a filed statement of authority granting that person authority may deliver to the [Secretary of State] for filing a statement of denial that:

(1)   provides the name of the limited liability company and the caption of the statement of authority to which the statement of denial pertains; and

(2)   denies the grant of authority.

Comment

For the effect of a statement of denial, see Section 302(k).

SECTION 304. LIABILITY OF MEMBERS AND MANAGERS.

(a)   The debts, obligations, or other liabilities of a limited liability company, whether arising in contract, tort, or otherwise:

(1)   are solely the debts, obligations, or other liabilities of the company; and

(2)   do not become the debts, obligations, or other liabilities of a member or manager solely by reason of the member acting as a member or manager acting as a manager.

(b)   The failure of a limited liability company to observe any particular formalities relating to the exercise of its powers or management of its activities is not a ground for imposing liability on the members or managers for the debts, obligations, or other liabilities of the company.

Comment

Subsection (a)(2) – This paragraph shields members and managers only against the debts, obligations and liabilities of the limited liability company and is irrelevant to claims seeking to hold a member or manager directly liable on account of the member's or manager's own conduct.

EXAMPLE: A manager personally guarantees a debt of a limited liability company. Subsection (a)(2) is irrelevant to the manager's liability as guarantor.

EXAMPLE: A member purports to bind a limited liability company while lacking any agency law power to do so. The limited liability company is not bound, but the member is liable for having breached the "warranty of authority" (an agency law doctrine).

Subsection (a)(2) does not apply. The liability is not *for* a "debt[], obligation[], [or] liabilit[y] of a limited liability company," but rather is the member's direct liability resulting because the limited liability company is *not* indebted, obligated or liable. RESTATEMENT (THIRD) OF AGENCY § 6.10 (2006).

EXAMPLE: A manager of a limited liability company defames a third party in circumstances that render the limited liability company vicariously liable under agency law. Under subsection (a)(2), the third party cannot hold the manager accountable for the *company's* liability, but that protection is immaterial. The manager is the tortfeasor and in that role is directly liable to the third party.

Subsection (a)(2) pertains only to claims by third parties and is irrelevant to claims by a limited liability company against a member or manager and vice versa. See e.g. Sections 408 (pertaining to a limited liability company's obligation to indemnify a member or manager), 409 (pertaining to management duties) and 901 (pertaining to a member's rights to bring a direct claim against a limited liability company).

Subsection (b) – This subsection pertains to the equitable doctrine of "piercing the veil"

–   i.e., conflating an entity and its owners to hold one liable for the obligations of the other. The doctrine of "piercing the corporate veil" is well-established, and courts regularly (and sometimes almost reflexively) apply that doctrine to limited liability companies. In the corporate realm, "disregard of corporate formalities" is a key factor in the piercing analysis. In the realm of LLCs, that factor is inappropriate, because informality of organization and operation is both common and desired.

This subsection does not preclude consideration of another key piercing factor – disregard by an entity's owners of the entity's economic separateness from the owners.

EXAMPLE: The operating agreement of a three-member, member-managed limited liability company requires formal monthly meetings of the members. Each of the members works in the LLC's business, and they consult each other regularly. They have forgotten or ignore the requirement of monthly meetings. Under subsection (b), that fact is irrelevant to a piercing claim.

EXAMPLE: The sole owner of a limited liability company uses a car titled in the company's name for personal purposes and writes checks on the company's account to pay for personal expenses. These facts are relevant to a piercing claim; they pertain to economic separateness, not subsection (b) formalities.

This subsection has no relevance to a member's claim of oppression under Section 701(a)(5)(B). In some circumstances, disregard of agreed-upon formalities can be a "freeze out" mechanism. Likewise, this section has no relevance to a member's claim that the disregard of agreed-upon formalities is a breach of the operating agreement.

Provisions of regulatory law may impose liability by status on a member or manager. *See*

CARTER G. BISHOP AND DANIEL S. KLEINBERGER, LIMITED LIABILITY COMPANIES: TAX AND BUSINESS LAW, ¶ 6.04(4) (Statutory Liability).

[ARTICLE] 4

RELATIONS OF MEMBERS TO EACH OTHER AND TO LIMITED LIABILITY COMPANY

SECTION 401. BECOMING MEMBER.

(a)   If a limited liability company is to have only one member upon formation, the person becomes a member as agreed by that person and the organizer of the company. That person and the organizer may be, but need not be, different persons. If different, the organizer acts on behalf of the initial member.

(b)   If a limited liability company is to have more than one member upon formation, those persons become members as agreed by the persons before the formation of the company. The organizer acts on behalf of the persons in forming the company and may be, but need not be, one of the persons.

(c)   If a filed certificate of organization contains the statement required by Section 201(b)(3), a person becomes an initial member of the limited liability company with the consent of a majority of the organizers. The organizers may consent to more than one person simultaneously becoming the company's initial members.

(d)   After formation of a limited liability company, a person becomes a member:

(1)   as provided in the operating agreement;

(2)   as the result of a transaction effective under [Article] 10;

(3)   with the consent of all the members; or

(4)   if, within 90 consecutive days after the company ceases to have any members:

(A)   the last person to have been a member, or the legal representative of that person, designates a person to become a member; and

(B)   the designated person consents to become a member.

(e)   A person may become a member without acquiring a transferable interest and without making or being obligated to make a contribution to the limited liability company.

Comment

Most LLC statutes address in separate provisions: (i) how an LLC obtains its initial member or members; and (ii) how additional persons might later become members. This Act follows that approach. Subsections (a) and (b) address the most common circumstances under which a limited liability company is formed – with one or more persons becoming members

upon formation. Subsection (c) addresses how a person becomes the initial member of an LLC whose certificate of organization was filed without there being any members. Subsection (d) addresses how persons become members after an LLC has had at least one member.

For a discussion of the concept of a "shelf LLC" and this Act's requirement that a limited liability company have at least one member upon formation, see the Comment to Section 201.

Subsection (d)(4) – The personal representative of the last member may designate her-, him-, or itself as the new member.

Subsection (e) – To accommodate business practices and also because a limited liability company need not have a business purpose, this subsection permits so-called "non-economic members."

SECTION 402. FORM OF CONTRIBUTION. A contribution may consist of tangible or intangible property or other benefit to a limited liability company, including money, services performed, promissory notes, other agreements to contribute money or property, and contracts for services to be performed.

Comment

Source – ULPA (2001) § 501, which derived from ULLCA § 401.

SECTION 403. LIABILITY FOR CONTRIBUTIONS.

(a)   A person's obligation to make a contribution to a limited liability company is not excused by the person's death, disability, or other inability to perform personally. If a person does not make a required contribution, the person or the person's estate is obligated to contribute money equal to the value of the part of the contribution which has not been made, at the option of the company.

(b)   A creditor of a limited liability company which extends credit or otherwise acts in reliance on an obligation described in subsection (a) may enforce the obligation.

Comment

Source: ULLCA § 402, which is taken from RULPA § 502(b), which also gave rise to ULPA (2001) § 502.

Subsection (a) – The reference to "perform personally" is not limited to individuals but rather may refer to any legal person (including an entity) that has a non-delegable duty.

SECTION 404. SHARING OF AND RIGHT TO DISTRIBUTIONS BEFORE DISSOLUTION.

(a)   Any distributions made by a limited liability company before its dissolution and winding up must be in equal shares among members and dissociated members, except to the extent necessary to comply with any transfer effective under Section 502 and any charging order in effect under Section 503.

(b)   A person has a right to a distribution before the dissolution and winding up of a limited liability company only if the company decides to make an interim distribution. A person's dissociation does not entitle the person to a distribution.

(c)   A person does not have a right to demand or receive a distribution from a limited liability company in any form other than money. Except as otherwise provided in Section 708(c), a limited liability company may distribute an asset in kind if each part of the asset is fungible with each other part and each person receives a percentage of the asset equal in value to the person's share of distributions.

(d)   If a member or transferee becomes entitled to receive a distribution, the member or transferee has the status of, and is entitled to all remedies available to, a creditor of the limited liability company with respect to the distribution.

Comment

This Act follows both the original ULLCA and ULPA (2001) in omitting any default rule for allocation of losses. The Comment to ULPA (2001), § 503 explains that omission as follows:

This Act has no provision allocating profits and losses among the partners. Instead, the Act directly apportions the right to receive distributions. Nearly all limited partnerships will choose to allocate profits and losses in order to comply with applicable tax, accounting and other regulatory requirements. Those requirements, rather than this Act, are the proper source of guidance for that profit and loss allocation.

Subsection (b) – The second sentence of this subsection accords with Section 603(a)(3) – upon dissociation a person is treated as a mere transferee of its own transferable interest. Like most inter se rules in this Act, this one is subject to the operating agreement. See Comment to Section 603(a)(3).

SECTION 405. LIMITATIONS ON DISTRIBUTION.

(a)   A limited liability company may not make a distribution if after the distribution:

(1)   the company would not be able to pay its debts as they become due in the ordinary course of the company's activities; or

(2)   the company's total assets would be less than the sum of its total liabilities plus the amount that would be needed, if the company were to be dissolved, wound up, and terminated at the time of the distribution, to satisfy the preferential rights upon dissolution, winding up, and termination of members whose preferential rights are superior to those of persons receiving the distribution.

(b)   A limited liability company may base a determination that a distribution is not prohibited under subsection (a) on financial statements prepared on the basis of accounting practices and principles that are reasonable in the circumstances or on a fair valuation or other method that is reasonable under the circumstances.

(c)   Except as otherwise provided in subsection (f), the effect of a distribution under subsection (a) is measured:

(1)   in the case of a distribution by purchase, redemption, or other acquisition of a transferable interest in the company, as of the date money or other property is transferred or debt incurred by the company; and

(2)   in all other cases, as of the date:

(A)   the distribution is authorized, if the payment occurs within 120 days after that date; or

(B)   the payment is made, if the payment occurs more than 120 days after the distribution is authorized.

(d)   A limited liability company's indebtedness to a member incurred by reason of a distribution made in accordance with this section is at parity with the company's indebtedness to its general, unsecured creditors.

(e)   A limited liability company's indebtedness, including indebtedness issued in connection with or as part of a distribution, is not a liability for purposes of subsection (a) if the terms of the indebtedness provide that payment of principal and interest are made only to the extent that a distribution could be made to members under this section.

(f)   If indebtedness is issued as a distribution, each payment of principal or interest on the indebtedness is treated as a distribution, the effect of which is measured on the date the payment is made.

(g)   In subsection (a), "distribution" does not include amounts constituting reasonable compensation for present or past services or reasonable payments made in the ordinary course of business under a bona fide retirement plan or other benefits program.

Comment

Source – ULPA (2001) § 508, which was derived from ULLCA § 406, which was in turn derived from MBCA § 6.40.

Subsection (b) – This subsection appears to involve a pure standard of ordinary care, in contrast with the more complicated approach stated in Section 409(c).

Subsection (g) – This exception applies only for the purposes of this section. See the Comment to Section 503(b)(2). The exception is derived from existing statutory provisions. See, e.g., DEL. CODE ANN., tit. 6, § 18-607(a) (2006) and VA. CODE ANN. § 13.1-1035(E) (West 2006). See also In re Tri-River Trading, LLC, 329 B.R. 252, 266, (8th Cir. BAP 2005), aff'd . 452 F.3d 756 (8th Cir. 2006) ("We know of no principle of law which suggests that a manager of a company is required to give up agreed upon salary to pay creditors when business turns bad.")

SECTION 406. LIABILITY FOR IMPROPER DISTRIBUTIONS.

(a)   Except as otherwise provided in subsection (b), if a member of a member-managed limited liability company or manager of a manager-managed limited liability company consents to a distribution made in violation of Section 405 and in consenting to the distribution fails to comply with Section 409, the member or manager is personally liable to the company for the amount of the distribution that exceeds the amount that could have been distributed without the violation of Section 405.

(b)   To the extent the operating agreement of a member-managed limited liability company expressly relieves a member of the authority and responsibility to consent to distributions and imposes that authority and responsibility on one or more other members, the liability stated in subsection (a) applies to the other members and not the member that the operating agreement relieves of authority and responsibility.

(c)   A person that receives a distribution knowing that the distribution to that person was made in violation of Section 405 is personally liable to the limited liability company but only to the extent that the distribution received by the person exceeded the amount that could have been properly paid under Section 405.

(d)   A person against which an action is commenced because the person is liable under subsection (a) may:

(1)   implead any other person that is subject to liability under subsection (a) and seek to compel contribution from the person; and

(2)   implead any person that received a distribution in violation of subsection (c) and seek to compel contribution from the person in the amount the person received in violation of subsection (c).

(e)   An action under this section is barred if not commenced within two years after the distribution.

Comment

Source – Same derivation as Section 405.

Liability under this section is not affected by a person ceasing to be a member, manager or transferee after the time that the liability attaches.

Subsection (b) – The operating agreement could not accomplish the "switch" in liability provided by this subsection, because the "switch" implicates the rights of third parties under this Act. Section 110(c)(11).

Subsections (c) and (d)(2) – Liability could apply to a person who receives a distribution under a charging order, but only if the person meets the knowledge requirement. That situation is very unlikely unless the person with the charging order is also a member or manager.

SECTION 407. MANAGEMENT OF LIMITED LIABILITY COMPANY.

(a)   A limited liability company is a member-managed limited liability company unless the operating agreement:

    (1)   expressly provides that:

        (A)   the company is or will be "manager-managed";

        (B)   the company is or will be "managed by managers"; or

        (C)   management of the company is or will be "vested in managers"; or

    (2)   includes words of similar import.

(b)   In a member-managed limited liability company, the following rules apply:

    (1)   The management and conduct of the company are vested in the members.

    (2)   Each member has equal rights in the management and conduct of the company's activities.

    (3)   A difference arising among members as to a matter in the ordinary course of the activities of the company may be decided by a majority of the members.

    (4)   An act outside the ordinary course of the activities of the company may be undertaken only with the consent of all members.

    (5)   The operating agreement may be amended only with the consent of all

members.

(c)   In a manager-managed limited liability company, the following rules apply:

    (1)   Except as otherwise expressly provided in this [act], any matter relating to the activities of the company is decided exclusively by the managers.

    (2)   Each manager has equal rights in the management and conduct of the activities of the company.

    (3)   A difference arising among managers as to a matter in the ordinary course of the activities of the company may be decided by a majority of the managers.

    (4)   The consent of all members is required to:

        (A)   sell, lease, exchange, or otherwise dispose of all, or substantially all, of the company's property, with or without the good will, outside the ordinary course of the company's activities; activities; and

(B)   approve a merger, conversion, or domestication under [Article] 10;

(C)   undertake any other act outside the ordinary course of the company's

(D)   amend the operating agreement.

(5)   A manager may be chosen at any time by the consent of a majority of the members and remains a manager until a successor has been chosen, unless the manager at an earlier time resigns, is removed, or dies, or, in the case of a manager that is not an individual, terminates. A manager may be removed at any time by the consent of a majority of the members without notice or cause.

(6)   A person need not be a member to be a manager, but the dissociation of a member that is also a manager removes the person as a manager. If a person that is both a manager and a member ceases to be a manager, that cessation does not by itself dissociate the person as a member.

(7)   A person's ceasing to be a manager does not discharge any debt, obligation, or other liability to the limited liability company or members which the person incurred while a manager.

(d) An action requiring the consent of members under this [act] may be taken without a meeting, and a member may appoint a proxy or other agent to consent or otherwise act for the member by signing an appointing record, personally or by the member's agent.

(e) The dissolution of a limited liability company does not affect the applicability of this section. However, a person that wrongfully causes dissolution of the company loses the right to participate in management as a member and a manager.

(f) This [act] does not entitle a member to remuneration for services performed for a member-managed limited liability company, except for reasonable compensation for services rendered in winding up the activities of the company.

Comment

Subsection (a) – This subsection follows implicitly from the definitions of "manager- managed" and "member-managed" limited liability companies, Section 102(10) and (12), but is included here for the sake of clarity. Although this Act has eliminated the link between management structure and statutory apparent authority, Section 301, the Act retains the manager- managed and member-managed constructs as options for members to use to structure their inter se relationship.

Subsection (b) – The subsection states default rules that, under Section 110, are subject to the operating agreement.

Subsection (c) – Like subsection (b), this subsection states default rules that, under Section 110, are subject to the operating agreement. For example, a limited liability company's operating agreement might state "This company is manager-managed," Section 102(10)(i), while providing that managers must submit specified ordinary matters for review by the members.

The actual authority of an LLC's manager or managers is a question of agency law and depends fundamentally on the contents of the operating agreement and any separate management contract between the LLC and its manager or managers. These agreements are the primary source of the manifestations of the LLC (as principal) from which a manager (as agent) will form the reasonable beliefs that delimit the scope of the manager's actual authority. RESTATEMENT (THIRD) OF AGENCY § 3.01 (2006). *See also* RESTATEMENT (SECOND) OF AGENCY §§ 15, 26.

Other information may be relevant as well, such as the course of dealing within the LLC, unless the operating agreement effectively precludes consideration of that information. See Section 110(a)(4) (stating that the operating agreement governs "the means and conditions for amending the operating agreement") and the comment to that subparagraph, which states that:

[Although this] Act does not specially authorize the operating agreement to limit the sources in which terms of the operating agreement might be found or limit amendments to specified modes ... Paragraph (a)(4) could be read to encompass such authorization. Also, under Section 107 the parol evidence rule will apply to a written operating agreement containing an appropriate merger provision.

If the operating agreement and a management contract conflict, the reasonable manager will know that the operating agreement controls the extent of the manager's rightful authority to act for the LLC–despite any contract claims the manager might have. See Section 111(a)(2) (stating that the operating agreement governs "the rights and duties under this [act] of a person in the capacity of manager") and the comment to that paragraph, which states:

Because the term "[o]perating agreement . . . . includes the agreement as amended or restated," Section 102(13), this paragraph gives the members the ongoing power to define the role of an LLC's managers. Power is not the same as right, however, and exercising the power provided by this paragraph might constitute a breach of a separate contract between the LLC and the manager.

See also RESTATEMENT (THIRD) OF AGENCY § 8.13, cmt. b (2006) and RESTATEMENT (SECOND) OF AGENCY, § 432, cmt. b (stating that, when a principal's instructions to an agent contravene a contract between the principal and agent, the agent may have a breach of contract claim but has no right to act contrary to the principal's instructions).

If (i) an LLC's operating agreement merely states that the LLC is manager-managed and does not further specify the managerial responsibilities, and (ii) the LLC has only one manager, the actual authority analysis is simple. In that situation, this subsection:

- serves as "gap filler" to the operating agreement; and thereby
- constitutes the LLC's manifestation to the manager as to the scope of the manager's authority; and thereby
- delimits the manager's actual authority, subject to whatever subsequent manifestations the LLC may make to the manager (e.g., by a vote of the members, or an amendment of the operating agreement).

If the operating agreement states only that the LLC is manager-managed and the LLC has more than one manager, the question of actual authority has an additional aspect. It is necessary to determine what actual authority any one manager has to act alone.

Paragraphs (c)(2), (3), and (4) combine to provide the answer. A single manager of a multi-manager LLC:

- has no actual authority to commit the LLC to any matter "outside the ordinary course of the activities of the company," paragraph (c)(4)(C), or any matter encompassed in paragraph (c)(4); and

- has the actual authority to commit the LLC to any matter "in the ordinary course of the activities of the company," paragraph (c)(3), unless the manager has reason to know that other managers might disagree or the manager has some other reason to know that consultation with fellow managers is appropriate.

The first point follows self-evidently from the language of paragraphs (c)(3) and (c)(4). In light of that language, no manager could reasonably believe to the contrary (unless the operating agreement provided otherwise).

The second point follows because:

- Subsection (c) serves as the gap-filler manifestation from the LLC to its managers, and subsection (c) does <u>not</u> require managers of a multi-manager LLC to act <u>only</u> in concert or after consultation.
- To the contrary, subject to the operating agreement:
  - paragraph (c)(2) expressly provides that "each manager has equal rights in the management and conduct of the activities of the company," and
  - paragraph (c)(3) suggests that several (as well as joint) activity is appropriate on ordinary matters, so long as the manager acting in the matter has no reason to believe that the matter will be controversial among the managers and therefore requires a decision under paragraph (c)(3).

While the individual members of a corporate board of directors lack actual authority to bind the corporation, 2 WILLIAM MEADE FLETCHER, FLETCHER CYCLOPEDIA OF THE LAW OF

CORPORATIONS, § 392 (noting "the overwhelming weight of authority"), subsection (c) does not describe "board" management. Instead, subsection (c) provides management rules derived from those that govern the members of a general partnership and multiple general partners of a limited partnership. RUPA, § 401 and ULPA (2001), § 406.

The common law of agency will also determine the apparent authority of an LLC's manager or managers, and in that analysis what the particular third party knows or has reason to know about the management structure and business practices of the particular LLC will always be relevant. RESTATEMENT (THIRD) OF AGENCY § 3.03 cmt. d (2006) ("The nature of an organization's business or activity is relevant to whether a third party could reasonably believe that a [manager] is authorized to commit the organization to a particular transaction.").

As a general matter, however – i.e., as to the apparent authority of the position of LLC manager under this Act – courts may view the position as clothing its occupants with the apparent authority to take actions that reasonably appear within the ordinary course of the company's business. The actual authority analysis stated above supports that proposition; absent a reason to believe to the contrary, a third party could reasonably believe a manager to possess the authority contemplated by the gap-fillers of the statute. But see Section 102(9), cmt. (stating that "confusion around the term 'manager' is common to almost all LLC statutes").

Subsection (c)(5) – Under the default rule stated in this paragraph, dissolution of an entity that is a manager does not end the entity's status as manager. Contrast Section 602(4)(D) (referring to the expulsion of a member that is a partnership or limited liability company and authorizing the other members to expel, by unanimous consent, the dissolved partnership or limited liability company).

An LLC does not cease to be "manager-managed" simply because no managers are in place. In that situation, absent additional facts, the LLC is manager-managed and the manager position is vacant. Non-manager members who exercise managerial functions during the vacancy (or at any other time) will have duties as determined by other law, most particularly the law of agency.

Subsection (c)(7) – The obligation to safeguard trade secrets and other confidential or propriety information is incurred when the person is a manager, and a subsequent cessation does not entitle the person to usurp the information or use it to the prejudice of the LLC after the cessation.

Subsection (e) – Under the default rules of this Act, it is not possible for a person to wrongfully cause dissolution (as distinguished from wrongfully dissociating). Compare Section 701 with Section 601(b). However, the operating agreement might contemplate wrongful dissolution, and this subsection would then apply – unless the operating provides otherwise.

Under the second sentence of this subsection, a person might lose the rights to act as a manager without automatically and formally ceasing to be denominated as a manager.

Subsection (f) – This provision traces back to the 1914 Uniform Partnership Act, § 18(f) and is included for fear that its absence might be misinterpreted as implying a contrary rule.

This Act does not provide for remuneration to a manager of a manager-managed LLC. That issue is for the operating agreement, or a separate agreement between the LLC and the manager. A manager seeking compensation will have the burden of proving an agreement. For a case demonstrating how *not* to establish an agreement, see Jandrain v. Lovald, 351B.R. 679 (D. S.D. 2006).

SECTION 408. INDEMNIFICATION AND INSURANCE.

(a)   A limited liability company shall reimburse for any payment made and indemnify for any debt, obligation, or other liability incurred by a member of a member-managed company or the manager of a manager-managed company in the course of the member's or manager's activities on behalf of the company, if, in making the payment or incurring the debt, obligation, or other liability, the member or manager complied with the duties stated in Sections 405 and 409.

(b)   A limited liability company may purchase and maintain insurance on behalf of a member or manager of the company against liability asserted against or incurred by the member or manager in that capacity or arising from that status even if, under Section 110(g), the operating agreement could not eliminate or limit the person's liability to the company for the conduct giving rise to the liability.

Comment

Subsection (a) – This subsection states a default rule, which corresponds to the default rules on management duties. In the default mode, the correspondence is appropriate, because otherwise the statutory rule on indemnification could undercut or even vitiate the statutory rules on duty. Both this subsection and the rules on duty are subject to the operating agreement.

This subsection does not expressly require a limited liability company to provide advances to cover expenses. However, in some jurisdictions the indemnity obligation might be interpreted to include an obligation to make advances.

This subsection concerns only managers of manager-managed limited liability companies and members of member-managed companies. The definite article in the phrases "the member's" [paragraph (1)] and "the member" [paragraph (2)] refers back to the original phrase "A limited liability company shall reimburse . . . and indemnify . . . a member of a member- managed company . . . ." A limited liability company's obligation, if any, to reimburse or indemnify others (including non-managing members of a manager-managed LLC and LLC employees) is a question for other law, including the law of agency.

Subsection (b) – In contrast to subsection (a), this subsection encompasses all members, not just members in a member-managed LLC.

This subsection's language is very broad and authorizes an LLC to purchase insurance to cover, e.g., a manager's intentional misconduct. It is unlikely that such insurance would be available. For restrictions on the power of an operating agreement to provide for indemnification, see Section 110, particularly subsection (g).

SECTION 409. STANDARDS OF CONDUCT FOR MEMBERS AND MANAGERS.

(a)   A member of a member-managed limited liability company owes to the company and, subject to Section 901(b), the other members the fiduciary duties of loyalty and care stated in subsections (b) and (c).

(b)   The duty of loyalty of a member in a member-managed limited liability company includes the duties:

(1)   to account to the company and to hold as trustee for it any property, profit, or benefit derived by the member:

(A)   in the conduct or winding up of the company's activities;

(B)   from a use by the member of the company's property; or

(C)   from the appropriation of a limited liability company opportunity;

(2)   to refrain from dealing with the company in the conduct or winding up of the company's activities as or on behalf of a person having an interest adverse to the company; and

(3)   to refrain from competing with the company in the conduct of the company's activities before the dissolution of the company.

(c) Subject to the business judgment rule, the duty of care of a member of a member- managed limited liability company in the conduct and winding up of the company's activities is to act with the care that a person in a like position would reasonably exercise under similar circumstances and in a manner the member reasonably believes to be in the best interests of the company. In discharging this duty, a member may rely in good faith upon opinions, reports, statements, or other information provided by another person that the member reasonably believes is a competent and reliable source for the information.

(d)   A member in a member-managed limited liability company or a manager-managed limited liability company shall discharge the duties under this [act] or under the operating agreement and exercise any rights consistently with the contractual obligation of good faith and fair dealing.

(e)   It is a defense to a claim under subsection (b)(2) and any comparable claim in equity or at common law that the transaction was fair to the limited liability company.

(f)   All of the members of a member-managed limited liability company or a manager- managed limited liability company may authorize or ratify, after full disclosure of all material facts, a specific act or transaction that otherwise would violate the duty of loyalty.

(g)   In a manager-managed limited liability company, the following rules apply:

(1)   Subsections (a), (b), (c), and (e) apply to the manager or managers and not the embers. completed.

(2)   The duty stated under subsection (b)(3) continues until winding up is

(3)   Subsection (d) applies to the members and managers.

(4)   Subsection (f) applies only to the members.

(5)   A member does not have any fiduciary duty to the company or to any other member solely by reason of being a member.

Comment

This section follows the structure of many LLC acts, first stating the duties of members in a member-managed limited liability company and then using that statement and a "switching" mechanism, subsection (g), to allocate duties in a manager-managed company. The duties stated in this section are subject to the operating agreement, but Section 110 contains important limitations on the power of the operating agreement to affect fiduciary duties and the obligation of good faith.

This section contains several noteworthy developments in the law of unincorporated business organizations:

- fiduciary duty is "uncabined" – see the Comment to subsections (a) and (b);

- the duty of care is not set at gross negligence – see the Comment to subsection (c); and

- the statutory endorsement of self-interest is omitted – see the Comment to section (e)

The standards, duties, and obligations of this Section are subject to delineation, restriction, and, to some extent, elimination by the operating agreement. See Section 110.

Subsections (a) and (b) – Until the promulgation of RUPA, it was almost axiomatic that:

(i) fiduciary duties reflect judge-made law; and (ii) statutory formulations can express some of that law but do not exhaustively codify it. The original UPA was a prime example of this approach.

In an effort to respect freedom of contract, bolster predictability, and protect partnership agreements from second-guessing, the Conference decided that RUPA should fence or "cabin in" all fiduciary duties within a statutory formulation. That decision was followed without re- consideration in ULLCA and ULPA (2001).

This Act takes a different approach. After lengthy discussion in the drafting committee and on the floor of the 2006 Annual Meeting, the Conference decided that: (i) the "corral" created by RUPA does not fit in the very complex and variegated world of LLCs; and (ii) it is impracticable to cabin all LLC-related fiduciary duties within a statutory formulation.

As a result, this Act: (i) eschews "only" and "limited to" – the words RUPA used in an effort to exhaustively codify fiduciary duty; (ii) codifies the core of the fiduciary duty of loyalty; but (iii) does not purport to discern every possible category of overreaching. One important consequence is to allow courts to continue to use fiduciary duty concepts to police disclosure obligations in member-to-member and member-LLC transactions.

Subsection (c) – Although ULLCA, § 409(c) followed RUPA, § 404(c) and provided a gross negligence standard of care, at least a plurality of LLC statutes use an ordinary care standard. Sandra K. Miller, *The Role of the Court in Balancing Contractual Freedom With the Need For Mandatory Constraints on Opportunistic and Abusive Conduct in the* LLC, 152 U. PA.

L. REV 1609, 1658 (May 2004) (containing two tables characterizing the standard of care under LLC statutes: 21 states with "good faith prudent person" language and 19 states using "gross negligence or willful misconduct" language); Elizabeth S. Miller and Thomas E. Rutledge, *The Duty of Finest Loyalty and Reasonable Decisions: The Business Judgment Rule in Unincorporated Business Organizations,* 30 DEL. J. CORP. L. 343, 366- 368 (2005) (stating that "[a]pproximately eighteen state LLC statutes parallel language formerly used in the MBCA and require managers and managing members to act in good faith and exercise the care of an ordinarily prudent person in a like position under similar circumstances"). See also William J. Callison, *"The Law Does Not Perfectly Comprehend . . . .": The Inadequacy of the Gross*

Negligence Duty of Care Standard in Unincorporated Business Organizations, 94 KY. L.J. 451, 452 (2005-2006) ("examin[ing] the gross negligence standard and find[ing] it wanting, particularly as it has intruded, largely unexamined and by drafting osmosis, into subsequent uniform acts governing limited partnerships and limited liability companies").

In some circumstances, an unadorned standard of ordinary care is appropriate for those in charge of a business organization or similar, non-business enterprise. In others, the proper application of the duty of care must take into account the difficulties inherent in establishing an enterprise's most fundamental policies, supervising the enterprise's overall activities, or making complex business judgments. Corporate law subdivides circumstances somewhat according to the formal role exercised by the person whose conduct is later challenged (e.g., distinguishing the duties of directors from the duties of officers). LLC law cannot follow that approach, because a hallmark of the LLC entity is its structural flexibility.

This subsection, therefore, seeks "the best of both worlds" – stating a standard of ordinary care but subjecting that standard to the business judgment rule to the extent circumstances warrant. The content and force of the business judgment rule vary across jurisdictions, and therefore the meaning of this subsection may vary from jurisdiction to jurisdiction.

That result is intended. In any jurisdiction, the business judgment rule's application will vary depending on the nature of the challenged conduct. There is, for example, very little (if any) judgment involved when a person with managerial power acts (or fails to act) on an essentially ministerial matter. Moreover, under the law of many jurisdictions, the business judgment rule applies similarly across the range of business organizations. That is, the doctrine is sufficiently broad and conceptual so that the formality of organizational choice is less important in shaping the application of the rule than are the nature of the challenged conduct and the responsibilities and authority of the person whose conduct is being challenged.

This Act seeks therefore to invoke rather than unsettle whatever may be each jurisdiction's approach to the business judgment rule.

Subsection (d) – This subsection refers to the "contractual obligation of good faith and fair dealing" to emphasize that the obligation is not an invitation to re-write agreements among the members. As explained in the Comment to ULPA (2001), § 305(b):

The obligation of good faith and fair dealing is not a fiduciary duty, does not command altruism or self-abnegation, and does not prevent a partner from acting in the partner's own self-interest. Courts should not use the obligation to change ex post facto the parties' or this Act's allocation of risk and power. To the contrary, in light of the nature of a limited partnership, the obligation should be used only to protect agreed-upon arrangements from conduct that is manifestly beyond what a reasonable person could have contemplated when the arrangements were made…. In sum, the purpose of the obligation of good faith and fair dealing is to protect the arrangement the partners have chosen for themselves, not to restructure that arrangement under the guise of safeguarding it.

At first glance, it may seem strange to apply a contractual obligation to statutory duties and rights – i.e., duties and rights "under this [act]." However, for the most part those duties and rights apply to relationships inter se the members and the LLC and function only to the extent not displaced by the operating agreement. In the contract-based organization that is an LLC, those statutory default rules are intended to function like a contract. Therefore, applying the contractual notion of good faith makes sense.

As to whether the obligation stated in this subsection applies to transferees, see the Comment to Section 112(b).

Subsection (e) – Section 409 omits a noteworthy provision, which, beginning with RUPA, has been standard in the uniform business entity acts. RUPA, ULLCA, ULPA (2001) each placed the following language in the subsection following the formulation of the obligation of good faith:

A member ... does not violate a duty or obligation under this [act] or under the operating agreement merely because the member's conduct furthers the member's own interest.

This language is inappropriate in the complex and variegated world of LLCs. As a proposition of contract law, the language is axiomatic and therefore unnecessary. In the context of fiduciary duty, the language is at best incomplete, at worst wrong, and in any event confusing.

This Act's subsection (e) takes a very different approach, stating a well-established principle of judge-made law. Despite Section 107, the statement is not surplusage. Given this Act's very detailed treatment of fiduciary duties and especially the Act's very detailed treatment of the power of the operating agreement to modify fiduciary duties, the statement is important because its absence might be confusing. (An ex post fairness justification is not the same as an ex ante agreement to modify, but the topics are sufficiently close for a danger of the affirmative pregnant.)

This Act also omits, as anachronistic and potentially confusing, any provision resembling ULLCA, § 409(f) ("A member of a member-managed company may lend money to and transact other business with the company. As to each loan or transaction, the rights and obligations of the member are the same as those of a person who is not a member, subject to other applicable law.") See also ULPA (2001), § 112 ("A partner may lend money to and transact other business with the limited partnership and has the same rights and obligations with respect to the loan or other transaction as a person that is not a partner.")

Those provisions originated to combat the notion that debts to partners were categorically inferior to debts to non-partner creditors. That notion has never been part of LLC law, and so a modern uniform LLC act need not include language combating the notion. Moreover, to the uninitiated the language can be confusing, because the words might: (i) seem to undercut the duty of loyalty, which they do not; and (ii) deflect attention from bankruptcy law and the law of fraudulent transfer, which assuredly can look askance at transactions between an entity and an "insider."

Subsection (f) –The operating agreement can provide additional or different methods of authorization or ratification, subject to the strictures of Section 110(e). See the Comment to that subsection.

Subsection (g) – This is the "switching" mechanism, referred to in the introduction to this Comment.

Subsection (g)(2) – On the assumption that the members of a manager-managed LLC are dependent on the manager, this paragraph extends the duty longer than in a member-managed LLC.

Subsection (g)(5) – This paragraph merely negates a claim of fiduciary duty that is exclusively status-based and does not immunize misconduct.

EXAMPLE: Although a limited liability company is manager-managed, one member who is not a manager owns a controlling interest and effectively, albeit indirectly, controls the company's activities. A member owning a minority interest brings an action for dissolution under Section 701(a)(5)(B) (oppression by "the managers or those members in control of the company"). The court wishes to understand a claim as one alleging a breach of fiduciary duty by the controlling member. Subsection (g)(5) does not preclude that approach.

SECTION 410. RIGHT OF MEMBERS, MANAGERS, AND DISSOCIATED MEMBERS TO INFORMATION.

(a)   In a member-managed limited liability company, the following rules apply:

(1)   On reasonable notice, a member may inspect and copy during regular business hours, at a reasonable location specified by the company, any record maintained by the company regarding the company's activities, financial condition, and other circumstances, to the extent the information is material to the member's rights and duties under the operating agreement or this [act].

(2)   The company shall furnish to each member:

(A)   without demand, any information concerning the company's activities, financial condition, and other circumstances which the company knows and is material to the proper exercise of the member's rights and duties under the operating agreement or this [act], except to the extent the company can establish that it reasonably believes the member already knows the information; and

(B)   on demand, any other information concerning the company's activities, financial condition, and other circumstances, except to the extent the demand or information demanded is unreasonable or otherwise improper under the circumstances.

(3)   The duty to furnish information under paragraph (2) also applies to each member to the extent the member knows any of the information described in paragraph (2).

(b)   In a manager-managed limited liability company, the following rules apply:

(1)   The informational rights stated in subsection (a) and the duty stated in subsection (a)(3) apply to the managers and not the members.

(2)   During regular business hours and at a reasonable location specified by the company, a member may obtain from the company and inspect and copy full information regarding the activities, financial condition, and other circumstances of the company as is just and reasonable if:

(A)   the member seeks the information for a purpose material to the member's interest as a member;

(B)   the member makes a demand in a record received by the company, describing with reasonable particularity the information sought and the purpose for seeking the information; and

(C)   the information sought is directly connected to the member's purpose.

(3)   Within 10 days after receiving a demand pursuant to paragraph (2)(B), the company shall in a record inform the member that made the demand:

(A)   of the information that the company will provide in response to the demand and when and where the company will provide the information; and

(B)   if the company declines to provide any demanded information, the company's reasons for declining.

(4)   Whenever this [act] or an operating agreement provides for a member to give or withhold consent to a matter, before the consent is given or withheld, the company shall, without demand, provide the member with all information that is known to the company and is material to the member's decision.

(c)   On 10 days' demand made in a record received by a limited liability company, a dissociated member may have access to information to which the person was entitled while a member if the information pertains to the period during which the person was a member, the person seeks the information in good faith, and the person satisfies the requirements imposed on a member by subsection (b)(2). The company shall respond to a demand made pursuant to this subsection in the manner provided in subsection (b)(3).

(d)   A limited liability company may charge a person that makes a demand under this section the reasonable costs of copying, limited to the costs of labor and material.

(e)   A member or dissociated member may exercise rights under this section through an agent or, in the case of an individual under legal disability, a legal representative. Any restriction or condition imposed by the operating agreement or under subsection (g) applies both to the agent or legal representative and the member or dissociated member.

(f)   The rights under this section do not extend to a person as transferee.

(g)   In addition to any restriction or condition stated in its operating agreement, a limited liability company, as a matter within the ordinary course of its activities, may impose reasonable restrictions and conditions on access to and use of information to be furnished under this section, including designating information confidential and imposing nondisclosure and safeguarding obligations on the recipient. In a dispute concerning the reasonableness of a restriction under this subsection, the company has the burden of proving reasonableness.

Comment

This section is derived from ULPA (2001), §§ 304 (rights to information of limited partners and former limited partners) and 407 (same re: general partners and former general partners). The rules stated here are what might be termed "quasi-default rules" – subject to some change by the operating agreement. Section 110(c)(6) (prohibiting unreasonable restrictions on the information rights stated in this section).

Although the rights and duties stated in this section are extensive, they may not necessarily be exhaustive. In some situations, some courts have seen owners' information rights as reflecting a fiduciary duty of those with management power. This Act's statement of fiduciary duties is not exhaustive. See Comment to Section 409 (explaining that this Act does not seek to "cabin in" all fiduciary duties). In contrast, the operating agreement has considerable "cabining in" power of its own. Section 110(d)(4).

Subsection (a) – Paragraph 1 states the rule pertaining to information memorialized in "records maintained by the company". Paragraph 2 applies to information not in such a record. Appropriately, paragraph (2) sets a more demanding standard for those seeking information.

Subsection (a)(2) and (3) – In appropriate circumstances, violation of either or both of these provisions might cause a court to enjoin or even rescind action taken by the LLC, especially when the violation has interfered with an approval or veto mechanism involving member consent. *E.g. Blue Chip Emerald LLC v. Allied Partners Inc.*, 299 A.D.2d 278, 279-280 (N.Y. App. Div. 2002) (invoking partnership law precedent as reflecting a duty of full disclosure and holding that "[a]bsent such full disclosure, the transaction is voidable).

Subsection (a)(2) – Violation of this paragraph could give rise to a claim for damages against a member or manager [see subsection (b)(1)] who breaches the duties stated in Section 409 in causing or suffering the LLC to violate this paragraph.

Subsection (a)(3) – A member's violation of this paragraph is actionable in damages without need to show a violation of a duty stated in Section 409.

Subsection (b)(1) – This is a switching provision. A manager's violation of the duty stated in subsection (a)(3) is actionable in damages without need to show a violation of a duty stated in Section 409.

Subsection (b)(2) – This paragraph refers to "information" rather than "records maintained by the company" – compare subsection (a) – so in some circumstances the company might have an obligation to memorialize information. Such circumstances will likely be rare or at least unusual. Section 410 generally concerns providing existing information, not creating it. In any event, a member does not trigger the company's obligation under this paragraph merely by satisfying subparagraphs (A) through (C). The member must also satisfy the "just and reasonable" requirement.

Subsection (c) – This section does not control the rights of the estate of a member who dissociates by dying. In that circumstance, Section 504 controls.

Subsection (g) – The phrase "as a matter within the ordinary course of its activities" means that a mere majority consent is needed to impose a restriction or condition. See Section 407(b)(3) and (c)(3). This approach is necessary, lest a requesting member (or manager- member) have the power to block imposition of a reasonable restriction or condition needed to prevent the requestor from abusing the LLC.

The burden of proof under this subsection contrasts with the burden of proof when someone claims that a term of an operating agreement violates Section 110(c)(6). Under that subsection, as a matter of ordinary procedural law, the burden is on the person making the claim.

[ARTICLE] 5

TRANSFERABLE INTERESTS AND RIGHTS OF TRANSFEREES AND CREDITORS
SECTION 501. NATURE OF TRANSFERABLE INTEREST. A transferable interest is personal property.

Comment

Source – This Article most directly follows ULPA (2001), Article 7, because ULPA (2001) reflects the Conference's most recent thinking on the issues addressed here. However, ULPA (2001), Article 7 is quite similar in substance to ULLCA, Article 5, and both those Articles derive from Article 5 of RUPA.

Whether a transferable interest pledged as security is governed by Article 8 or 9 of the Uniform Commercial Code depends on the facts and the rules stated in those Articles.

This Act does not include ULLCA § 501(a), which provided: "A member is not a co- owner of, and has no transferable interest in, property of a limited liability company." That language was a vestige of the "aggregate" notion of the law of general partnerships, and in a modern LLC statute would be at least surplusage and perhaps confusing as well.

SECTION 502. TRANSFER OF TRANSFERABLE INTEREST.

(a)   A transfer, in whole or in part, of a transferable interest:

(1)   is permissible;

(2)   does not by itself cause a member's dissociation or a dissolution and winding up of the limited liability company's activities; and

(3)   subject to Section 504, does not entitle the transferee to:

(A)   participate in the management or conduct of the company's activities;

or

(B)   except as otherwise provided in subsection (c), have access to records

or other information concerning the company's activities.

(b)   A transferee has the right to receive, in accordance with the transfer, distributions to which the transferor would otherwise be entitled.

(c)   In a dissolution and winding up of a limited liability company, a transferee is entitled to an account of the company's transactions only from the date of dissolution.

(d)   A transferable interest may be evidenced by a certificate of the interest issued by the limited liability company in a record, and, subject to this section, the interest represented by the certificate may be transferred by a transfer of the certificate.

(e)   A limited liability company need not give effect to a transferee's rights under this section until the company has notice of the transfer.

(f)   A transfer of a transferable interest in violation of a restriction on transfer contained in the operating agreement is ineffective as to a person having notice of the restriction at the time of transfer.

(g)   Except as otherwise provided in Section 602(4)(B), when a member transfers a transferable interest, the transferor retains the rights of a member other than the interest in distributions transferred and retains all duties and obligations of a member.

(h)   When a member transfers a transferable interest to a person that becomes a member with respect to the transferred interest, the transferee is liable for the member's obligations under Sections 403 and 406(c) known to the transferee when the transferee becomes a member.

Comment

One of the most fundamental characteristics of LLC law is its fidelity to the "pick your partner" principle. This section is the core of the Act's provisions reflecting and protecting that principle.

A member's rights in a limited liability company are bifurcated into economic rights (the transferable interest) and governance rights (including management rights, consent rights, rights to information, rights to seek judicial intervention). Unless the operating agreement otherwise provides, a member acting without the consent of all other members lacks both the power and the right to: (i) bestow membership on a non-member, Section 401(d); or (ii) transfer to a non- member anything other than some or all of the member's transferable interest. Section 502(a)(3). However, consistent with current law, a member may transfer governance rights to another member without obtaining consent from the other members. Thus, this Act does not itself protect members from control shifts that result from transfers among members (as distinguished from transfers to non-members who seek thereby to become members).

This section applies regardless of whether the transferor is a member, a transferee of a member, a transferee of a transferee, etc. See Section 102(21) (defining "transferable interest" in terms of a right "originally associated with a person's capacity as a member" regardless of "whether or not the person remains a member or continues to own any part of the right").

Subsection (a) – The definition of "transfer," Section 102(20), and this subsection's reference to "in whole or in part" combine to mean that this section encompasses not only unconditional, permanent, and complete transfers but also temporary, contingent, and partial ones as well. Thus, for example, a charging order under Section 504 effects a transfer of part of the judgment debtor's transferable interest, as does the pledge of a transferable interest as collateral for a loan and the gift of a life-interest in a member's rights to distribution.

Subsection (a)(2) – Section 602(4)(B) creates a risk of dissociation via expulsion when a member transfers all of the member's transferable interest.

Subsection (a)(3) – Mere transferees have no right to intrude as the members carry on their activities as members. When a member dies, other law may effect a transfer of the member's interest to member's estate or personal representative. Section 504 contains special rules applicable to that situation.

Subsection (b) – Amounts due under this subsection are of course subject to offset for any amount owed to the limited liability company by the member or dissociated member on whose account the distribution is made. As to whether an LLC may properly offset for claims against a transferor that was never a member is matter for other law, specifically the law of contracts dealing with assignments.

Subsection (d) – The use of certificates can raise issues relating to Articles 8 and 9 of the Uniform Commercial Code.

SECTION 503. CHARGING ORDER.

(a)   On application by a judgment creditor of a member or transferee, a court may enter a charging order against the transferable interest of the judgment debtor for the unsatisfied amount of the judgment. A charging order constitutes a lien on a judgment debtor's transferable interest and requires the limited liability company to pay over to the person to which the charging order was issued any distribution that would otherwise be paid to the judgment debtor.

(b)   To the extent necessary to effectuate the collection of distributions pursuant to a charging order in effect under subsection (a), the court may:

(1)   appoint a receiver of the distributions subject to the charging order, with the power to make all inquiries the judgment debtor might have made; and

(2)   make all other orders necessary to give effect to the charging order.

(c)   Upon a showing that distributions under a charging order will not pay the judgment debt within a reasonable time, the court may foreclose the lien and order the sale of the transferable interest. The purchaser at the foreclosure sale obtains only the transferable interest, does not thereby become a member, and is subject to Section 502.

(d)   At any time before foreclosure under subsection (c), the member or transferee whose transferable interest is subject to a charging order under subsection (a) may extinguish the charging order by satisfying the judgment and filing a certified copy of the satisfaction with the court that issued the charging order.

(e)   At any time before foreclosure under subsection (c), a limited liability company or one or more members whose transferable interests are not subject to the charging order may pay to the judgment creditor the full amount due under the judgment and thereby succeed to the rights of the judgment creditor, including the charging order.

(f)   This [act] does not deprive any member or transferee of the benefit of any exemption laws applicable to the member's or transferee's transferable interest.

(g)   This section provides the exclusive remedy by which a person seeking to enforce a judgment against a member or transferee may, in the capacity of judgment creditor, satisfy the judgment from the judgment debtor's transferable interest.

Comment

Charging order provisions appear in various forms in UPA, ULPA, RULPA, RUPA, ULLCA, and ULPA (2001). This section builds on those acts, while: (i) modernizing the language: (ii) making explicit certain points that have been at best implicit; and (iii) seeking to delineate more precisely the types of extraordinary circumstances that would have to exist before a court enforcing a charging order would be justified in interfering with an LLC's management or activities.

This section balances the needs of a judgment creditor of a member or transferee with the needs of the limited liability company and the members. The section achieves that balance by allowing the judgment creditor to collect on the judgment through the transferable interest of the judgment debtor while prohibiting interference in the management and activities of the limited liability company.

Under this section, the judgment creditor of a member or transferee is entitled to a charging order against the relevant transferable interest. While in effect, that order entitles the judgment creditor to whatever distributions would otherwise be due to the member or transferee whose interest is subject to the order. However, the judgment creditor has no say in the timing or amount of those distributions. The charging order does not entitle the judgment creditor to accelerate any distributions or to otherwise interfere with the management and activities of the limited liability company.

The operating agreement has no power to alter the provisions of this section to the prejudice of third parties. Section 110(c)(11).

Subsection (a) – The phrase "judgment debtor" encompasses both members and transferees. As a matter of civil procedure and due process, an application for a charging order must be served both on the limited liability company and the member or transferee whose transferable interest is to be charged.

Subsection (b) – Paragraph (2) refers to "other orders" rather than "additional orders".

Therefore, given appropriate circumstances, a court may invoke either paragraph (1) or (2) or both.

Subsection (b)(1) – The receiver contemplated here is not a receiver for the limited liability company, but rather a receiver for the distributions. The principal advantage provided by this paragraph is an expanded right to information. However, that right goes no further than "the extent necessary to effectuate the collections of distributions pursuant to a charging order."

Subsection (b)(2) – This paragraph must be understood in the context of the balance described in the introduction to this section's Comment. In particular, the court's power to make orders "that the circumstances may of the case may require" is limited to "giv[ing] effect to the charging order."

Example: A judgment creditor with a charging order believes that the limited liability company should invest less of its surplus in operations, leaving more funds for distributions. The creditor moves the court for an order directing the limited liability company to restrict re-investment. Subsection (b)(2) does not authorize the court to grant the motion.

Example: A judgment creditor with a judgment for $10,000 against a member obtains a charging order against the member's transferable interest. Having been properly served with the order, the limited liability company nonetheless fails to comply and makes a $3000 distribution to the member.

The court has the power to order the limited liability company to pay $3000 to the judgment creditor to "give effect to the charging order."

Under subsection (b)(2), the court also has the power to decide whether a particular payment is a distribution, because that decision determines whether the payment is part of a transferable interest subject to a charging order. To the extent a payment is not a distribution, it is not part of the transferable interest and is not subject to subsection (g). The payment is therefore subject to whatever other creditor remedies may apply.

Section 405(g) states a special exception to the definition of "distribution," but that exception applies only "[f]or purposes of subsection (a)" of Section 405. Therefore, whether a charging order applies to "amounts constituting reasonable compensation for present or past services or reasonable payments made in the ordinary course of business under a bona fide retirement plan or other benefits program," Section 405(g), is a question determined under this section, without regard to Section 405(g). To date, case law is scant, but there is authority holding that compensation is a distribution. PB Real Estate, Inc. v. Dem II Properties, 719 A.2d 73, 75 (Conn. App. Ct. 1998) (rejecting the defendants' claim that the payments at issue were merely compensation for their services to their law firm, which was organized as an LLC; noting that the defendants' characterization was at odds with the firm's business records and tax returns; holding that the payments received were distributions subject to the charging order).

This Act has no specific rules for determining the fate or effect of a charging order when the limited liability company undergoes a merger, conversion, or domestication under [Article]

10.   In the proper circumstances, such an organic change might trigger an order under subsection (b)(2).

Subsection (c) –The phrase "that distributions under the charging order will not pay the judgment debt within a reasonable period of time" comes from case law. See, e.g., Nigri v. Lotz, 453 S.E.2d 780, 783 (Ga. Ct. App. 1995).

Subsection (e) – This Act jettisons the confusing concept of redemption and substitutes an approach that more closely parallels the modern, real-world possibility of the LLC or its members buying the underlying judgment (and thereby dispensing with any interference the judgment creditor might seek to inflict on the LLC). When possible, buying the judgment remains superior to the mechanism provided by this subsection, because: (i) this subsection requires full satisfaction of the underlying judgment, (ii) while the LLC or the other members might be able to buy the judgment for less than face value. On the other hand, this subsection operates without need for the judgment creditor's consent, so it remains a valuable protection in the event a judgment creditor seeks to do mischief to the LLC.

Whether an LLC's decision to invoke this subsection is "ordinary course" or "outside the ordinary course," Section 407(b)(3) and (4) and (c)(3) and (4)(C), depends on the circumstances. However, the involvement of this subsection does not by itself make the decision "outside the ordinary course."

Subsection (g) – This subsection does not override Article 9, which may provide different remedies for a secured creditor acting in that capacity. A secured creditor with a judgment might decide to proceed under Article 9 alone, under this section alone, or under both Article 9 and this section. In the last-mentioned circumstance, the constraints of this section would apply to the charging order but not to the Article 9 remedies.

This subsection is not intended to prevent a court from effecting a "reverse pierce" where appropriate. In a reverse pierce, the court conflates the entity and its owner to hold the entity liable for a debt of the owner. Litchfield Asset Mgmt. Corp. v. Howell, 799 A.2d 298, 312 (Conn. App. Ct. 2002) (approving a reverse pierce where a judgment debtor had established a limited liability company in a patent attempt frustrate the judgment creditor).

SECTION 504. POWER OF PERSONAL REPRESENTATIVE OF DECEASED

MEMBER. If a member dies, the deceased member's personal representative or other legal representative may exercise the rights of a transferee provided in Section 502(c) and, for the purposes of settling the estate, the rights of a current member under Section 410.

Comment

Source: ULPA (2001) § 704.

Section 410 pertains only to information rights.

[ARTICLE] 6

MEMBER'S DISSOCIATION

SECTION 601. MEMBER'S POWER TO DISSOCIATE; WRONGFUL DISSOCIATION.

(a)   A person has the power to dissociate as a member at any time, rightfully or wrongfully, by withdrawing as a member by express will under Section 602(1).

(b)   A person's dissociation from a limited liability company is wrongful only if the dissociation:

(1)   is in breach of an express provision of the operating agreement; or

(2)   occurs before the termination of the company and:

(A)   the person withdraws as a member by express will;

(B)   the person is expelled as a member by judicial order under Section 602(5);

(C)   the person is dissociated under Section 602(7)(A) by becoming a debtor in bankruptcy; or

(D)   in the case of a person that is not a trust other than a business trust, an estate, or an individual, the person is expelled or otherwise dissociated as a member because it willfully dissolved or terminated.

(c)   A person that wrongfully dissociates as a member is liable to the limited liability company and, subject to Section 901, to the other members for damages caused by the dissociation. The liability is in addition to any other debt, obligation, or other liability of the member to the company or the other members.

Comment

Source – ULPA (2001) § 604, which is based on RUPA Section 602. ULLCA § 602 is functionally identical in some respects but is not a good overall source, because that section presupposes the term/at-will paradigm.

SECTION 602. EVENTS CAUSING DISSOCIATION. A person is dissociated as a member from a limited liability company when:

(1)   the company has notice of the person's express will to withdraw as a member, but, if the person specified a withdrawal date later than the date the company had notice, on that later date;

(2)   an event stated in the operating agreement as causing the person's dissociation occurs;

(3)   the person is expelled as a member pursuant to the operating agreement;

(4)   the person is expelled as a member by the unanimous consent of the other members if:

    (A)   it is unlawful to carry on the company's activities with the person as a member;

    (B)   there has been a transfer of all of the person's transferable interest in the company, other than:

        (i)   a transfer for security purposes; or

        (ii)   a charging order in effect under Section 503 which has not been foreclosed;

    (C)   the person is a corporation and, within 90 days after the company notifies the person that it will be expelled as a member because the person has filed a certificate of dissolution or the equivalent, its charter has been revoked, or its right to conduct business has been suspended by the jurisdiction of its incorporation, the certificate of dissolution has not been revoked or its charter or right to conduct business has not been reinstated; or

    (D)   the person is a limited liability company or partnership that has been dissolved and whose business is being wound up;

(5)   on application by the company, the person is expelled as a member by judicial order because the person:

    (A)   has engaged, or is engaging, in wrongful conduct that has adversely and materially affected, or will adversely and materially affect, the company's activities;

    (B)   has willfully or persistently committed, or is willfully and persistently committing, a material breach of the operating agreement or the person's duties or obligations under Section 409; or

    (C)   has engaged in, or is engaging, in conduct relating to the company's activities which makes it not reasonably practicable to carry on the activities with the person as a member;

(6)   in the case of a person who is an individual:

    (A)   the person dies; or

(B)   in a member-managed limited liability company:

   (i)   a guardian or general conservator for the person is appointed; or

   (ii)   there is a judicial order that the person has otherwise become incapable of performing the person's duties as a member under [this act] or the operating agreement;

(7)   in a member-managed limited liability company, the person:

(A)   becomes a debtor in bankruptcy;

(B)   executes an assignment for the benefit of creditors; or

(C)   seeks, consents to, or acquiesces in the appointment of a trustee, receiver, or liquidator of the person or of all or substantially all of the person's property;

(8)   in the case of a person that is a trust or is acting as a member by virtue of being a trustee of a trust, the trust's entire transferable interest in the company is distributed;

(9)   in the case of a person that is an estate or is acting as a member by virtue of being a personal representative of an estate, the estate's entire transferable interest in the company is distributed;

(10)   in the case of a member that is not an individual, partnership, limited liability company, corporation, trust, or estate, the termination of the member;

(11)   the company participates in a merger under [Article] 10, if:

(A)   the company is not the surviving entity; or

(B)   otherwise as a result of the merger, the person ceases to be a member;

(12)   the company participates in a conversion under [Article] 10;

(13)   the company participates in a domestication under [Article] 10, if, as a result of the domestication, the person ceases to be a member; or

(14)   the company terminates.

Comment

Source – ULLCA § 601; RUPA Section 601; ULPA (2001) §§ 601 and 603.

Paragraph (4)(B) –Under this paragraph (unless the operating agreement provides otherwise), a member's transferee can protect itself from the vulnerability of "bare transferee" status by obligating the member/transferor to retain a 1% interest and then to exercise its governance rights (including the right to bring a derivative suit) to protect the transferee's interests.

SECTION 603. EFFECT OF PERSON'S DISSOCIATION AS MEMBER.

(a)   When a person is dissociated as a member of a limited liability company:

(1)   the person's right to participate as a member in the management and conduct of the company's activities terminates;

(2)   if the company is member-managed, the person's fiduciary duties as a member end with regard to matters arising and events occurring after the person's dissociation; and

(3)   subject to Section 504 and [Article] 10, any transferable interest owned by the person immediately before dissociation in the person's capacity as a member is owned by the person solely as a transferee.

(b)   A person's dissociation as a member of a limited liability company does not of itself discharge the person from any debt, obligation, or other liability to the company or the other members which the person incurred while a member.

Comment

Source – ULPA (2001) § 605, which was drawn from RUPA Section 603(b).

Subsection (a) – This provision makes no reference to power-to-bind matters, because the Act provides that a member qua member has no power to bind the LLC. Section 301.

Subsection (a)(2) – This provision applies only when the limited liability company is member-managed, because in a manager-managed LLC these duties do not apply to a member qua member. Section 409(g)(5).

Subsection (a)(3) – This paragraph accords with Section 404(b) – dissociation does not entitle a person to any distribution. Like most inter se rules in this Act, this one is subject to the operating agreement. For example, the operating agreement has the power to provide for the buy out of a person's transferable interest in connection with the person's dissociation.

Subsection (b) – In a member-managed limited liability company, the obligation to safeguard trade secrets and other confidential or proprietary information is incurred when a person is a member. A subsequent dissociation does not entitle the person to usurp the information or use it to the prejudice of the LLC after the dissociation. (In a manager-managed LLC, any obligations of a non-manager member viz a viz proprietary information would be a matter for the operating agreement, the obligation of good faith, or other law.)

[ARTICLE] 7

DISSOLUTION AND WINDING UP

SECTION 701. EVENTS CAUSING DISSOLUTION.

(a)   A limited liability company is dissolved, and its activities must be wound up, upon the occurrence of any of the following:

(1)   an event or circumstance that the operating agreement states causes dissolution;

(2)   the consent of all the members;

(3)   the passage of 90 consecutive days during which the company has no members;

(4)   on application by a member, the entry by [appropriate court] of an order dissolving the company on the grounds that:

    (A)   the conduct of all or substantially all of the company's activities is

unlawful; or

    (B)   it is not reasonably practicable to carry on the company's activities in

conformity with the certificate of organization and the operating agreement; or

(5)   on application by a member, the entry by [appropriate court] of an order dissolving the company on the grounds that the managers or those members in control of the company:

    (A)   have acted, are acting, or will act in a manner that is illegal or fraudulent; or

    (B)   have acted or are acting in a manner that is oppressive and was, is, or will be directly harmful to the applicant.

(b)   In a proceeding brought under subsection (a)(5), the court may order a remedy other than dissolution.

Comment

Subsection(a)(4) – The standard stated here is conventional, and this subsection (a)(4) is non-waivable. Section 110(c)(7).

Subsection (a)(5) – ULLCA § 801(4)(v) contains a comparable provision, although that provision also gives standing to dissociated members. Even in non-ULLCA states, courts have begun to apply close corporation "oppression" doctrine to LLCs.

This provision's reference to "those members in control of the company" implies that such members have a duty to avoid acting oppressively toward fellow members.

Subsection (a)(5) is non-waivable. See Section 110(c)(7).

Subsection (b) – In the close corporation context, many courts have reached this position without express statutory authority, most often with regard to court-ordered buyouts of oppressed shareholders. This subsection saves courts and litigants the trouble of re-inventing that wheel in the LLC context. However, unlike, subsection (a)(4) and (5), subsection (b) can be overridden by the operating agreement. Thus, the members may agree to a restrict or eliminate a court's power to craft a lesser remedy, even to the extent of confining the court (and themselves) to the all-or-nothing remedy of dissolution.

SECTION 702. WINDING UP.

(a)   A dissolved limited liability company shall wind up its activities, and the company continues after dissolution only for the purpose of winding up.

(b)   In winding up its activities, a limited liability company:

(1)   shall discharge the company's debts, obligations, or other liabilities, settle and close the company's activities, and marshal and distribute the assets of the company; and

(2)   may:

(A)   deliver to the [Secretary of State] for filing a statement of dissolution stating the name of the company and that the company is dissolved;

(B)   preserve the company activities and property as a going concern for a reasonable time; or administrative;

(C)   prosecute and defend actions and proceedings, whether civil, criminal,

(D)   transfer the company's property;

(E)   settle disputes by mediation or arbitration;

(F)   deliver to the [Secretary of State] for filing a statement of termination stating the name of the company and that the company is terminated; and

(G)   perform other acts necessary or appropriate to the winding up.

(c)   If a dissolved limited liability company has no members, the legal representative of the last person to have been a member may wind up the activities of the company. If the person does so, the person has the powers of a sole manager under Section 407(c) and is deemed to be a manager for the purposes of Section 304(a)(2).

(d)   If the legal representative under subsection (c) declines or fails to wind up the company's activities, a person may be appointed to do so by the consent of transferees owning a majority of the rights to receive distributions as transferees at the time the consent is to be effective. A person appointed under this subsection:

(1)   has the powers of a sole manager under Section 407(c) and is deemed to be a manager for the purposes of Section 304(a)(2); and

(2)   shall promptly deliver to the [Secretary of State] for filing an amendment to the company's certificate of organization to:

(A)   state that the company has no members;

(B)   state that the person has been appointed pursuant to this subsection to wind up the company; and

(C)   provide the street and mailing addresses of the person.

(e)   The [appropriate court] may order judicial supervision of the winding up of a dissolved limited liability company, including the appointment of a person to wind up the company's activities:

(1)   on application of a member, if the applicant establishes good cause;

(2)   on the application of a transferee, if:

(A)   the company does not have any members;

(B)   the legal representative of the last person to have been a member declines or fails to wind up the company's activities; and

(C)   within a reasonable time following the dissolution a person has not been appointed pursuant to subsection (d); or

(3)   in connection with a proceeding under Section 701(a)(4) or (5).

Comment

Source – ULPA (2001) § 803, which was based on RUPA Sections 802 and 803.

Because under this Act the power to bind a limited liability company to a third party is primarily a matter of agency law, Section 301, Comment, this Act has no need of provisions delineating the effect of dissolution on a member or manager's power to bind.

Subsection (b)(2)(A) and (F) – For the constructive notice effect of a statement of dissolution or termination, see Section 103(d)(2)(A) and (B).

SECTION 703. KNOWN CLAIMS AGAINST DISSOLVED LIMITED LIABILITY COMPANY.

(a)   Except as otherwise provided in subsection (d), a dissolved limited liability company may give notice of a known claim under subsection (b), which has the effect as provided in subsection (c).

(b)   A dissolved limited liability company may in a record notify its known claimants of the dissolution. The notice must:

(1)   specify the information required to be included in a claim;

(2)   provide a mailing address to which the claim is to be sent;

(3)   state the deadline for receipt of the claim, which may not be less than 120 days after the date the notice is received by the claimant; and

(4)   state that the claim will be barred if not received by the deadline.

(c)   A claim against a dissolved limited liability company is barred if the requirements of subsection (b) are met and:

(1)   the claim is not received by the specified deadline; or

(2)   if the claim is timely received but rejected by the company:

(A)   the company causes the claimant to receive a notice in a record stating that the claim is rejected and will be barred unless the claimant commences an action against the company to enforce the claim within 90 days after the claimant receives the notice; and

(B)   the claimant does not commence the required action within the 90

days.

(d)   This section does not apply to a claim based on an event occurring after the effective

date of dissolution or a liability that on that date is contingent.

Comment

Source – ULPA (2001) § 806, which was based on ULLCA § 807, which in turn was based on MBCA § 14.06.

SECTION 704. OTHER CLAIMS AGAINST DISSOLVED LIMITED LIABILITY COMPANY.

(a)   A dissolved limited liability company may publish notice of its dissolution and request persons having claims against the company to present them in accordance with the notice.

(b)   The notice authorized by subsection (a) must:

(1)   be published at least once in a newspaper of general circulation in the [county] in this state in which the dissolved limited liability company's principal office is located or, if it has none in this state, in the [county] in which the company's designated office is or was last located;

(2)   describe the information required to be contained in a claim and provide a mailing address to which the claim is to be sent; and

(3)   state that a claim against the company is barred unless an action to enforce the claim is commenced within five years after publication of the notice.

(c)   If a dissolved limited liability company publishes a notice in accordance with subsection (b), unless the claimant commences an action to enforce the claim against the company within five years after the publication date of the notice, the claim of each of the following claimants is barred:

(1)   a claimant that did not receive notice in a record under Section 703;

(2)   a claimant whose claim was timely sent to the company but not acted on; and

(3)   a claimant whose claim is contingent at, or based on an event occurring after, the effective date of dissolution.

(d)   A claim not barred under this section may be enforced:

(1)   against a dissolved limited liability company, to the extent of its undistributed

assets; and

(2)   if assets of the company have been distributed after dissolution, against a member or transferee to the extent of that person's proportionate share of the claim or of the assets distributed to the member or transferee after dissolution, whichever is less, but a person's total liability for all claims

under this paragraph does not exceed the total amount of assets distributed to the person after dissolution.

Comment

Source – ULPA (2001) § 807, which was based on ULLCA § 808, which in turn was based on MBCA § 14.07.

Subsection (d)(2) – Liability under this paragraph extends to those who have received distributions under a charging order. See Comment to 502(a) (explaining that the beneficiary of a charging order is a transferee). Unlike Section 406(c) (recapture of improper interim distributions), this paragraph contains no "knowledge" element.

SECTION 705. ADMINISTRATIVE DISSOLUTION.

(a)   The [Secretary of State] may dissolve a limited liability company administratively if the company does not:

(1)   pay, within 60 days after the due date, any fee, tax, or penalty due to the [Secretary of State] under this [act] or law other than this [act]; or

(2)   deliver, within 60 days after the due date, its annual report to the [Secretary of State].

(b)   If the [Secretary of State] determines that a ground exists for administratively dissolving a limited liability company, the [Secretary of State] shall file a record of the determination and serve the company with a copy of the filed record.

(c)   If within 60 days after service of the copy pursuant to subsection (b) a limited liability company does not correct each ground for dissolution or demonstrate to the reasonable satisfaction of the [Secretary of State] that each ground determined by the [Secretary of State] does not exist, the [Secretary of State] shall dissolve the company administratively by preparing, signing, and filing a declaration of dissolution that states the grounds for dissolution. The [Secretary of State] shall serve the company with a copy of the filed declaration.

(d)   A limited liability company that has been administratively dissolved continues in existence but, subject to Section 706, may carry on only activities necessary to wind up its activities and liquidate its assets under Sections 702 and 708 and to notify claimants under Sections 703 and 704.

(e)   The administrative dissolution of a limited liability company does not terminate the authority of its agent for service of process.

Comment

Source – ULPA (2001) § 809, which was based on ULLCA §§ 809 and 810. See also

RMBCA §§ 14.20 and 14.21.

SECTION 706. REINSTATEMENT FOLLOWING ADMINISTRATIVE DISSOLUTION.

(a)   A limited liability company that has been administratively dissolved may apply to the [Secretary of State] for reinstatement within two years after the effective date of dissolution. The application must be delivered to the [Secretary of State] for filing and state:

    (1)   the name of the company and the effective date of its dissolution;

    (2)   that the grounds for dissolution did not exist or have been eliminated; and

    (3)   that the company's name satisfies the requirements of Section 108.

(b)   If the [Secretary of State] determines that an application under subsection (a) contains the required information and that the information is correct, the [Secretary of State] shall prepare a declaration of reinstatement that states this determination, sign and file the original of the declaration of reinstatement, and serve the limited liability company with a copy.

(c)   When a reinstatement becomes effective, it relates back to and takes effect as of the effective date of the administrative dissolution and the limited liability company may resume its activities as if the dissolution had not occurred.

Comment

Source – ULPA (2001) § 810, which was based on ULLCA § 811. See also RMBCA Section 14.22.

SECTION 707. APPEAL FROM REJECTION OF REINSTATEMENT.

(a)   If the [Secretary of State] rejects a limited liability company's application for reinstatement following administrative dissolution, the [Secretary of State] shall prepare, sign, and file a notice that explains the reason for rejection and serve the company with a copy of the notice.

(b)   Within 30 days after service of a notice of rejection of reinstatement under subsection (a), a limited liability company may appeal from the rejection by petitioning the [appropriate court] to set aside the dissolution. The petition must be served on the [Secretary of State] and contain a copy of the [Secretary of State's] declaration of dissolution, the company's application for reinstatement, and the [Secretary of State's] notice of rejection.

(c)   The court may order the [Secretary of State] to reinstate a dissolved limited liability company or take other action the court considers appropriate.

Comment

Source – ULPA (2001) § 811, which was based on ULLCA § 812.

This section uses "rejection" rather than "denial" (the word used by both ULPA (2001) and ULLCA). The change is to avoid confusion with a "statement of denial" under Section 302.

SECTION 708. DISTRIBUTION OF ASSETS IN WINDING UP LIMITED LIABILITY COMPANY'S ACTIVITIES.

(a)   In winding up its activities, a limited liability company must apply its assets to discharge its obligations to creditors, including members that are creditors.

(b)   After a limited liability company complies with subsection (a), any surplus must be distributed in the following order, subject to any charging order in effect under Section 503:

(1)   to each person owning a transferable interest that reflects contributions made by a member and not previously returned, an amount equal to the value of the unreturned contributions; and

(2)   in equal shares among members and dissociated members, except to the extent necessary to comply with any transfer effective under Section 502.

(c)   If a limited liability company does not have sufficient surplus to comply with subsection (b)(1), any surplus must be distributed among the owners of transferable interests in proportion to the value of their respective unreturned contributions.

(d)   All distributions made under subsections (b) and (c) must be paid in money.

Comment

Source: ULLCA § 806, restyled.

Subsection (a) – This section is mostly not a default rule. See Section 110(c)(11) (stating that "except as provided in Section 112(b), [the operating agreement may not] restrict the rights under this [act] of a person other than a member or manager"). However, if the creditors are willing, a dissolved limited liability company may certainly make agreements with them specifying the terms under which the LLC will "discharge its obligations to creditors."

Subsections (b), (c) and (d) – These subsections provide default rules. Distributions under these subsections (or otherwise under the operating agreement) are subject to Section 503 (charging orders).

[ARTICLE] 8

FOREIGN LIMITED LIABILITY COMPANIES

SECTION 801. GOVERNING LAW.

(a)   The law of the state or other jurisdiction under which a foreign limited liability company is formed governs:

(1)   the internal affairs of the company; and

(2)   the liability of a member as member and a manager as manager for the debts, obligations, or other liabilities of the company.

(b) A foreign limited liability company may not be denied a certificate of authority by reason of any difference between the law of the jurisdiction under which the company is formed and the law of this state.

(c) A certificate of authority does not authorize a foreign limited liability company to engage in any business or exercise any power that a limited liability company may not engage in or exercise in this state.

Comment

Subsection (a) – This Section parallels the formulation stated in Section 106 for a domestic limited liability company.

Subsection (a)(2) – This provision does not pertain to the "internal shields" of a foreign "series" LLC, because those shields do not concern the liability of members or managers for the obligations of the LLC. Instead, those shields seek to protect specified assets of the LLC (associated with one series) from being available to satisfy specified obligations of the LLC (associated with another series). See the Prefatory Note, No Provision for "Series" LLCs.

SECTION 802. APPLICATION FOR CERTIFICATE OF AUTHORITY.

(a) A foreign limited liability company may apply for a certificate of authority to transact business in this state by delivering an application to the [Secretary of State] for filing. The application must state:

(1) the name of the company and, if the name does not comply with Section 108, an alternate name adopted pursuant to Section 805(a);

(2) the name of the state or other jurisdiction under whose law the company is formed;

(3) the street and mailing addresses of the company's principal office and, if the law of the jurisdiction under which the company is formed requires the company to maintain an office in that jurisdiction, the street and mailing addresses of the required office; and

(4) the name and street and mailing addresses of the company's initial agent for service of process in this state.

(b) A foreign limited liability company shall deliver with a completed application under subsection (a) a certificate of existence or a record of similar import signed by the [Secretary of State] or other official having custody of the company's publicly filed records in the state or other jurisdiction under whose law the company is formed.

Comment

Source – ULPA (2001) § 902, which was based on ULLCA § 1002.

SECTION 803. ACTIVITIES NOT CONSTITUTING TRANSACTING BUSINESS.

(a) Activities of a foreign limited liability company which do not constitute transacting business in this state within the meaning of this [article] include:

(1)   maintaining, defending, or settling an action or proceeding;

(2)   carrying on any activity concerning its internal affairs, including holding meetings of its members or managers;

(3)   maintaining accounts in financial institutions;

(4)   maintaining offices or agencies for the transfer, exchange, and registration of the company's own securities or maintaining trustees or depositories with respect to those securities;

(5)   selling through independent contractors;

(6)   soliciting or obtaining orders, whether by mail or electronic means or through employees or agents or otherwise, if the orders require acceptance outside this state before they become contracts;

(7)   creating or acquiring indebtedness, mortgages, or security interests in real or personal property;

(8)   securing or collecting debts or enforcing mortgages or other security interests in property securing the debts and holding, protecting, or maintaining property so acquired;

(9)   conducting an isolated transaction that is completed within 30 days and is not in the course of similar transactions; and

(10)   transacting business in interstate commerce.

(b)   For purposes of this [article], the ownership in this state of income-producing real property or tangible personal property, other than property excluded under subsection (a), constitutes transacting business in this state.

(c)   This section does not apply in determining the contacts or activities that may subject a foreign limited liability company to service of process, taxation, or regulation under law of this state other than this [act].

Comment

Source – ULPA (2001) § 903, which was based on ULLCA § 1003.

SECTION 804. FILING OF CERTIFICATE OF AUTHORITY.

Unless the [Secretary of State] determines that an application for a certificate of authority does not comply with the filing requirements of this [act], the [Secretary of State], upon payment of all filing fees, shall file the application of a foreign limited liability company, prepare, sign, and file a certificate of authority to transact business in this state, and send a copy of the filed certificate, together with a receipt for the fees, to the company or its representative.

Comment

Source – ULPA (2001) § 904, which was based on ULLCA § 1004 and RULPA § 903.

SECTION 805. NONCOMPLYING NAME OF FOREIGN LIMITED LIABILITY COMPANY.

(a)   A foreign limited liability company whose name does not comply with Section 108 may not obtain a certificate of authority until it adopts, for the purpose of transacting business in this state, an alternate name that complies with Section 108. A foreign limited liability company that adopts an alternate name under this subsection and obtains a certificate of authority with the alternate name need not comply with [fictitious or assumed name statute]. After obtaining a certificate of authority with an alternate name, a foreign limited liability company shall transact business in this state under the alternate name unless the company is authorized under [fictitious or assumed name statute] to transact business in this state under another name.

(b)   If a foreign limited liability company authorized to transact business in this state changes its name to one that does not comply with Section 108, it may not thereafter transact business in this state until it complies with subsection (a) and obtains an amended certificate of authority.

Comment

Source – ULPA (2001) § 905, which was based on ULLCA § 1005.

SECTION 806. REVOCATION OF CERTIFICATE OF AUTHORITY.

(a)   A certificate of authority of a foreign limited liability company to transact business in this state may be revoked by the [Secretary of State] in the manner provided in subsections (b) and (c) if the company does not:

(1)   pay, within 60 days after the due date, any fee, tax, or penalty due to the [Secretary of State] under this [act] or law other than this [act];

(2)   deliver, within 60 days after the due date, its annual report required under Section 209; 113(b); or

(3)   appoint and maintain an agent for service of process as required by Section

(4)   deliver for filing a statement of a change under Section 114 within 30 days after a change has occurred in the name or address of the agent.

(b)   To revoke a certificate of authority of a foreign limited liability company, the [Secretary of State] must prepare, sign, and file a notice of revocation and send a copy to the company's agent for service of process in this state, or if the company does not appoint and maintain a proper agent in this state, to the company's designated office. The notice must state:

(1)   the revocation's effective date, which must be at least 60 days after the date the [Secretary of State] sends the copy; and

(2)   the grounds for revocation under subsection (a).

(c)   The authority of a foreign limited liability company to transact business in this state ceases on the effective date of the notice of revocation unless before that date the company cures each ground or revocation stated in the notice filed under subsection (b). If the company cures each ground, the [Secretary of State] shall file a record so stating.

Comment

Source – ULPA (2001) § 906, which was based on ULLCA § 1006.

SECTION 807. CANCELLATION OF CERTIFICATE OF AUTHORITY.

To cancel its certificate of authority to transact business in this state, a foreign limited liability company must deliver to the [Secretary of State] for filing a notice of cancellation stating the name of the company and that the company desires to cancel its certificate of authority. The certificate is canceled when the notice becomes effective.

SECTION 808. EFFECT OF FAILURE TO HAVE CERTIFICATE OF AUTHORITY.

(a)   A foreign limited liability company transacting business in this state may not maintain an action or proceeding in this state unless it has a certificate of authority to transact business in this state.

(b)   The failure of a foreign limited liability company to have a certificate of authority to transact business in this state does not impair the validity of a contract or act of the company or prevent the company from defending an action or proceeding in this state.

(c)   A member or manager of a foreign limited liability company is not liable for the debts, obligations, or other liabilities of the company solely because the company transacted business in this state without a certificate of authority.

(d)   If a foreign limited liability company transacts business in this state without a certificate of authority or cancels its certificate of authority, it appoints the [Secretary of State] as its agent for service of process for rights of action arising out of the transaction of business in this state.

Comment

Source – ULPA (2001) § 907, which was based on RULPA § 907(d) and ULLCA § 1008.

SECTION 809. ACTION BY [ATTORNEY GENERAL].

The [Attorney General] may maintain an action to enjoin a foreign limited liability company from transacting business in this state in violation of this [article].

Comment

Source – ULPA (2001) § 908, which was based on RULPA § 908 and ULLCA § 1009.

[ARTICLE] 9

ACTIONS BY MEMBERS

SECTION 901. DIRECT ACTION BY MEMBER.

(a)   Subject to subsection (b), a member may maintain a direct action against another member, a manager, or the limited liability company to enforce the member's rights and otherwise protect the member's interests, including rights and interests under the operating agreement or this [act] or arising independently of the membership relationship.

(b)   A member maintaining a direct action under this section must plead and prove an actual or threatened injury that is not solely the result of an injury suffered or threatened to be suffered by the limited liability company.

Comment

Subsection (a) – Source: ULPA (2001) § 1001(a), which was based on RUPA Section 405(b). The subsection has been somewhat re-styled from the ULPA version, and the phrase "for legal or equitable relief" has been deleted as unnecessary. ULPA's reference to "with or without an accounting" has been deleted because the reference: (i) was to the partnership remedy of accounting, which reflected the aggregate nature of a partnership and is inapposite for an entity such as an LLC; and (ii) generated some confusion with the equitable claim for an accounting (in the nature of a constructive trust). The "entity-analog" to the partnership-as- aggregate notion of an accounting is the distinction between a direct and derivative claim.

The last phrase of this subsection ("or arising independently . . .") comes from RUPA

§ 405(b)(3), does not create any new rights, obligations, or remedies, and is included merely to emphasize that a person's membership in an LLC does not preclude the person from enforcing rights existing "independently or the membership relationship."

Subsection (b) – Source: ULPA (2001) § 1001(b). The Comment to that subsection explains:

In ordinary contractual situations it is axiomatic that each party to a contract has standing to sue for breach of that contract. Within a limited partnership, however, different circumstances may exist. A partner does not have a direct claim against another partner merely because the other partner has breached the partnership agreement. Likewise, a partner's violation of this Act does not automatically create a direct claim for every other partner. To have standing in his, her, or its own right, a partner plaintiff must be able to show a harm that occurs independently of the harm caused or threatened to be caused to the limited partnership.

SECTION 902. DERIVATIVE ACTION. A member may maintain a derivative action to enforce a right of a limited liability company if:

(1)   the member first makes a demand on the other members in a member-managed limited liability company, or the managers of a manager-managed limited liability company, requesting that they cause the company to bring an action to enforce the right, and the managers or other members do not bring the action within a reasonable time; or

(2)   a demand under paragraph (1) would be futile.

Comment

Source – ULPA (2001) § 1002, which was a re-styled version RULPA § 1001.

SECTION 903. PROPER PLAINTIFF.

(a)   Except as otherwise provided in subsection (b), a derivative action under Section 902 may be maintained only by a person that is a member at the time the action is commenced and remains a member while the action continues.

(b)   If the sole plaintiff in a derivative action dies while the action is pending, the court may permit another member of the limited liability company to be substituted as plaintiff.

Comment

This section abandons the traditional "contemporaneous ownership" rule, on the theory that the protections of that rule are unnecessary given the closely-held nature of most limited liability companies and the built-in, statutory restrictions on persons becoming members.

Subsection (b) – This subsection will be inapposite if the limited liability company has only two members, one of whom is the derivative plaintiff. In that limited circumstance, the plaintiff's death would cause the derivative action to abate. The "pick your partner" principal enshrined in Section 502 would prevent the decedent's heirs from succeeding to plaintiff status in the derivative action. This Act does not take a position on whether the death of member abates a <u>direct</u> claim against the LLC or a fellow member.

SECTION 904. PLEADING. In a derivative action under Section 902, the complaint must state with particularity:

(1)   the date and content of the plaintiff's demand and the response to the demand by the managers or other members; or

(2)   if a demand has not been made, the reasons a demand under Section 902(1) would be futile.

Comment

Source – ULPA (2001) § 1004, which was a re-styled version RULPA § 1003.

SECTION 905. SPECIAL LITIGATION COMMITTEE.

(a)   If a limited liability company is named as or made a party in a derivative proceeding, the company may appoint a special litigation committee to investigate the claims asserted in the proceeding and determine whether pursuing the action is in the best interests of the company. If the company appoints a special litigation committee, on motion by the committee made in the name of the company, except for good cause shown, the court shall stay discovery for the time reasonably necessary to permit the committee to make its investigation. This subsection does not prevent the court from enforcing a person's right to information under Section 410 or, for good cause shown, granting extraordinary relief in the form of a temporary restraining order or preliminary injunction.

(b)   A special litigation committee may be composed of one or more disinterested and independent individuals, who may be members.

(c)   A special litigation committee may be appointed:

(1)   in a member-managed limited liability company:

(A)   by the consent of a majority of the members not named as defendants or plaintiffs in the proceeding; and

(B)   if all members are named as defendants or plaintiffs in the proceeding, by a majority of the members named as defendants; or

(2)   in a manager-managed limited liability company:

(A)   by a majority of the managers not named as defendants or plaintiffs in the proceeding; and

(B)   if all managers are named as defendants or plaintiffs in the proceeding,

by a majority of the managers named as defendants.

(d)   After appropriate investigation, a special litigation committee may determine that it is in the best interests of the limited liability company that the proceeding:

(1)   continue under the control of the plaintiff;

(2)   continue under the control of the committee;

(3)   be settled on terms approved by the committee; or

(4)   be dismissed.

(e)   After making a determination under subsection (d), a special litigation committee shall file with the court a statement of its determination and its report supporting its determination, giving notice to the plaintiff. The court shall determine whether the members of the committee were disinterested and independent and whether the committee conducted its investigation and made its recommendation in good faith, independently, and with reasonable care, with the committee having the burden of proof. If the court finds that the members of the committee were disinterested and independent and that the committee acted in good faith, independently, and with reasonable care, the court shall enforce the determination of the committee. Otherwise, the court shall dissolve the stay of discovery entered under subsection (a) and allow the action to proceed under the direction of the plaintiff.

Comment

Although special litigation committees are best known in the corporate field, they are no more inherently corporate than derivative litigation or the notion that an organization is a person distinct from its owners. An "SLC" can serve as an ADR mechanism, help protect an agreed upon arrangement from strike suits, protect the interests of members who are neither plaintiffs nor defendants (if any), and bring to any judicial decision the benefits of a specially tailored business judgment.

This section's approach corresponds to established law in most jurisdictions, modified to fit the typical governance structures of a limited liability company.

Subsection (a) – On the availability of Section 410 remedies pending the SLC's investigation, compare *Kaufman v. Computer Assoc. Int'l., Inc.*, No. Civ.A. 699-N, 2005 WL 3470589 at *1 (Del.Ch. Dec. 21, 2005, as revised) (presenting "the question of whether to stay a books and records action under 8 Del. C. § 220 at the request of a special litigation committee when a derivative action encompassing substantially the same allegations of wrongdoing filed by different plaintiffs is pending in another jurisdiction;" concluding "[f]or reasons that have much to do with the light burden imposed by the plaintiff's demand in this case . . . that the special litigation committee's motion to stay the books and records action should be denied")

Subsection (d) – The standard stated for judicial review of the SLC determination follows *Auerbach v. Bennett*, 47 N.Y.2d 619, 419 N.Y.S.2d 920 (N.Y. 1979) rather than *Zapata Corp. v. Maldonado*, 430 A.2d 779 (Del. 1981), because the latter's reference to a court's business judgment has generally not been followed in other states.

Houle v. Low, 407 Mass. 810, 822, 556 N.E.2d 51, 58 (Mass. 1990) contains an excellent explanation of the court's role in reviewing an SLC decision:

The value of a special litigation committee is coextensive with the extent to which that committee truly exercises business judgment. In order to ensure that special litigation committees do act for the [entity]'s best interest, a good deal of judicial oversight is necessary in each case. At the same time, however, courts must be careful not to usurp the committee's valuable role in exercising business judgment. . . . . [A] special litigation committee must be independent, unbiased, and act in good faith. Moreover, such a committee must conduct a thorough and careful analysis regarding the plaintiff's derivative suit, ... The burden of proving that these procedural requirements have been met must rest, in all fairness, on the party capable of making that proof--the [entity].

For a discussion of how a court should approach the question of independence, see *Einhorn v. Culea*, 612 N.W.2d 78, 91 (Wis.2000).

SECTION 906. PROCEEDS AND EXPENSES.

(a)   Except as otherwise provided in subsection (b):

(1)   any proceeds or other benefits of a derivative action under Section 902, whether by judgment, compromise, or settlement, belong to the limited liability company and not to the plaintiff; and

(2)   if the plaintiff receives any proceeds, the plaintiff shall remit them immediately to the company.

(b)   If a derivative action under Section 902 is successful in whole or in part, the court may award the plaintiff reasonable expenses, including reasonable attorney's fees and costs, from the recovery of the limited liability company.

Comment

Source – ULPA (2001) § 1005, which was a re-styled version RULPA § 1004.

[ARTICLE] 10

MERGER, CONVERSION, AND DOMESTICATION

SECTION 1001. DEFINITIONS. In this [article]:

(1)   "Constituent limited liability company" means a constituent organization that is a limited liability company.

(2)   "Constituent organization" means an organization that is party to a merger.

(3)   "Converted organization" means the organization into which a converting organization converts pursuant to Sections 1006 through 1009.

(4)   "Converting limited liability company" means a converting organization that is a limited liability company.

(5)   "Converting organization" means an organization that converts into another organization pursuant to Section 1006.

(6)   "Domesticated company" means the company that exists after a domesticating foreign limited liability company or limited liability company effects a domestication pursuant to Sections 1010 through 1013.

(7)   "Domesticating company" means the company that effects a domestication pursuant to Sections 1010 through 1013.

(8)   "Governing statute" means the statute that governs an organization's internal affairs.

(9)   "Organization" means a general partnership, including a limited liability partnership, limited partnership, including a limited liability limited partnership, limited liability company, business trust, corporation, or any other person having a governing statute. The term includes a domestic or foreign organization regardless of whether organized for profit.

(10) "Organizational documents" means:

(A)   for a domestic or foreign general partnership, its partnership agreement;

(B)   for a limited partnership or foreign limited partnership, its certificate of limited partnership and partnership agreement;

(C)   for a domestic or foreign limited liability company, its certificate or articles of organization and operating agreement, or comparable records as provided in its governing statute;

(D)   for a business trust, its agreement of trust and declaration of trust;

(E)   for a domestic or foreign corporation for profit, its articles of incorporation, bylaws, and other agreements among its shareholders which are authorized by its governing statute, or comparable records as provided in its governing statute; and

(F)   for any other organization, the basic records that create the organization and determine its internal governance and the relations among the persons that own it, have an interest in it, or are members of it.

(11) "Personal liability" means liability for a debt, obligation, or other liability of an organization which is imposed on a person that co-owns, has an interest in, or is a member of the organization:

(A)   by the governing statute solely by reason of the person co-owning, having an interest in, or being a member of the organization; or

(B)   by the organization's organizational documents under a provision of the governing statute authorizing those documents to make one or more specified persons liable for all or specified debts, obligations, or other liabilities of the organization solely by reason of the person or persons co-owning, having an interest in, or being a member of the organization.

(12) "Surviving organization" means an organization into which one or more other organizations are merged whether the organization preexisted the merger or was created by the merger.

Comment

This article is based on Article 11 of ULPA (2001) and differs principally in treating domestications as a separate type of organic transaction rather than as a subset of conversions.

SECTION 1002. MERGER.

(a)   A limited liability company may merge with one or more other constituent organizations pursuant to this section, Sections 1003 through 1005, and a plan of merger, if:

(1)   the governing statute of each of the other organizations authorizes the merger;

(2)   the merger is not prohibited by the law of a jurisdiction that enacted any of the governing statutes; and

(3)   each of the other organizations complies with its governing statute in effecting

the merger.

(b)   A plan of merger must be in a record and must include:

(1)   the name and form of each constituent organization;

(2)   the name and form of the surviving organization and, if the surviving organization is to be created by the merger, a statement to that effect;

(3)   the terms and conditions of the merger, including the manner and basis for converting the interests in each constituent organization into any combination of money, interests in the surviving organization, and other consideration;

(4)   if the surviving organization is to be created by the merger, the surviving organization's organizational documents that are proposed to be in a record; and

(5)   if the surviving organization is not to be created by the merger, any amendments to be made by the merger to the surviving organization's organizational documents that are, or are proposed to be, in a record.

SECTION 1003. ACTION ON PLAN OF MERGER BY CONSTITUENT LIMITED LIABILITY COMPANY.

(a)   Subject to Section 1014, a plan of merger must be consented to by all the members of a constituent limited liability company.

(b)   Subject to Section 1014 and any contractual rights, after a merger is approved, and at any time before articles of merger are delivered to the [Secretary of State] for filing under Section 1004, a constituent limited liability company may amend the plan or abandon the merger:

(1)   as provided in the plan; or

(2)   except as otherwise prohibited in the plan, with the same consent as was required to approve the plan.

SECTION 1004. FILINGS REQUIRED FOR MERGER; EFFECTIVE DATE.

(a)   After each constituent organization has approved a merger, articles of merger must be signed on behalf of:

(1)   each constituent limited liability company, as provided in Section 203(a); and

(2)   each other constituent organization, as provided in its governing statute.

(b)   Articles of merger under this section must include:

(1)   the name and form of each constituent organization and the jurisdiction of its governing statute;

(2)   the name and form of the surviving organization, the jurisdiction of its governing statute, and, if the surviving organization is created by the merger, a statement to that effect; organization;

(3)   the date the merger is effective under the governing statute of the surviving

(4)   if the surviving organization is to be created by the merger:

(A)   if it will be a limited liability company, the company's certificate of

organization; or

(B)   if it will be an organization other than a limited liability company, the

organizational document that creates the organization that is in a public record;

(5)   if the surviving organization preexists the merger, any amendments provided for in the plan of merger for the organizational document that created the organization that are in a public record;

(6)   a statement as to each constituent organization that the merger was approved as required by the organization's governing statute;

(7)   if the surviving organization is a foreign organization not authorized to transact business in this state, the street and mailing addresses of an office that the [Secretary of State] may use for the purposes of Section 1005(b); and

(8)   any additional information required by the governing statute of any constituent

organization.

(c)   Each constituent limited liability company shall deliver the articles of merger for filing in the [office of the Secretary of State].

(d)   A merger becomes effective under this [article]:

(1)   if the surviving organization is a limited liability company, upon the later of:

(A)   compliance with subsection (c); or

(B)   subject to Section 205(c), as specified in the articles of merger; or

(2)   if the surviving organization is not a limited liability company, as provided by the governing statute of the surviving organization.

SECTION 1005. EFFECT OF MERGER.

(a)   When a merger becomes effective:

(1)   the surviving organization continues or comes into existence;

(2)   each constituent organization that merges into the surviving organization ceases to exist as a separate entity;

(3)   all property owned by each constituent organization that ceases to exist vests in the surviving organization;

(4)   all debts, obligations, or other liabilities of each constituent organization that ceases to exist continue as debts, obligations, or other liabilities of the surviving organization;

(5)   an action or proceeding pending by or against any constituent organization that ceases to exist may be continued as if the merger had not occurred;

(6)   except as prohibited by other law, all of the rights, privileges, immunities, powers, and purposes of each constituent organization that ceases to exist vest in the surviving organization;

(7)   except as otherwise provided in the plan of merger, the terms and conditions of the plan of merger take effect; and

(8)   except as otherwise agreed, if a constituent limited liability company ceases to exist, the merger does not dissolve the limited liability company for the purposes of [Article] 7;

(9)   if the surviving organization is created by the merger:

     (A)   if it is a limited liability company, the certificate of organization becomes effective; or

     (B)   if it is an organization other than a limited liability company, the organizational document that creates the organization becomes effective; and

(10)   if the surviving organization preexisted the merger, any amendments provided for in the articles of merger for the organizational document that created the organization become effective.

(b)   A surviving organization that is a foreign organization consents to the jurisdiction of the courts of this state to enforce any debt, obligation, or other liability owed by a constituent organization, if before the merger the constituent organization was subject to suit in this state on the debt, obligation, or other liability. A surviving organization that is a foreign organization and not authorized to transact business in this state appoints the [Secretary of State] as its agent for service of process for the purposes of enforcing a debt, obligation, or other liability under this subsection. Service on the [Secretary of State] under this subsection must be made in the same manner and has the same consequences as in Section 116(c) and (d).

SECTION 1006. CONVERSION.

(a)   An organization other than a limited liability company or a foreign limited liability company may convert to a limited liability company, and a limited liability company may convert to an organization other than a foreign limited liability company pursuant to this section, Sections 1007 through 1009, and a plan of conversion, if:

(1)   the other organization's governing statute authorizes the conversion;

(2)   the conversion is not prohibited by the law of the jurisdiction that enacted the other organization's governing statute; and

(3)   the other organization complies with its governing statute in effecting the conversion.

(b)   A plan of conversion must be in a record and must include:

(1)   the name and form of the organization before conversion;

(2)   the name and form of the organization after conversion;

(3)   the terms and conditions of the conversion, including the manner and basis for converting interests in the converting organization into any combination of money, interests in the converted organization, and other consideration; and

(4)   the organizational documents of the converted organization that are, or are proposed to be, in a record.

SECTION 1007. ACTION ON PLAN OF CONVERSION BY CONVERTING LIMITED LIABILITY COMPANY.

(a)   Subject to Section 1014, a plan of conversion must be consented to by all the members of a converting limited liability company.

(b)   Subject to Section 1014 and any contractual rights, after a conversion is approved, and at any time before articles of conversion are delivered to the [Secretary of State] for filing under Section 1008, a converting limited liability company may amend the plan or abandon the conversion:

(1)   as provided in the plan; or

(2)   except as otherwise prohibited in the plan, by the same consent as was required to approve the plan.

SECTION 1008. FILINGS REQUIRED FOR CONVERSION; EFFECTIVE DATE.

(a)   After a plan of conversion is approved:

(1)   a converting limited liability company shall deliver to the [Secretary of State] for filing articles of conversion, which must be signed as provided in Section 203(a) and must include: another organization; governing statute;

(A)   a statement that the limited liability company has been converted into

(B)   the name and form of the organization and the jurisdiction of its

(C)   the date the conversion is effective under the governing statute of the converted organization;

(D)   a statement that the conversion was approved as required by this [act];

(E)   a statement that the conversion was approved as required by the governing statute of the converted organization; and

(F)   if the converted organization is a foreign organization not authorized to transact business in this state, the street and mailing addresses of an office which the [Secretary of State] may use for the purposes of Section 1009(c); and

(2)   if the converting organization is not a converting limited liability company, the converting organization shall deliver to the [Secretary of State] for filing a certificate of organization, which must include, in addition to the information required by Section 201(b):

(A)   a statement that the converted organization was converted from another organization;

(B)   the name and form of that converting organization and the jurisdiction of its governing statute; and

(C)   a statement that the conversion was approved in a manner that complied with the converting organization's governing statute.

(b)   A conversion becomes effective:

(1)   if the converted organization is a limited liability company, when the certificate of organization takes effect; and

(2)   if the converted organization is not a limited liability company, as provided by the governing statute of the converted organization.

SECTION 1009. EFFECT OF CONVERSION.

(a)   An organization that has been converted pursuant to this [article] is for all purposes the same entity that existed before the conversion.

(b)   When a conversion takes effect:

(1)   all property owned by the converting organization remains vested in the converted organization;

(2)   all debts, obligations, or other liabilities of the converting organization continue as debts, obligations, or other liabilities of the converted organization;

(3)   an action or proceeding pending by or against the converting organization may be continued as if the conversion had not occurred;

(4)   except as prohibited by law other than this [act], all of the rights, privileges, immunities, powers, and purposes of the converting organization remain vested in the converted organization;

(5)   except as otherwise provided in the plan of conversion, the terms and conditions of the plan of conversion take effect; and

(6)   except as otherwise agreed, the conversion does not dissolve a converting limited liability company for the purposes of [Article] 7.

(c)   A converted organization that is a foreign organization consents to the jurisdiction of the courts of this state to enforce any debt, obligation, or other liability for which the converting limited liability company is liable if, before the conversion, the converting limited liability company was subject to suit in this state on the debt, obligation, or other liability. A converted organization that is a foreign organization and not authorized to transact business in this state appoints the [Secretary of State] as its agent for service of process for purposes of enforcing a debt, obligation, or other liability under this subsection. Service on the [Secretary of State] under this subsection must be made in the same manner and has the same consequences as in Section 116(c) and (d).

SECTION 1010. DOMESTICATION.

(a)   A foreign limited liability company may become a limited liability company pursuant to this section, Sections 1011 through 1013, and a plan of domestication, if:

(1)   the foreign limited liability company's governing statute authorizes the domestication;

(2)   the domestication is not prohibited by the law of the jurisdiction that enacted the governing statute; and

(3)   the foreign limited liability company complies with its governing statute in effecting the domestication.

(b)   A limited liability company may become a foreign limited liability company pursuant to this section, Sections 1011 through 1013, and a plan of domestication, if:

(1)   the foreign limited liability company's governing statute authorizes the domestication;

(2)   the domestication is not prohibited by the law of the jurisdiction that enacted the governing statute; and

(3)   the foreign limited liability company complies with its governing statute in effecting the domestication.

(c)   A plan of domestication must be in a record and must include:

(1)   the name of the domesticating company before domestication and the jurisdiction of its governing statute;

(2)   the name of the domesticated company after domestication and the jurisdiction of its governing statute;

(3)   the terms and conditions of the domestication, including the manner and basis for converting interests in the domesticating company into any combination of money, interests in the domesticated company, and other consideration; and

(4)   the organizational documents of the domesticated company that are, or are proposed to be, in a record.

SECTION 1011. ACTION ON PLAN OF DOMESTICATION BY DOMESTICATING LIMITED LIABILITY COMPANY.

(a)   A plan of domestication must be consented to:

(1)   by all the members, subject to Section 1014, if the domesticating company is a limited liability company; and

(2)   as provided in the domesticating company's governing statute, if the company is a foreign limited liability company.

(b)   Subject to any contractual rights, after a domestication is approved, and at any time before articles of domestication are delivered to the [Secretary of State] for filing under Section 1012, a domesticating limited liability company may amend the plan or abandon the domestication:

(1)   as provided in the plan; or

(2)   except as otherwise prohibited in the plan, by the same consent as was required to approve the plan.

SECTION 1012. FILINGS REQUIRED FOR DOMESTICATION; EFFECTIVE DATE.

(a)   After a plan of domestication is approved, a domesticating company shall deliver to the [Secretary of State] for filing articles of domestication, which must include:

(1)   a statement, as the case may be, that the company has been domesticated from or into another jurisdiction;

(2)   the name of the domesticating company and the jurisdiction of its governing statute; statute;

(3)   the name of the domesticated company and the jurisdiction of its governing

(4)   the date the domestication is effective under the governing statute of the domesticated company;

(5)   if the domesticating company was a limited liability company, a statement that the domestication was approved as required by this [act];

(6)   if the domesticating company was a foreign limited liability company, a statement that the domestication was approved as required by the governing statute of the other jurisdiction; and

(7)   if the domesticated company was a foreign limited liability company not authorized to transact business in this state, the street and mailing addresses of an office that the [Secretary of State] may use for the purposes of Section 1013(b).

(b)   A domestication becomes effective:

(1)   when the certificate of organization takes effect, if the domesticated company is a limited liability company; and

(2)   according to the governing statute of the domesticated company, if the domesticated organization is a foreign limited liability company.

SECTION 1013. EFFECT OF DOMESTICATION.

(a)   When a domestication takes effect:

(1)   the domesticated company is for all purposes the company that existed before the domestication;

(2)   all property owned by the domesticating company remains vested in the domesticated company;

(3)   all debts, obligations, or other liabilities of the domesticating company continue as debts, obligations, or other liabilities of the domesticated company;

(4)   an action or proceeding pending by or against a domesticating company may be continued as if the domestication had not occurred;

(5)   except as prohibited by other law, all of the rights, privileges, immunities, powers, and purposes of the domesticating company remain vested in the domesticated company;

(6)   except as otherwise provided in the plan of domestication, the terms and conditions of the plan of domestication take effect; and

(7)   except as otherwise agreed, the domestication does not dissolve a domesticating limited liability company for the purposes of [Article] 7.

(b)   A domesticated company that is a foreign limited liability company consents to the jurisdiction of the courts of this state to enforce any debt, obligation, or other liability owed by the domesticating company, if, before the domestication, the domesticating company was subject to suit in this state on the debt, obligation, or other liability. A domesticated company that is a foreign limited liability company and not authorized to transact business in this state appoints the [Secretary of State] as its agent for service of process for purposes of enforcing a debt, obligation, or other liability under this subsection. Service on the [Secretary of State] under this subsection must be made in the same manner and has the same consequences as in Section 116(c) and (d).

(c)   If a limited liability company has adopted and approved a plan of domestication under Section 1010 providing for the company to be domesticated in a foreign jurisdiction, a statement surrendering the company's certificate of organization must be delivered to the [Secretary of State] for filing setting forth:

(1)   the name of the company;

(2)   a statement that the certificate of organization is being surrendered in connection with the domestication of the company in a foreign jurisdiction;

(3)   a statement the domestication was approved as required by this [act]; and

(4)   the jurisdiction of formation of the domesticated foreign limited liability company.

SECTION 1014. RESTRICTIONS ON APPROVAL OF MERGERS, CONVERSIONS, AND DOMESTICATIONS.

(a)   If a member of a constituent, converting, or domesticating limited liability company will have personal liability with respect to a surviving, converted, or domesticated organization, approval or amendment of a plan of merger, conversion, or domestication is ineffective without the consent of the member, unless:

(1)   the company's operating agreement provides for approval of a merger, conversion, or domestication with the consent of fewer than all the members; and

(2)   the member has consented to the provision of the operating agreement.

(b)   A member does not give the consent required by subsection (a) merely by consenting to a provision of the operating agreement that permits the operating agreement to be amended with the consent of fewer than all the members.

SECTION 1015. [ARTICLE] NOT EXCLUSIVE. This [article] does not preclude an entity from being merged, converted, or domesticated under law other than this [act].

[ARTICLE] 11

MISCELLANEOUS PROVISIONS

SECTION 1101. UNIFORMITY OF APPLICATION AND CONSTRUCTION.

In applying and construing this uniform act, consideration must be given to the need to promote uniformity of the law with respect to its subject matter among states that enact it.

SECTION 1102. RELATION TO ELECTRONIC SIGNATURES IN GLOBAL AND NATIONAL COMMERCE ACT. This [act] modifies, limits, and supersedes the federal Electronic Signatures in Global and National Commerce Act, 15 U.S.C. Section 7001 et seq., but does not modify, limit, or supersede Section 101(c) of that act, 15 U.S.C. Section 7001(c), or authorize electronic delivery of any of the notices described in Section 103(b) of that act, 15 U.S.C. Section 7003(b).

SECTION 1103. SAVINGS CLAUSE. This [act] does not affect an action commenced, proceeding brought, or right accrued before this [act] takes effect.

SECTION 1104. APPLICATION TO EXISTING RELATIONSHIPS.

(a)   Before [all-inclusive date], this [act] governs only:

(1)   a limited liability company formed on or after [the effective date of this act];

and

(2)   except as otherwise provided in subsection (c), a limited liability company

formed before [the effective date of this act] which elects, in the manner provided in its operating agreement or by law for amending the operating agreement, to be subject to this [act].

(b)   Except as otherwise provided in subsection (c), on and after [all-inclusive date] this [act] governs all limited liability companies.

(c)   For the purposes applying this [act] to a limited liability company formed before [the effective date of this act]:

      (1)   the company's articles of organization are deemed to be the company's certificate of organization; and

      (2)   for the purposes of applying Section 102(10) and subject to Section 112(d), language in the company's articles of organization designating the company's management structure operates as if that language were in the operating agreement.

Legislative Note: It is recommended that the "all-inclusive" date should be at least one year after the date of enactment but no longer than two years.

Each enacting jurisdiction should consider whether: (i) this Act makes material changes to the "default" (or "gap filler") rules of jurisdiction's predecessor statute; and (ii) if so, whether subsection (c) should carry forward any of those rules for pre-existing limited liability companies. In this assessment, the focus is on pre-existing limited liability companies that have left default rules in place, whether advisedly or not. The central question is whether, for such limited liability companies, expanding subsection (c) is necessary to prevent material changes to the members' "deal."

For an example of this type of analysis in the context of another business entity act, see the Uniform Limited Partnership Act (2001), § 1206(c).

Section 301 (de-codifying statutory apparent authority) does not require any special transition provisions, because: (i) applying the law of agency, as explained in the Comments to Sections 301 and 407, will produce appropriate results; and (ii) the notion of "lingering apparent authority" will protect any third party that has previously relied on the statutory apparent authority of a member of a particular member-managed LLC or a manager of a particular manager-managed LLC. RESTATEMENT (THIRD) OF AGENCY § 3.11, cmt. c (2006).

It is unnecessary to expand subsection (c) of this Act if the state's predecessor act is the original Uniform Limited Liability Company Act, revised to provide for perpetual duration.

Comment

Subsection (c) – When a pre-existing limited liability company becomes subject to this Act, the company ceases to be governed by the predecessor act, including whatever requirements that act might have imposed for the contents of the articles of organization.

SECTION 1105. REPEALS. Effective [all-inclusive date], the following acts and parts of acts are repealed: [the state limited liability company act, as amended, and in effect immediately before the effective date of this act].

SECTION 1106. EFFECTIVE DATE. This [act] takes effect on July 1, 2009.

ABOUT THE AUTHOR

Vincent Cornelius is the founder of Georgia LLC Direct, a company designed to help prospective entrepreneurs form and maintain successful legal business entities. He is also the Chairman of the non-profit community development association, Riverdale Economic Development Mastermind (RED Mastermind). He is an advocate for entrepreneurship, and strongly believes that anyone who desires to own their own business, should. Vincent also conducts free seminars throughout Clayton County Georgia on "How to Start Your Own Business".

www.ingramcontent.com/pod-product-compliance
Lightning Source LLC
Chambersburg PA
CBHW080525220326
41599CB00032B/6207